OBAMA'S SECRETS

How to Speak and Communicate with Power and a Little Magic

Gil and Nili Peretz

OBAMA'S SECRETS
How to Speak and Communicate with Power and a Little Magic

Copyright © 2011 by Gil and Nili Peretz
All rights reserved.
ISBN: 978-1-4565-0636-0
Library of Congress Control Number: 2011900319
CreateSpace, North Charleston, SC

For translation rights please contact rights@ObamasSecrets.com

To explore the possibilities of bringing the power of international speaker Gil Peretz to your organization, contact international@ObamasSecrets.com

No part of this publication may be reproduced, stored in a retrieval system, or transmitted in any form or by any means electronic, mechanical, photocopied, recorded, or otherwise, without the prior written permission of the copyright owners.

This book is in no way affiliated with, sponsored by, or otherwise intended to express the views of Barack Obama.

Printed in the United States of America

www.ObamasSecrets.com

To Kim, Dor, and Shaked.

Each one of you can.

Love you to the heavens and back.

CONTENTS

Foreword i
How Is The Book Structured? vii

Part One: Street Smarts

1. Obama's Story – How It All Began 1
2. The Secrets Behind The Magic – Three Secrets Obama Takes With Him Everywhere 7
3. When We Reach The Bridge – How Mediation Capability Influences People 21
4. Like A Ballet Dancer – How To Persuade By Using A Flexible Transition Between Positions ... 31

Part Two: Obama's Brain Power

5. It's All In Your Mind – You Are What You Think 47
6. A Wall Or A Cathedral – Obama's Vision 53
7. Who Am I – Obama's Identity 59
8. Yes, I Can – Obama's Winning Personal Beliefs 63
9. What Really Matters – Obama's Values 75
10. Awakening The Communicator Within – Fulfilling Inner Capabilities And Strategies 83

Part Three: Engineering Winning Messages

11. The Core Messages – How To Use And Instill Optimistic Messages 91
12. The Winning Topics – How To Speak About What Motivates People 101
13. True, It's Difficult – How To Handle Potential Objections 105
14. It's Simple – How To Make Complex Messages Clear And Catchy 119
15. You Can Be A Star – How To Speak On Stage With Confidence, Like Obama 129
16. Uhh, Uhhmm… – The Secret Of Quiet Charisma 137

Part Four: The Magic of Intimate Communication

17. A Love Story – How To Create An Intimate Relationship When You Communicate 145
18. Dance With Them – How To Connect And Stimulate Action By Using The "Pacing And Leading" Technique 169
19. Inspire People Like A Personal Coach – How To Compliment, Empower, And Conquer Audiences 175
20. The Power Of Humor – How To Laugh At Your Own Weaknesses And Win 181

Part Five: The Power of the Mind in Communication

21. Under The Radar – How To Penetrate Your Audience's Right Brain With Power Stories 189
22. Don't Say It, Paint It! – How To Make Messages Stick With Simple Metaphors 211
23. The Mind As A Super Computer – How To Connect To The Thinking Strategies Of Your Audience 217

Part Six: Linguistic Patterns Tool Box

24. Why Does It Work? – How To Ask Questions And Lead To The Desired Direction........ 245
25. 1,2,3 – How To Exploit The Mind's Preference For The Magic Number 3 251
26. Repetition, Repetition, Repetition – How To Help Your Target Internalize Your Key Messages 257
27. Black And White – How To Use Contrasts To Emphasize Key Messages........................ 265
28. Kennedy Said – How To Influence By Using Great People Quotes................................. 269
29. Verbal Aikido – How To Exploit The Opponent's Momentum And Verbally Subdue Him 271
30. Who Said It? – Hand In Hand With The Subconscious 275

Part Seven: The Magic of Nonverbal Communication

31. Without Words – How To Use Movements, Gestures, And Empowering Body Language 285
32. All The World Is A Stage – How To Use The Surroundings, The Setting, And Props To Empower Your Messages 303
33. Voice Power – How To Thrill And Influence An Audience By Varying Voice Tones........ 309

Afterword... 321
International Speaker Gil Peretz 325
NLP Expert Nili Peretz.. 327
Recommendations... 329

FOREWORD

"Public speaking is a skill that can be studied, polished, perfected. Not only can you get good at it, you can get damn good at it and it makes a heck of a difference."

– **Tom Peters**
Best-selling author and leadership guru

Thank you for choosing to read *Obama's Secrets: How to Speak and Communicate with Power and a Little Magic.*

The book you are holding is *not* about President Barack Obama. It is about *you*. It's about how *you* can hone your presentation and communication skills based on the communication secrets of Barack Obama.

You are invited to upgrade your "communication IQ" and hone your presentation skills by implementing the secrets we had found when we cracked the code of Obama's formula for engineering and delivering effective messages.

Magnetizing. Charismatic. Eloquent. Captivating. Natural talent. Energetic. Exciting. Persuasive. Heart- piercing. The master of words. There has always been sweeping agreement regarding Obama's extraordinary communication skills, even among his opponents. This is why we have chosen him as our role model for effective communication. President Obama has an extraordinary ability for speaking, for conveying messages in an effective manner, and for influencing an audience. This ability is not disputed, and certainly helped him get elected as the 44th president of the United States.

Though words have enormous power, they cannot solve all the problems of the world. As our book goes to print in the middle of Obama's third year as president, one could claim that he did not solve many of America's economic challenges and as of September 2011, we can see that, indeed, a lot of hard work is still ahead of him. Therefore, please note that our book is by no means a political book. It's a professional "how-to" guide for anyone who wants to excel as an effective communicator.

Once you start to use Obama's secrets, you will communicate your messages like a pro, you will connect with your target audience using the secrets we reveal in this unique book, and you will inspire any audience and stimulate action. We are confident that anyone who reads and applies Obama's secrets will gain a competitive advantage – including you.

Have you ever been unfortunate enough to have to sit through, or even to have to make, a long and boring PowerPoint presentation? You should be aware that what makes the difference in any presentation is *you*, the presenter. You connect. You create a trust. You bond with your audience. You speak. You handle objections. You sell. You motivate. You are the message. *It's all about you.*

This book reveals Obama's secrets of communication and the manner in which he uses the power of words to influence, persuade, mesmerize, and, ultimately, garner people's support of his views. And as you will soon discover, Obama's ability to influence people is a skill that can be learned. Most of his secrets are easy to implement, and they will assist you in every area of your practice and career. As Peak Performance coach Anthony Robbins says, "The way we communicate with others and with ourselves ultimately determines the quality of our lives."

This book is the outcome of study, research, and thorough analysis that we have conducted for over three years. For the purpose of research, we have read, viewed, and analyzed over *three hundred* of Obama's speeches and media appearances. We started our analysis of the communication techniques he used in his speeches from the 1990s when he was still relatively unknown, we covered his campaign for president in 2008, and we reviewed many of his speeches as president right up until August 2011.

In addition, we have analyzed, using diverse tools, Obama's personality and media profile as depicted in his first two books *Dreams from My Father: A Story of Race and Inheritance* and *The Audacity of Hope: Thoughts on Reclaiming the American Dream*.

In our research, we sought to break the code to Obama's special charisma - his extraordinary ability to connect with diverse audiences and influence them, while changing

Foreword

attitudes and behaviors of people worldwide. Though we have not yet met President Obama face to face, we believe that, during our mutual journey, we have managed to decipher the majority of his secrets of communication and influence. Our view is based on our systematic and in-depth analysis of the vast array of research material, and on our own professional experience.

༄

Before we give you a short description of the book, you might want to know some important facts about us, the coauthors.

International speaker **Gil Peretz** is one of the world's leading authorities on communication and sales training. With more than 25 years of experience, Gil has coached and trained thousands of CEOs, entrepreneurs, sales experts, coaches, political leaders, and diplomats.

Since 1986, Gil has delivered more than 2,600 keynote speeches, presentations, and seminars. He is considered both a "motiv-actional" speaker and a results-driven trainer covering a range of topics including communication, presentation skills, whole-brain selling, negotiation, intimate marketing, and training for impact.

Gil has helped a wide range of organizations unleash their sales teams' potential. Global Fortune 500 companies engage Gil for their keynote addresses, breakout sessions, and to coach executives on their presentations.

Gil's clients include international organizations such as Microsoft, Motorola, Coca-Cola, IBM, Allergan, Merck, Teva, Pfizer, Philip Morris International, Swiss International Air Lines, HP, Hertz, Orange, Ericsson, Hilton, British American Tobacco, Manpower, Dun & Bradstreet, M-systems, Comverse, Peugeot, Citroen, Lee Cooper, Delta, and many more.

As a highly respected member of the American National Speakers Association, Gil has been invited to deliver his *"unforgettable presentations"* many times across the globe at conventions and conferences attended by thousands of participants.

Since 2009, Gil has been invited to deliver his seminars about *Obama's effective secrets of communication* and the ways in which they can be utilized for presentations, sales calls, and even in education.

Gil is considered a high-energy, virtuoso intimate speaker with rare presentation talents and a special ability to bond with any audience. Participants at his lectures feel that he speaks to each of them, individually, as if it were an intimate talk. The participants always leave with ideas for immediate implementation and, no less important, with a sense that they have taken part in a special intellectual and emotional experience.

He has been teaching marketing and presentation skills at the University of Tel-Aviv's Faculty of Management – The Leon Recanati Graduate School of Business Administration.

Gil is the author of the best-selling instructional novel *Intimate Marketing*.

Nili Peretz has brought to this joint writing endeavor her experience of over a decade as a business attorney, during which time she has worked as Defense Attorney, preparing dozens of defendants for the most important presentation of their lives—the one that would determine their innocence in front of a judge.

In addition to her BA and MA degrees in Law (completed with honors) and her training as a certified mediator, Nili has contributed her expertise as a Master Practitioner NLP (Neuro-Linguistic Programming) to the research, as well as the knowledge and hands-on experience she has accumulated in helping people make significant changes in various areas of their lives through the use of NLP tools.

Nili also conducts "Excellence Studies" projects–as a role model and as a means to improve business performance.

We both share a common worldview based on the assumption that we can learn from others' success. Malcolm Gladwell's book *Outliers: The Story of Success,* as well as many studies, shows that most successful people, in any field, achieve success after a lot of hard work and not necessarily as a result of good genes or natural talent.

It is important to reiterate that anyone can learn what Obama has learned to do as a communicator. Yes, anyone. Anyone can apply the tools provided in this book.

Our book is the result of a unique combination of our shared professional experience. Together, we wrote this book out of love. We wrote a practical book for you, which is based on Obama's secrets. It includes dozens of tools from the arenas of persuasion, communication, presentation, psychology, and recent studies in the field of brain science. **Our goal is to help you to use the tools presented here to convey your messages in a better way: more sincerely, more persuasively.**

We have no doubt that this book will be useful for any individual who wants to have a successful career. Therefore, whether you are a CEO, a corporate president, an entrepreneur, or a business owner, whether you are in sales and marketing, or you are a lawyer, a teacher, or a politician—you can benefit significantly from Obama's secrets.

Please send us your feedback. Visit us at www.ObamasSecrets.com.

We hope to meet you in our keynotes and seminars around the world.

Gil and Nili Peretz
Authors@ObamasSecrets.com
September 2011

HOW IS THE BOOK STRUCTURED?

In the *first part* of the book, you will be exposed to several secrets that Obama brings with him from his personal life: the "street smarts" that transform his media messages or speeches from a collection of eloquently-formulated theoretical ideas into terms that penetrate the hearts and souls of his listeners.

In the *second part*, you will discover how Obama thinks and how his way of thinking helps him to influence and persuade. Many people whom we encountered during our work, who had acquired effective presentation skills, focused primarily on tactics and methods, but we discovered that tactics alone are not enough. Something more is required beyond tactics; something much more basic and profound that is related to our way of thinking.

In the *third part*, you will become acquainted with Obama's "Message Engineering." You will be provided with a simple implementation toolkit that will enable you to improve the way you convey your messages in all areas. You will discover that what seems a lighthearted performance by Obama is, in fact, a well-timed musical composition in which various and diverse instruments are played, each of which possesses vast power.

You will see how Obama writes his speeches and discover what he does to join the ranks of charismatic speakers, such as Martin Luther King Jr., Winston Churchill, John F. Kennedy, Ronald Reagan, and Bill Clinton, and business leaders such as Steve Jobs, Harvey Mackay, Jack Welch, Stephen Covey, Mark Victor Hansen, and Ken Blanchard.

In the *fourth part*, you will discover how Obama makes people fall in love with him and become enthralled by his messages, and you will get to know how he activates these secrets of infatuation. He creates human chemistry and intimate closeness with a heterogeneous audience, which sometimes consists of tens of thousands of people.

In the *fifth part*, you will be provided with effective tools to communicate with the "right brain" and the subconscious mind of your listeners. This is a very important part because it presents the power of stories and metaphors of which many of the executives and politicians we have trained were unaware. You will be exposed to the naturalness with which the mind absorbs stories and metaphors, and the way in which they directly penetrate the subconscious. After that, you will see how Obama uses "thought programs" to "program" the audience's mind and "glue" messages thereto.

In the *sixth part*, you will learn how Obama uses effective linguistic patterns to convey messages. Here, too, you will be provided a very useful toolbox, with emphasis not only on the tools themselves but also the reasons why these tools are effective.

The *last part* focuses on the power of nonverbal communication, which is an integral part of any interpersonal communication.

For your convenience, we have added a brief and concise summary on the last page of most of the chapters, which will allow you to use the book quickly and efficiently when preparing for presentations and speeches.

PART ONE
Street Smarts

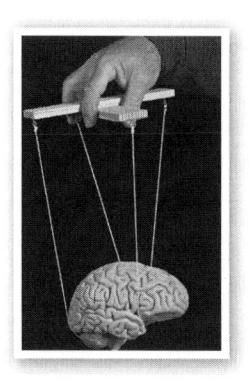

CHAPTER 1

OBAMA'S STORY – HOW IT ALL BEGAN

Mahatma Gandhi was one of the world's most respected leaders of the twentieth century. Gandhi was the leader of India's Independence Movement in its peaceful and nonviolent struggle against the British Empire, and advocated nonviolence and truth. During a political gathering in India, a participant turned to Gandhi and said, "I am a simple man and I don't understand much. Could you tell me in simple terms what your message is?" Gandhi responded, "I am my message."

President Barack Obama is a living example of the use of Gandhi's message. In fact, each one of us can magnetize, influence, and lead people if we remember that a man is primarily his own message. Charisma is within us. However, not everyone knows how to uncover it and realize it. Obama did both and, later in this book, we will reveal his secrets of power communication, charisma, and influence.

The circumstances of Obama's life impacted, and continue to impact, his messages. In his youth, he understood that the true raw materials of life can be found in the street, among the people, and in the stories people tell.

His street smarts weren't acquired in universities, libraries, or laboratories. It was accumulated one experience after another. Obama is well aware that it is only what he experiences himself that he can convey to others. He accumulated wisdom through rich personal experience and by listening to people's stories and what motivates them. He was raised on the perception that only when one walks in another's shoes can one truly understand how the other person feels, what drives him. When Obama speaks before an audience, he can predict how his audience will feel, and he will know how to motivate it. This knowledge is based on a virtually intimate familiarity with stories from the street and with what motivates people.

Obama moves with extraordinary flexibility between diverse standpoints and perceptions and examines every situation from several perspectives. His ability to bridge the gaps between the various parts of society, while striving to find common interests, is a result of his extraordinary life-story and his close interaction with the person on the street. The books Obama wrote provide an opportunity to learn firsthand about his personality, and when meticulously analyzed, his secrets can be uncovered.

Before we reveal Obama's secrets, let's review his life and see how it all began.

Barack Hussein Obama was born on August 4, 1961 in Honolulu, Hawaii, to a white mother and black father. His father immigrated to Hawaii from Kenya as a foreign student on a learning scholarship. His mother came with her parents from Kansas. Intermarriage of a black man and a white woman was unusual at the time in the United States, and was even illegal in some states.

When Obama was two years old, his parents separated. His father left to study at Harvard and never returned to his family. He remarried and returned to Kenya. His mother remarried also, an exchange student from Indonesia.

Obama's biological father did not function as a parent, after Obama turned two years old. Though Obama knew him from the stories his mother told, his life was shaped as a direct result of his absence rather than his presence. After his parents had separated, he met his father only once in Hawaii. When he was ten years old, his father visited him at Christmas. This encounter was their first and last. His father was killed in 1982 in a car accident.

When he was six years old, Obama moved with his mother and stepfather to Jakarta, the capital of Indonesia, his stepfather's homeland. He lived there and learned how to read and write Indonesian in the local school.

When he was ten years old, he returned to Honolulu on his own and studied at a private school. He lived with his grandparents, who assumed the role of his parents.

Only in 1986, when he was twenty-five years old, did Obama visit his father's family in Kenya for the first time during a trip in search of his family roots.

As you can see, in his early childhood, Obama experienced changes in the family setting, in parental figures, residential setting, culture, language—and even in his personal identity. From the moment he was born, he lived a dynamic reality, and he grew up and was shaped into an open-minded youth who flowed with life and its inherent surprises.

Obama's biography is a story of change and of overcoming hardships. Not by chance did the word "change" become his presidential campaign motto. Obama is an expert when it comes to change. He went through many changes in his life and, remarkably, overcame most of them. This is precisely what provides him the inner power to feel he has a legitimate right to lead his country, and the entire world, towards change.

Due to his unique identity, as the son of a black father and white mother, as a youth who looked black but grew up and was educated among white people, Obama could relate to being unlike others, to being different. Who, of all people, knows what it's like to feel that one doesn't belong? To always feel somewhat different—not really white but not quite black, either? Throughout his entire life both black and white people regarded him as different, not one of their own. Obama referred to this in his speeches.

> At various stages in the campaign, some commentators have deemed me either "too black" or "not black enough."
>
> "A More Perfect Union" speech
> Philadelphia, Pennsylvania
> March 2008

No wonder the boy Obama grew up to be a liberal and tolerant man, striving to bridge gaps; he was forced to bridge the inner gaps in his identity to reach internal wholeness. In his autobiography, *Dreams from My Father*, he wrote of himself:

> That my father looked nothing like the people around me—that he was black as pitch, my mother white as milk—barely registered in my mind…Their very image together would have been considered lurid and perverse, a handy retort to the handful of softheaded liberals who supported a civil rights agenda.

In 1979, after graduating from high school, Obama moved to Los Angeles and studied for two years in college. Afterwards, he went on to Columbia University in New York, where he majored in political science with a specialty in international relations.

After graduation in 1983, he worked in New York for a year as an analyst at a consulting firm for companies whose center of business was overseas. Then he moved to Chicago, where he became a community organizer. In the framework of this position, he was involved in, among other activities, training local leaders in the projects and initiating and leading social projects. One can learn about his work as a community organizer, and through this about his worldview, from an article he wrote in 1988, published in August of that year in the magazine of Illinois University in Springfield. In the article, he tells of several reasons why he deals with people in an area perceived by many as ungrateful:

> Over the past five years, I've often had a difficult time explaining my profession to folks. Typical is a remark a public school administrative aide made to me one bleak January morning, while I waited to deliver some flyers to a group of confused and angry parents, who had discovered the presence of asbestos in their school.
>
> "Listen, Obama," she began. "You're a bright young man, Obama. You went to college, didn't you?"
>
> I nodded.
>
> "I just cannot understand why a bright young man like you would go to college, get that degree, and become a community organizer."
>
> "Why's that?"
>
> "Cause the pay is low, the hours are long, and don't nobody appreciate you." She shook her head in puzzlement as she wandered back to attend to her duties.
>
> I've thought back on that conversation more than once during the time I've organized with the Developing Communities Project, based in Chicago's far south side. Unfortunately, the answers that come to mind haven't been as simple as her question. Probably the shortest one is this: It needs to be done, and not enough folks are doing it.

As a community organizer, Obama realized that, to create real change, one must strive for change in politics and law. That same year, he began studying law at Harvard and made history when he was chosen as the first African-American editor of the prestigious *Harvard Law Review*.

He was certified in 1991, and after graduating, turned down tempting offers from law firms and returned to Chicago, where he began working as a civil rights attorney. At the same time, he taught legislative law at the University of Chicago. In those years, he handled cases of workers who suffered from discrimination, unemployed individuals who were evacuated from their homes, and cases of other people from the margins of society. These experiences provided Obama with the street smarts that, in later years, he transformed into a springboard into the White House.

In 1995, when he was already married to Michelle, he published his autobiography *Dreams from My Father*, which became a bestseller nine years later after he made his historic speech in 2004 at the Democratic National Convention.

Shortly thereafter, in 1996, Obama began his public career. He was elected to the Illinois State Senate, and served there between 1997 and 2004.

On his way to the presidency, Obama suffered some failures, as well.

In 2000, he managed an unsuccessful election campaign for the US House of Representatives and lost to his opponent, Bobby Rush, who won by a landslide of 2:1.

However, four years later, in 2004, he was given the opportunity of a lifetime when he delivered the keynote speech at the Democratic National Convention, a speech that is considered historic and inspiring.

After the speech, he became a respected politician and not only among the Democrats.

At the end of that year, he was also elected to the United States Senate and became the fifth African-American senator in history.

Two years later, in 2006, he published his second book, *The Audacity of Hope*, which also became a bestseller. The name of the book is taken from a sermon given by Reverend Jeremiah Wright in 1988, the reverend to whose church Obama belonged, the same reverend whose statements later caused Obama quite a bit of embarrassment, during the presidential campaign in 2008.

The Audacity of Hope was also the name of the speech Obama made two years earlier at the 2004 Democratic National Convention (DNC).

In the freezing cold of February 2007, in Springfield, Illinois, Obama announced his intention to run for president of the United States and, in August 2008, he was elected as the candidate of the Democratic Party for the presidential election, after having defeated Hillary Clinton, who had been the forerunner of the party several months earlier.

On November 4, 2008, Obama was elected as the next president of the USA. That was the peak of a long journey, and a historic moment in America. The majority of the American people voted for the first black president.

In October 2009, Obama was named the 2009 Nobel Peace Prize laureate.

In the first two years as president, Obama signed economic stimulus legislation, the "Obama Care" health resolution (Patient Protection and Affordable Care Act), and the Don't Ask, Don't Tell Repeal Act of 2010. Obama also promoted the "Race to the Top" education program. He gradually withdrew combat troops from Iraq, increased troop levels in Afghanistan, and signed an arms control treaty with Russia.

On May 1, 2011, Obama announced, in an address to the American nation, that a small team of American military forces, acting on his direct order, had killed Osama bin Laden in Pakistan.

That is Obama's story. Now, let's see three secrets Barack Obama takes with him everywhere.

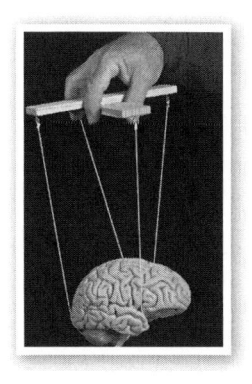

CHAPTER 2

The Secrets Behind The Magic – Three Secrets Obama Takes With Him Everywhere

"Speakers who talk about what life has taught them never fail to keep the attention of their listeners."

—**Dale Carnegie**

After reviewing Obama's biography, let's get to know three basic secrets.

Secret #1: Conveying Messages based on the Power of Personal Experience

> I don't know what kind of lives John McCain thinks that celebrities lead, but this has been mine.
> These are my heroes.
> Theirs are the stories that shaped me.
> And it is on their behalf that I intend to win this election
> and keep our promise alive as President of the United States.
>
> "The American Promise"
> Democratic National Convention
> August 28, 2008
> Denver, Colorado

Obama's Secrets

When his grandmother's health declined at the height of the presidential election campaign, Obama went to be with her for a few days. She passed away shortly before the polls opened.

This fact proves above all else that the true heroes of Obama's life story are members of his family. His grandmother, mother, father, wife, daughters, and the people he encountered along the way are the real heroes of his story. They are the force that motivates him to lead, change, and influence.

Let's see how he shares a story about his grandmother. On October 5, 2010, he spoke at the 2010 Fortune Most Powerful Women Summit:

> As some of you know, I was raised in part by my grandmother. She just passed away a couple of years ago. When I was born, she got a job as a secretary to help provide for our family. Now, she only had a high school education. She had grown up in a generation where women weren't necessarily encouraged to pursue a college degree, and certainly not after they had gotten married and had a child. But she had an incredible mind and sound judgment. And so, over the years, she worked her way up—without a college degree, just a high school degree—to become one of the first woman bank vice presidents in the state of Hawaii. And that was an amazing accomplishment, but that position was also her glass ceiling. For nearly two decades, she watched, as men no more qualified than she was—in fact, usually men whom she had trained— would get promoted up the corporate ladder ahead of her.
>
> Now, I know that if given the chance, she would have run that bank better than anybody. But she never got that opportunity. And she never complained. She hardly ever took a vacation. She just kept getting up and giving her best every single day.

As we saw, Obama did not grow up in a "stable" family. His life was fraught with hardships, changes, tragedies, and confrontations with a virtually impossible reality. His ability to mesmerize, lead, and influence, despite all these challenges, stems from the way in which he harnessed the harsh circumstances of his life to his advantage. This is how he describes it in his own words:

> I should not be here today.
> I was not born into money or status.
> I was born to a teenage mom in Hawaii,

and my dad left us when I was two.
But my family gave me love,
they gave me education,
and most of all they gave me hope—hope that in America,
no dream is beyond our grasp if we reach for it,
and fight for it,
and work for it.

Madison, WI
February 12, 2008

Meet the Teleprompter

Some of the quotes from Obama's speeches appear in the book, in the form of short lines. This is so you can read these speeches in a similar manner to the way Obama read and delivered them with the aid of a teleprompter. While reading, you can get a feel for the power of pausing, when speaking, and identify musical motifs in the speeches.

In this speech, he conveys the message of his life: anyone can learn to turn problems and hardships into opportunities. And so Obama hurdled over the hardships, soared above the tragedies, and became stronger, thanks to the changes. Therefore, when he said the words, "Yes we can," it was easy to relate to his message as early as in 2004, the message that later became his motto in his 2008 presidential election campaign.

Obama makes us think that his success is related to the hardships he experienced in life that he succeeded as a result of the hardships, not despite them. He uses messages that originate from his personal experiences, words that trigger emotion and a sense of affinity among his listeners.

He proves in his speeches that he believes in the promise of America, because that is the way he was raised and educated:

> That's why I'm in this race.
>
> I love this country too much to see it divided and distracted at this moment in history.

I believe in our ability to perfect this union because it's the only reason I'm standing here today.

And I know the promise of America because I have lived it.

—May 6, 2008, Raleigh, NC

🔍 Tell Your Story

Obama's message is that if he triumphed over the hardships in his personal life and realized the American dream, anyone can. Your life story can also be used as raw material when you want to influence, convey messages, persuade, and sell.

Your personal experiences, the people you met along the way, the hardships you overcame—all these instill life in the words you choose and messages you convey.

Consider how your life story can become a force that motivates you, how it is related to issues you deem important to promote, how an experience you went through is relevant to your message.

Anything you experienced in your life can be relevant when it comes to influencing and conveying messages. There is no good or bad life experience; there is no interesting or uninteresting life story—every life experience can be relevant in order to persuade and influence, as long as it is based on real life.

Real communication is based on real-life stories.

If you want people to listen to your messages, reconnect with the experiences you went through yourself.

Your true heroes are the people who accompanied you along the way. What did you learn from them?

Obama got to where he is by using street smarts and messages based on his life experience. Yes, you can too. What is your story?

Secret #2: Listening in order to Influence

> "Courage is what it takes to stand up and speak; courage is also what it takes to sit down and listen."
>
> —**Winston Churchill**

Obama reveals in his books the second and simple secret to success. The secret is listening. In his book, *The Audacity of Hope*, he writes:

> I tried my best to keep my mouth shut and hear what they had to say. I listened to people talk about their jobs, their businesses, the local school; their anger at Bush and their anger at Democrats; their dogs, their back pain, their war service, and the things they remembered from childhood.

Ten years earlier, in his book, *Dreams from My Father*, Obama indicated that he loves people:

> A measure of what we sacrificed for technology and mobility, but that here… remained essentially intact: the insistent pleasure of other people's company, the joy of human warmth.

He knows that listening is one of the most important secrets of communication and influence and that it is a powerful tool for gathering information that will help him understand what motivates people. He believes God gave us two ears and one mouth, so that we listen at least twice as much as we talk.

When Obama says, "Let's *talk* to some people," he means, "Let's *listen* to some people." He regards listening as a vital component with which to create relationships, and relationships—as we will see later on—are the cornerstones of his communication and influence theory. Here is what he said at his Facebook town hall meeting:

> And historically, part of what makes for a healthy democracy, what is good politics, is when you've got citizens who are informed, who are engaged. And what Facebook allows us to do is make sure this isn't just a one-way conversation; makes sure that not only am I speaking to you but you're also speaking back and we're in a conversation, we're in a dialogue. So I love doing town hall meetings.

— April, 20, 2011

Throughout his career, private and public, Obama has always walked the streets among the people and listened to their life stories. He did this when he was a community organizer. He tells of this in his book, *Dreams from My Father*:

> That's what the leadership was teaching me, day by day: that the self-interest I was supposed to be looking for extended well beyond the immediacy of issues, that beneath the small talk and sketchy biographies and received opinions people carried within them some central explanation of themselves. Stories full of terror and wonder, studded with events that still haunted or inspired them. Sacred stories.

Obama never stopped listening, even when he became a respected politician. He always maintained a direct affinity for the people.

> In spite of this absence of leadership from Washington, I have seen a new generation of Americans begin to take up the call. I meet them everywhere I go, young people involved in the project of American renewal.
>
> — "The America We Love" speech, June 30, 2008, Independence, Missouri

Obama adeptly keeps in touch with the people in the age of Internet-based social networks, as well. In his 2008 presidential election campaign, he was smart enough to involve the voters in the online social communication channels. In fact, he transformed the world of elections, thanks to the strategic moves he made while using the Internet.

Bill Clinton was the first US president whose second inaugural address in 1997 was broadcast online, and Obama had determined, in no uncertain terms, that to win the elections, he should win online. To that end, Obama used a combination of Facebook and Google campaigns, among others.

One of the consultants, whose advice Obama abides, is Eric Schmidt, former CEO of Google, the company that changed the Internet world with its search technology. (Schmidt is also a former member of the board of directors of Apple). His other consultant, Chris Hughes, is a brilliant young man who was born in 1983 and was a founder and spokesperson of Facebook. He left the company to develop Obama's online presence. Obama knew that to listen to the young generation he had to know its language—the language of the Internet and the social networks.

The number of entries to Obama's website throughout the 2008 campaign was much larger than the number of entries to the website of his Republican opponent John McCain. Obama's speech, "A More Perfect Union," from March 2008, became almost as popular online as a Victoria's Secret fashion show. Within twenty-four hours, it had been viewed by over a million people on YouTube.

Obama also made sure to create a YouTube channel with hundreds of video clips, which millions have watched.

To understand Obama's power, it is worthwhile to compare his numbers to those of his opponents: the viewing volume of his channel was nine times greater than Hillary Clinton's channel, and twenty-one times greater than John McCain's.

For many Americans, as in most countries in the 21st century, the Internet is not only a tool for conveying information; it is also a social network. Obama took advantage of this. He opened a profile on every leading social network and even had an avatar created for him in the Second Life virtual game. At the time, his Facebook friends numbered over 2.5 million. Today, these initiatives seem obvious, but in 2008, they were innovative.

The Internet helped Obama create ties with voters and supporters and enabled him to motivate them. He listened to the many messages that were sent to him, as no other politician had ever done before. Obama's secret of listening changed the perception about online influence.

In terms of fundraising, Obama implemented what is known in online economics as "The Long Tail theory." Instead of receiving large donations from traditional donators, he recruited many donations of less than one hundred dollars. Thus, he created the beginning of a binding relationship, based on listening to hundreds of thousands of supporters. For those people–for whom a donation such as this was significant–voting for Obama was only natural and obvious.

Obama continued to pursue the secret of listening, using the Internet as a basis for relationships and maintaining direct contact with the American people, but he also does this as president of the USA. In March 2009, he became the first American president to speak online and provided surfers an opportunity to ask questions with no sifting, no teleprompter, no White House spokesperson, and no filtering mechanisms.

Listening is at the heart of who Obama is. He speaks to youths at eye level, i.e., online. The Internet is the street of the 21st century. Obama uses his good old street smarts and merely applies them to a new format.

Obama knows that the Internet is a strategic tool with which to connect people with common interests to each other. In addition, the Internet provides him with lists of new email addresses for the 2012 elections, and Obama certainly knows how to activate strategic thinking. His 2012 campaign started with a Facebook town hall meeting from Facebook headquarters in Palo Alto, California (April 20, 2011).

Shortly after he was elected, during the one hundred days of grace, he and Michelle found time to conduct a story hour for second-grade children at an elementary school in northwest Washington. This was at a time when the number of challenges inside America and outside its borders was enormous. Obama also informed people of his intention to invite guests to the White House on weekends.

He doesn't want to live in an ivory tower, detached from the people. His unwillingness to part with his Blackberry was a clear indication of his desire to stay in touch with the street. Obama wanted to keep listening to the people and communicate with them as president, without any filtering by external entities, something that generally happens immediately after the president is elected.

Obama knows how to listen, even when listening becomes complex. An example of a simple solution to complex listening can be seen at a press conference conducted at the end of his one hundred days of grace. *A New York Times* reporter asked Obama a long, four-part question. Instead of remembering the entire question, Obama removed a pen and said, "Allow me to write the question down." He also made the reporter repeat the question, without being accused of forgetfulness, and he generated a burst of laughter among the other reporters, who liked how Obama handled their colleague's "speech." This is elegant handling of a question, which projects professionalism and true listening.

On another occasion, Obama tackled a long question in a different manner. At a joint press conference in Tokyo, after meeting with the prime minister of Japan, Yukio Hatoyama, in November 2009, he gave an amusing answer to a question one of the reporters asked that was especially long:

> Well, first of all, I am impressed that the Japanese journalists use the same strategy as American journalists—in asking multiple questions.

Many people listen, as long as they hear what they want to hear: things that don't contradict their opinions. Another aspect of listening is to listen, even if we don't agree with what is being said. Obama listens, even when he doesn't agree. He listens, even when the situation is tough, and he listens to people who are not political supporters.

In February 2010, Obama proved this again when he implemented another innovation: he summoned congressional members to a political debate between himself and opponents of the health reform, which was televised live for several hours on all news channels in the USA. Every American could see and hear a lengthy debate for and against the reform. Obama has no fear of listening to people with views that contradict his own.

He said as much during his 2008 presidential election victory speech. Here is what he said in an attempt to influence and lead:

> There will be setbacks and false starts.
> There are many who won't agree
> with every decision or policy I make as president,
> and we know that government can't solve every problem.
> But I will always be honest with you about the challenges we face.
> I will listen to you, especially when we disagree.
> And above all, I will ask you join in the work of remaking this nation the only way it's been done in America for two-hundred and twenty-one years—
> block by block, brick by brick, calloused hand by calloused hand…
> … And to those Americans whose support I have yet to earn—
> I may not have won your vote,
> but I hear your voices,
> I need your help,
> and I will be your president, too.
>
> —Election Night Victory Speech, November 4, 2008,
> Chicago, Illinois

Transforming a Grain of Sand into a Pearl

Listening is easy to do, but many people don't know how significant it is. The ears are a primary tool of influence. When you listen, you obtain vast information and understand better. Also, the other party will be willing to listen to you, in return. The secret is simple: before you open your mouth—open your ears.

Look around you and take note of how many people you know who truly listen. Many relationships would do better if both parties would implement this rule.

When you ask someone a question, you can see and hear if he or she knows how to listen. It can be during a presentation, a sales pitch, a speech, a press conference, or the Q&A part of a presentation. In all these cases, active listening is required, while focusing entirely on the question and the individual asking the question, throughout.

Before you answer the question, it's best that you repeat it, both to ensure you understood it and to convey to the other party that you had listened well.

There is a lot of power in listening. To influence people, allow yourself first to be influenced by them. Listening precedes influence, and it is vital to attain it. Here's an example from nature:

For a pearl to form in a shell, the shell must be open so that a grain of sand can penetrate it. If it is not open, a pearl will not be formed.

The next time you have to give a speech, persuade, or sell—meet the public, study the topics about which you intend to talk, and the people to whom you intend to speak.

Remember to conduct a genuine and continuous relationship with people; meet them face-to-face, listen to their stories, learn to appreciate the pleasure of human warmth, as Obama says. Listen, even when you don't agree or when other difficulties arise. Listen in particular to someone who does not support you. That is where the potential lies to pick up things that will enable you to influence people.

Apply Obama's secret of listening; look how far he came with this truly basic human skill!

Secret #3: Putting Yourself in Someone else's Shoes

Two years before he was elected president, and six months before he announced his candidacy as president, Obama shared one of his secrets of success—the ability to create empathy and put himself in someone else's shoes. Empathy is one of the cornerstones that shaped Obama's personality:

> You know, there's a lot of talk in this country about the federal deficit.
> But I think we should talk more about our empathy deficit—
> the ability to put ourselves in someone else's shoes;
> to see the world through the eyes of those who are different from us—
> the child who's hungry,
> the steelworker who's been laid-off,
> the family who lost the entire life they built together
> when the storm came to town.
>
> Xavier University Commencement Address
August 11, 2006
New Orleans, Louisiana

When Obama listens, he does not remain passive. He takes the process a step further and puts himself in the other person's shoes. He tries to see the world through the eyes of that person, to hear through his or her ears, and to sense his or her feelings. He changes roles with that person, placing himself in the other person's position.

Why is this important? Once you see, hear, and feel things from the other person's perspective, as opposed to merely your own, you can plan the way you will communicate your messages, so that you can suitably influence the other party.

You will see later that there are *four perceptual positions*, which we will expand on in the upcoming chapters. At this time, we will touch upon them to clarify Obama's perceptual position.

The **"first position"** is *your* position: when you see, hear, and feel everything from your own perspective.

The **"second position"** is the *other person's* perception: when you see, hear, and feel things from the other person's point of view.

The **"third position"** is when you see things from the *outside*: from the perspective of a fly on the wall. You see all sides, you remain uninvolved, and you are able to analyze the situation in an unfettered and creative way.

The **"fourth position"** is the *mediating* position. You can experience this position only after having experienced all the others, because it unites all the aspects that all the positions have in common. This is the position that characterizes mediation processes.

Obama knows how to put himself in the other person's shoes and adeptly use the second perceptual position. This skill, which is the basis for human empathy, is one of the most effective skills for persuasion, for mesmerizing people, and for leadership.

You could say Obama had learned it from his mother, as she raised him on the values of decency, listening, and helping one's fellow man.

Daniel Pink, author of *A Whole New Mind – Why Right Brainers will Rule the Future*, stresses that empathy is an incredible action of penetrating the other person's mind, in order to experience the world from his or her point of view.

Empathy, like many other skills that comprise our emotional intelligence, is an acquired skill. After all, we know that from the moment a baby is born, it is focused on itself and its needs. It wants everyone to wait on it; it needs them to wait on it. It cries and expects a reaction. When the child grows up and learns to speak, it says, "This!" and expects to get its wish then and there. It sees everything from its own perspective. This doesn't change entirely when we grow up. Everyone sees, hears, and feels things through his or her own prism. Everyone has perceptions, beliefs, concerns, feelings, and prejudices. All these influence the way in which people see the world and take it in.

For Obama, empathy is a key skill and a core belief, and in order for you to communicate better, you should work on developing your empathy too. Let's see how Obama talks as a leader of the USA.

On January 12, 2011, at a memorial service for the victims of the shooting in Tucson, Arizona, he said:

> Rather than pointing fingers or assigning blame,
> let's use this occasion to expand our moral imaginations,
> to listen to each other more carefully,

to sharpen our instincts for empathy
and remind ourselves of all the ways
that our hopes and dreams are bound together.

Three and a half years before, on July 17, 2007, while speaking at the Planned Parenthood conference in DC, Obama expressed his own intention to appoint justices with empathy:

> We need somebody who's got the heart, the empathy to recognize what it's like to be a young teenage mom. The empathy to understand what it's like to be poor, or African-American, or gay, or disabled, or old. And that's the criteria by which I'm going to be selecting my judges.

To be an effective communicator, you should be able to put yourself in the other person's shoes and try to understand his or her perception and feelings. Obama's empathy also relates to his outlook, according to which people are connected to one another and are responsible for one another.

In his 2004 speech at the Democratic National Convention, which paved his way to the presidency, he demonstrated this well and was afforded great acclaim. This is what happens when you know how to be not only empathic but to convey your message clearly to the people around you, as Obama did:

> For alongside our famous individualism,
> there's another ingredient in the American saga.
> A belief that we are connected as one people.
> If there's a child on the south side of Chicago who can't read,
> that matters to me, even if it's not my child.
> If there's a senior citizen somewhere who can't pay for her prescription and has
> to choose between medicine and the rent,
> that makes my life poorer, even if it's not my grandmother…
> It's that fundamental belief—
> I am my brother's keeper,
> I am my sister's keeper—
> that makes this country work.

This kind of message recurs in many of Obama's speeches and reveals an aspect of his inner world. You cannot remain indifferent to the suffering of others when you put yourself in their shoes. It is difficult not to help, to get up and take action, when you really and truly feel the other person's distress. And when the other person's problem becomes your problem, this motivates you into action.

Obama's third secret is, in fact, a strategy that is not overt, but is always behind the scenes. At first, he listens to people, then he changes places with them and studies their motives and feelings, while applying the *second perceptual position*. He is able to understand what is important to them and how they feel, and thus the road is paved to influence them, while joining them and leading them in the desired direction.

As we will see later on, Obama uses this secret very often. Since this secret and the two others we have revealed are simple to apply—you too can adopt them easily in every inter-personal communication.

Crossing the Bridge

Empathy is more than a professional skill to be used if you want to survive the employment market in the 21st century. It is an important part of a meaningful life. To persuade others and motivate them into action, you should first put yourself in their shoes. The next time you listen to someone, take it one step further: see the experience through his or her eyes, hear what he or she hears, and feel that person's feelings. Thus, you will be able to better understand what motivates and triggers him or her, and you will be able to use everything you learned about that person to join and lead him or her in the desired direction.

When you want to influence or persuade someone, or sell an idea, product, or service you are standing on one side of the bridge, while the other party is standing on the other. If we see communication as a negotiation of ideas, we should use effective negotiation skills when we communicate.

Cofounder of the Harvard Law School Program on Negotiation, William Ury, said it clearly in his book, *Getting Past No: Negotiating with Difficult People*. If you want to persuade, do not make the mistake many people make: don't try to shift the other party to your side by force. Instead, cross the bridge mentally, go to the other side, and then you can return with the target audience to your side of the bridge.

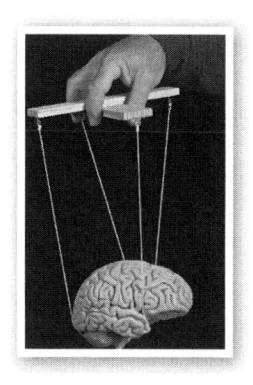

CHAPTER 3

When We Reach The Bridge – How Mediation Capability Influences People

"We build too many walls and not enough bridges."

—Isaac Newton

After revealing Obama's three basic secrets, we will see how he uses them to bridge gaps and unite people. When you know how Obama does it, you can do it yourself.

Look at his statement after meeting with bipartisan leadership (November 30, 2010):

> As I told the leaders at the beginning of the meeting,
> the next election is two years away,
> and there will be plenty of time for campaigning.
> But right now we're facing some very serious challenges.
> We share an obligation to meet them.
> And that will require choosing the best of our ideas over the worst of our politics.

In a speech in Richmond, Virginia, Obama conveyed his street smarts clearly, while using supporting body language and variations in his tone of voice, cadence, and dramatics:

There are no real or fake parts of this country.
We are not separated by the pro-America and anti-America parts of this nation—
we all love this country,
no matter where we live or where we come from.
There are patriots who supported this war in Iraq
and patriots who opposed it;
patriots who believe in Democratic policies
and those who believe in Republican policies.
The men and women from Virginia and all across America
who serve on our battlefields may be Democrats and Republicans and Independents,
but they have fought together
and bled together
and some died together under the same proud flag.
They have not served a Red America or a Blue America—
they have served the United States of America.

October 22, 2008
Richmond, VA

Throughout his campaign, Obama used positive messages and combined the personal stories of each and every individual into a universal uniting story. In Philadelphia, too, in his speech on race in March 2008, he emphasized that he chose to run for the presidency to shape a better future for children and grandchildren, regardless of the fact that voters all have a different point of view:

> I chose to run for the presidency at this moment in history
> because I believe deeply that we cannot solve the challenges of our time
> unless we solve them together –
> unless we perfect our union by understanding that we may have different stories,
> but we hold common hopes;
> that we may not look the same and we may not have come from the same place,
> but we all want to move in the same direction –
> towards a better future for of children and our grandchildren.
>
> —"A More Perfect Union" speech, March 18, 2008, Philadelphia, PA

You might have seen, in the last examples, the way Obama uses contrasts to build a strong message. There will be more on that effective tool in chapter 27. Obama conveys his fine mediation skills in his messages. He listens with sensitivity, supports, helps others, and is patient and tolerant. He respects the different parties and their problems, maintains a neutral stand, and he is creative. Obama has an aptitude for thinking and analyzing diverse subjects, and he is skillful at conveying verbal and nonverbal messages in accordance with the situation.

He identifies the main topics that are in conflict, but also the topics that can be agreed upon.

Let's see what he said on December 17, 2010, before signing the Middle-Class Tax Cuts Bill, only a few weeks after the midterm elections in the US (and after the Democrats were defeated by the Republicans):

> Now, candidly speaking,
> there are some elements of this legislation that *I don't like.*
> There are some elements that *members of my party don't like.*
> There are some elements that *Republicans here today don't like.*
> That's the nature of compromise—
> yielding on something each of us cares about to move forward on what all of us care about.
> And right now, *what all of us care about* is growing the American economy and creating jobs for the American people.

Let's see what he said on July 30, 2011, while trying to solve the problem of the national debt crisis:

> Any solution to avoid default must be bipartisan.
> It must have the support of both parties that were sent here to represent the American people –
> not just one faction of one party.
> There are multiple ways to resolve this problem.
> Congress must find common ground on a plan that can get support from both parties in the House.

The topics that can be agreed upon must not be taken for granted. In a study conducted by Prof. Leigh Thompson from the Kellogg School of Management at Northwestern

University, it was found that people who negotiate are generally unaware of what the majority of indisputable subjects are and which interests are mutual.

In an analysis of thirty-two studies on negotiating, in which some five thousand individuals took part, Thompson and her team discovered that negotiators failed at identifying the subjects over which there was no dispute 50 percent of the time and, often, negotiations ended with both parties losing out, or they "left money on the table," even though a solution could have been reached that would have enabled both parties to win.

Therefore, if you want to persuade and influence when you communicate in a negotiation, you should develop skills to identify the mutual and contradicting interests. This skill is the basis of Obama's communication success.

When analyzing Obama's life circumstances, it is apparent how he was prepared for the role of mediator. As an individual who is both black and white, he turned his life journey into what one could call an inner mediation process, whereby he consolidated his identity into one harmonious whole, while settling the structured contradictions in his dual identity. He experienced firsthand the need to live in peace between the different extremes, without merely becoming one or the other.

He also knew how to communicate this to potential voters. In Philadelphia, in March 2008, he expanded on this in the context of his life story:

> It's a story that hasn't made me the most conventional candidate. But it is a story that has seared into my genetic makeup the idea that this nation is more than the sum of its parts—that out of many, we are truly one.

To this is added the close-knit interaction Obama created with the people on the street, while listening attentively to the issues that motivated them and by putting himself in their shoes.

All these generated in Obama the capacity to mediate between diverse segments of society and to strive for agreement and a common ground. He constantly strives to bring this mediation to every situation and every conflict he encounters, in the USA and the world over.

In the previous chapter, we briefly mentioned the four perceptual positions, and we saw how Obama puts himself in the other person's shoes while applying the second perceptual position. However, Obama also applies the fourth perceptual position, the mediating position.

In this position, one puts on mental glasses that focus on what is common to us all.

According to this position, we are all one entity. This is a position shared by all parties, which includes the contents and values that everyone agrees upon. It is also the position that provides inspiration and motivation to rise above the differences, the social classes, and the gaps between the parties, and to observe the full and overall picture. *When you communicate from the fourth perceptual position, people feel you magnetize them, and see you as a leader with charisma.*

Me, Myself and I

Most people are unaware of the words they use. When you talk to people, the words you choose disclose your point of view.

Do you, like many others, often say the word "I" without even knowing it? Do you focus on yourself, or are you focused on others? No one likes to listen to someone who is focused exclusively on him or herself.

If you want to persuade others, it is important you know that, once the words have left your mouth, they no longer belong to you. Neither, undoubtedly, does their interpretation. The way in which your words are understood is affected by the experiences, concerns, fears, hopes, beliefs, and biases of the people that hear you.

Remember: it's not what you say. It's what people hear, see, and feel!

One of the prominent trademarks of applying the *fourth perceptual position* is the use of the words "We," "All of us," and "Together"—words that Obama often uses in his speeches and media appearances. An architect of words, Obama knows this very well, and he makes sure his speech writers are focused on the people he wants to lead—those he wants to influence, persuade, and sell his ideas to, as a salesman selling products or services. Let's see some examples where the fourth perceptual position has been applied:

In his presidential inaugural address, in January 2009, Obama used the word "We" sixty-two times, as opposed to only the few times he used the word "I." If it seems simple to do, listen to the people around you. You will discover that, in most cases, they do the exact opposite. If you do it Obama's way, you will connect faster and better with your target audience.

In Obama's first speech as president of the United States to a Joint Session of Congress, once again he used words that focused for the most part on his audience, not himself.

Obama said the word "us" nineteen times, "you" forty times, "ours" one hundred and fifteen times, and "we" one hundred and thirty-eight times, compared to the number of times he said "I" (fifteen) and "me" (seven) in a speech that was six thousand words long. Sport commentators say, "The numbers don't lie." The same goes for the statistics in terms of the frequency of use of different words.

It sounds simple, but bear in mind how often you hear speeches in which the speaker or lecturer used the word "I" many times. How many times have you come across marketing and sales people who speak from their perspective alone, and how many times a week have *you* said "I" when you've spoken?

Obama knows to lead without saying "I, I, I," which creates antagonism. To be influential, every word matters. Every word has a positive or negative effect. Obama examines the words he uses with a magnifying glass, and this helps him be influential.

The use of the words "we" and "us" can be seen many times in other speeches he has made, even before he was elected president:

> **We** are the United States of America.
> **We** are a nation that's faced down war and depression, great challenges, and great threats.
> And at each and every moment,
> **we** have risen to meet these challenges—
> not as Democrats, not as Republicans, but as Americans.
>
> —October 22, 2008 Richmond, VA

Obama's life taught him that what unites people is stronger than what divides them. Remember—he was elected to be the President of the *United* States of America, not the *divided* states…

This insight became one of the central messages in his speeches and a cornerstone of his political philosophy, as he wrote in the foreword of his book *The Audacity of Hope*:

> A tradition based on the simple idea that we have a stake in one another, and that what binds us together is greater than what drives us apart, and that if enough people believe in the truth of that proposition and act on it, then we might not solve every problem, but we can get something meaningful done.

Despite the differences and the gaps, Obama believes most people all over the world share common dreams, common hopes, and a shared destiny. This way of speaking mesmerizes people, even those who dismissed him in the past. And this is what he says to readers of *The Audacity of Hope*.

> And we will need to remind ourselves, despite all our differences, just how much we share: common hopes, common dreams, a bond that will not break.

Obama applies his mediation skills to virtually all controversial subjects. He manages to isolate the issues that form the core of the conflict on the one hand, and focus on everyone's common interests on the other. He regards the power to bridge the gaps and to rise above the differences as not only an important skill, but also an integral part of the promise of American democracy and a vital component of proper leadership.

Obama's secret is that he knows how to use the skill of mediation, even when it comes to sensitive subjects such as abortions and same-sex relationships. He demonstrated this well at the Democratic National Convention in 2008:

> **We may not agree** on abortion,
>
> **but surely we can agree** on reducing the number of unwanted pregnancies in this country.
>
> The reality of gun ownership may be different for hunters in rural Ohio than for those plagued by gang violence in Cleveland,
>
> but don't tell me we can't uphold the Second Amendment while keeping AK-47s out of the hands of criminals.
>
> **I know there are differences** on same-sex marriage,
>
> **but surely we can agree** that our gay and lesbian brothers and sisters deserve to visit the person they love in the hospital and to live lives free of discrimination.

> Passions fly on immigration,
>
> but I don't know anyone who benefits when a mother is separated from her infant child or an employer undercuts American wages by hiring illegal workers.
>
> This too is part of America's promise—the promise of a democracy where we can find the strength and grace to bridge divides and unite in common effort.
>
> — "The American Promise"
Democratic National Convention
August 28, 2008, Denver, Colorado

What is Obama's communication secret when it comes to these sensitive issues? He uses a "magic formula," which he saves for issues just like these: a stylistic pattern designed to bridge gaps, and it is most effective for creating dialogue and new understandings: "We don't agree on… but we can surely agree on…"

We don't have to agree with all of resident Obama's views and decisions, but we can surely agree that he knows how to use this formula well. Can't we?

When you want to communicate and persuade effectively, you can use Obama's magic formula to change the point of reference in a conversation, as in the following example: "We don't agree on the price, but we can surely agree that quality and service are more important than anything else."

Based on his acknowledgment of differences and gaps, Obama invites his audience to prefer mediation. As early as his inaugural address, he directed a message to the enemies of America in a mediatory manner:

> We will not apologize for our way of life,
> nor will we waver in its defense,
> and for those who seek to advance their aims
> by inducing terror and slaughtering innocents,
> we say to you now that our spirit is stronger and cannot be broken;
> you cannot outlast us, and we will defeat you.
>
> For we know that our patchwork heritage is strength,
> not a weakness.

> We are a nation of Christians and Muslims, Jews and Hindus—and non-believers.
> We are shaped by every language and culture, drawn from every end of this Earth;
> and because we have tasted the bitter swill of civil war and segregation,
> and emerged from that dark chapter stronger and more united,
> we cannot help but believe that the old hatreds shall someday pass;
> that the lines of tribe shall soon dissolve;
> that as the world grows smaller,
> our common humanity shall reveal itself;
> and that America must play its role in ushering in a new era of peace.
>
> To the Muslim world, we seek a new way forward,
> based on mutual interest and mutual respect.
> To those leaders around the globe who seek to sow conflict,
> or blame their society's ills on the West—
> know that your people will judge you on what you can build,
> not what you destroy.
> To those who cling to power through corruption and deceit and the silencing of dissent,
> know that you are on the wrong side of history;
> but that we will extend a hand if you are willing to unclench your fist.
>
> —Inaugural Address, January 20, 2009, Washington, DC

Obama focuses on seeing the overall, common picture, beyond the details and differences, beyond the separation and rivalry.

Another example of the mediatory nature of Obama's words is associated with the objection to sending military forces to Iraq in 2002, long before the presidential election. Obama used this "ace in the hole" throughout the election campaign, and you can see the power in his words when he speaks as a mediator between the people that supported going to Iraq and those who objected:

> There are patriots who opposed the war in Iraq and patriots who supported it.
> We are one people, all of us pledging allegiance to the stars and stripes,
> all of us defending the United States of America.

—Keynote Address at the 2004 Democratic National Convention, July 27, 2004

When these words are read, one can understand that Obama spoke like a president four years before being elected president. In this way, he communicated to people that he was suited to the position. He allowed them to imagine him as leader of the nation. This was an important move in itself, especially when the challenge was to break the psychological barrier of a president of African-American origin.

When Obama talks about the beliefs, values, and contents that are shared by all, when he rises above the differences and gaps, he creates a convenient atmosphere with which to lead his audience to a new direction of thinking: a direction of creative solutions, dialogue, and consent, a situation where there are no winners and losers. Everyone wins.

It's *Us* - not *Me*

When you want to persuade others, it's not enough to consider and focus on your own opinion.

Put yourself in the other person's shoes; understand the way he or she perceives the world. Develop your mediation capacities.

Identify the subjects at the core of the conflict, as well as the subjects that can be agreed upon.

Develop the use of the fourth perceptual position, which focuses on what all parties have in common. Specify the common subjects, contents, and values everyone agrees upon. In this way, you will evoke inspiration and motivation to rise above the differences and observe the overall picture. One of the prominent trademarks of using the fourth perceptual position is using the words "we," "all of us," and "together." Integrate these words when you communicate. Remember, what unites people is stronger than what divides them. Communication is not broadcasting your messages. As a professional communicator, you do not want to talk *at* people. You do not want to speak *to* people. You want to communicate *with* them. You want to dance with them and lead them.

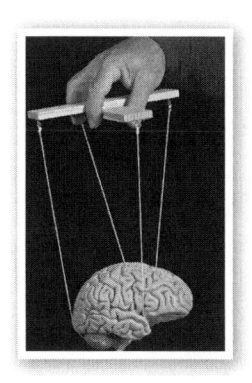

CHAPTER 4

LIKE A BALLET DANCER – HOW TO PERSUADE BY USING A FLEXIBLE TRANSITION BETWEEN POSITIONS

The three secrets we revealed in chapter 2—the power of personal experience, the power of listening, and the power of empathy—combined with the concept of mediation and focus on the common denominator, are the cornerstones of another aspect of Obama's *street smarts*: **thinking flexibility.** Thinking flexibility allows Obama to shift between the four perceptual positions and, as a result, influence people with great intensity.

If you would like to be a professional in the field of persuasion and influence, you should be familiar and adept with this skill of thinking flexibly. Observe how, in his speech in Virginia, Obama takes us through the time tunnel into the future, to future generations who will judge us in retrospect; who will assess our choices and the way we functioned when they look at us through time:

> This country and the dream it represents
> are being tested in a way that we haven't seen in nearly a century.
> And future generations will judge ours
> by how we respond to this test.
> Will they say that this was a time when America lost its way and its purpose?
> When we allowed the same divisions and fear tactics and our own petty differences
> to plunge this country into a dark and painful recession?

> Or will they say that this was another one of those moments when America overcame?
>
> When we battled back from adversity by recognizing that common stake that we have in each other's success?

Obama is a language wizard who applies diverse points of view and shifts between the four perceptual positions. He shifts with extraordinary flexibility from one position to another, based on the matter at hand, thus maximizing his capacity to influence, persuade, and lead to action.

He often speaks from within himself, and then he focuses on what he thinks, what he feels, and what he wants to do.

He often puts himself in the other person's shoes, and then focuses on the way the other feels what the other wants.

And he often analyzes the events as an observer, evaluating the situation by observing from the outside.

He also speaks primarily on behalf of everyone, while emphasizing everyone's common interests. Switching points of view enriches his ability to relate to an event and increases the quantity and quality of the information he has about that event.

One of the ways you can develop effective communication is to shift among points of view, among perceptual positions. People with the capacity to influence and communicate effectively, like Obama, are skilled at shifting between perceptual positions to create forces of motivation, persuasion, and influence.

As we mentioned, there are four perceptual positions or, as our young daughters say, four pairs of mental glasses that can be applied to look at the world. Now we will expand upon this topic.

As a communicator, the first perceptual position is related to *me* and *myself*. This is a perspective that is natural to every one of us. We see, hear, and feel events through our own eyes; we live our own personal experience. When we are in this position, we are focused on what matters to us, on what we want to accomplish, on what we believe in, on our values, and our authentic self. Egocentric people see everything from this first perceptual position. Do you let egocentric people convince you, persuade you, or sell you anything?

That's why people who are in sales understand this position, because it is, in fact, the customer's position. Your customers see the world from their perspective, through their senses and needs, and this is the way they'd like others to see it.

But if we remain fixed on this position, we will become egotistical, and we will fail to understand and motivate others.

For the most part, people do not listen to individuals who are focused on the first position (themselves) and do not want to "buy" their ideas. Obama knows this; therefore, he rarely uses the first position. He uses it mainly to tell a personal story and to persuade others that his optimism is indeed based on personal experience. This is what he did in Iowa, in May 2008:

> It's what I saw all those years ago on the streets of Chicago
> when I worked as an organizer—
> that in the face of joblessness,
> and hopelessness,
> and despair,
> a better day is still possible.
> if there are people willing to work for it,
> and fight for it,
> and believe in it.
> That's what I've seen here in Iowa.
> That's what is happening in America…

Obama also uses the first position to reveal his motives, his values, and his "credo," which led to the clincher at the end of the following paragraph:

> Throughout my life,
> I have always taken my deep and abiding love for this country as a given.
> It was how I was raised;
> it is what propelled me into public service;
> it is why I am running for president…
>
> —Florida, June 2008

The term IQ obviously refers to intelligence quotient, but a person whose "I" quotient in communication is high—meaning the number of the words "I" appears often in his or her speeches—is liable to wind up all alone.

Obama is generally focused on his listeners and conveys to them the sense that it is not he that is in the center, but it is they as well as the common good.

The second perceptual position is the perspective whereby one sees, hears, and feels the world from the other person's perspective. Therefore, one of the characteristics of applying this position is to use sentences in which the subject is the word "you." If you think and speak in this manner, you will be focused on the benefit of the other party, and you will influence him or her with greater intensity. And what is more intense than the following sentence, which Obama repeated in diverse variations many times:

> This election has never been about **me**
> It's been about **you.**

He went on to attribute the victory to the voters and not to himself, even after he was elected and gave his 2008 victory speech:

> But above all,
> I will never forget who this victory truly belongs to—
> it belongs to **you**…
> This is **your** victory.

When we revealed the concept of Obama's three basic secrets, we emphasized that the second perceptual position is manifested in the ability to put oneself in the other person's shoes and to imagine what it's like to be that person: to see through another's eyes, hear through his or her ears, and to feel what another feels. When you apply this position, your mind thinks like the other person's mind; you believe in the beliefs and values of the other person, you sense his desires, and you experience the situation as the other person experiences it. This position focuses on what's important to the other person and what he or she wants to achieve.

If you practice and apply this position correctly, you will be able to predict how the other person will react and what he or she will do. The shift to the other person's position helps to create a bond and will help you attain understanding and persuasion, because when you understand the other person, you build a bridge between both of you, a bridge that can be crossed to get to the other person's side.

Adopting the second perceptual position, whereby you are focused on the other person, also ensures you will value the other person, as we always tell participants in our sales seminars: "Selling is something you do *with* people, not something you do *to* them."

A professional "ballet dancer in communication," Obama very often uses the magic word "you." But this is not a natural talent, as one would think. Obama learned this tip the hard way. When he was just starting out on his political path, he didn't talk this way, and people sometimes accused him of focusing on himself, rather than the voters. But Obama, the master of listening to feedback, and a man who believes in consistent learning and constant improvement, adopted this secret the moment he realized its strength. During his 2008 election campaign, he made a point of saying in virtually every conversation:

"This election is not about me, it's about *you*"

The great communicator President Ronald Reagan also used the magic word "you" when, as a presidential candidate, he asked viewers during a televised debate: "Are *you* better off today than *you* were four years ago?"

Power Words You Want to Use

Marketing and advertising people use a list of power words to sell their products. You might recognize a few of these words:

Money, health, easy, save, results, proven, love, guarantee, safety, new, and…you.

The word considered the most influential is "you."

Companies adopt these words when they design campaigns or slogans that accompany the products and services they sell.

You will want to use some of these words if you want to communicate with power and a little magic.

You will see that using these words brings results.

It is guaranteed.

Here are more examples of how to influence by using the magic word "you". The most widely viewed video website in the world is YouTube; in September 2009, Yahoo announced a new global branding with the slogan "It's YOU," and Pringles potato chips' famous slogan is "Once you pop, you can't stop."

The word "you" has a "cousin" word: your.

Let's see it in action. Rio de Janeiro won the rights to host the 2016 Olympic Games, after beating out Chicago, Tokyo, and Madrid. Rio's slogan used the magic word, "Live *your* passion." M&Ms differentiated their marketing message with the slogan that includes the word twice, "Melts in your mouth, not in your hand."

When *you* use *"you"* and focus on the second perceptual position, *you* often make people in the audience feel as if *you* are reading their minds. This is what Obama does and with great success. Let's see an example from a speech in Virginia that illustrates this well:

> This is one of those moments.
> I realize *you're* cynical and fed up with politics.
> I understand that *you're* disappointed and even angry with *your* leaders.
> *You* have every right to be.

Here, too, you can see how Obama refers precisely to the objections, but he communicates what his audience feels. When you feel you are understood and that someone feels what you feel, you are willing to listen and open up to the messages directed at you.

Obama's intimate familiarity of the details and his ability to feel his audience is another secret of his influence. They help him lead the listeners to new, effective ways of thinking.

Obama made extensive use of the second perceptual position at the 2008 Democratic National Convention. He understood that people do not want to hear someone constantly saying "I, I, I." Therefore, his emphasis was, of course, on "you."

Note the power of the words every time Obama focuses on his listeners.

> For eighteen long months,
> you have stood up, one by one,
> and said enough to the politics of the past.
> You understand that in this election,

> the greatest risk we can take is to try the same old politics with the same old players and expect a different result.
> You have shown what history teaches us—that at defining moments like this one, the change we need doesn't come from Washington.
> Change comes to Washington.
> Change happens because the American people demand it—because they rise up and insist on new ideas and new leadership, a new politics for a new time.

If you can set your ego aside, like Obama, you will be able to focus on your listeners. Why is this effective? Because the other party feels better when you speak *from* his or her side, not *to* him or her, and surely not *above* him or her. The sense of togetherness, the sense you are understood, is the basis for changing perceptions and leading people from point A to point B.

If you want to get someone to see something from your perspective, first you must prove to him or her that you see things from his or her perspective.

Now, let's move forward with our ballet class: the third perceptual position is the position of observer, witnessing the event from the perspective of a fly on the wall in a room where people communicate with one another. This is an objective position, devoid of emotional involvement. As a result, it enables the viewer to reassess the situation. Anyone can become an observer and observe everything from the outside, even oneself.

If you position yourself in the third perceptual position and become an observer, you can see and hear yourself and others from an external standpoint.

This position allows you to express an opinion, give advice, judge, and evaluate.

Once you adopt this position, you will transform from an involved party into one of consultant or critic. From this position, you will be able to communicate creative ideas and solutions you never thought about before, and offer new and surprising modes of action.

Having said that, most people don't have the knowledge, training, and experience to put on the mental glasses of the third position. Therefore, they are forced to use a judge or mediator to solve problems and conflicts.

If a transition from the first position to the second position can be compared to the transition from standing in an upright position with legs closed to standing with legs open, then the transition to the third position can be compared to doing the splits.

And to be so flexible—one must practice.

The capacity to look at things from the outside enables you to detach yourself from the emotional situation you are in when trying to persuade others and influence them, especially in conflict situations. It enables you to be very creative, to involve less ego and emotions and be more matter of fact. When you observe from the outside, you can listen to the communication among the involved parties and analyze the situation in a reasonable fashion, without the pressure you feel when you are involved.

This skill is useful in all sorts of communication, and you will want to use it wisely during negotiations. Any time you feel you have reached a dead end, this is an opportunity to adopt the third position of the observer, to stop and ask yourself, "What would a wise consultant say if he could see us now?" "How would 'the fly' suggest we solve the conflict?"

Obama is an excellent role model for using the third perceptual position in communication. He demonstrates the verbal flexibility of a ballerina in an extraordinary fashion. He makes creative use of the third position when, in his speeches, he places another figure in the position of the observer every time. Sometimes, it's the future generations who will judge us in retrospect; at other times, it's himself becoming an observer who can rise above the details and see the big picture, while analyzing and assessing it. Sometimes, he observes past events; at other times, he observes present events. Sometimes, he simply observes himself from the outside and the manner in which he is coming across to the audience.

In September 2009, at the beginning of the school year, President Obama addressed the students of the United States and inspired them. He used the *third perceptual position* and asked them:

> What will a president who comes here in twenty, fifty, or one hundred years say about what all of you did for this country?

A year earlier, one week before the presidential election, Obama integrated this third position in a speech as he observed from the fly's view the past and present events and suggested improvements:

> That is why what we have lost in these last eight years cannot be measured by lost wages or bigger trade deficits alone.

> What has also been lost is the idea that, in this American story, each of us has a role to play.
> Each of us has a responsibility to work hard and look after ourselves and our families, and each of us has a responsibility to our fellow citizens.
> That's what's been lost these last eight years—our sense of common purpose, of higher purpose.
> And that's what we need to restore right now.

In another opportunity, three weeks before the 2008 presidential election, Obama examined the American story throughout history with the *third perceptual position*:

> We have seen our share of hard times.
> The American story has never been about things coming easy—it's been about rising to the moment when the moment is hard;
> About rejecting panicked division for purposeful unity;
> About seeing a mountaintop from the deepest valley.
> That's why we remember that some of the most famous words ever spoken by an American came from a president who took office in a time of turmoil…

Then he quoted President Roosevelt's famous phrase:

> The only thing we have to fear is fear itself.

As an observer placed at the third position, Obama can study himself from the outside, see his shortcomings, and incorporate them into his speech:

> I realize that I am not the likeliest candidate for this office.
> I don't fit the typical pedigree,
> and I haven't spent my career in the halls of Washington…
>
> — Speech at the 2008 Democratic National Convention

Obama knows that to influence and persuade people, they should hear what they think or what they talk about among themselves, thus creating credibility and leading to a change in position.

In his 2008 victory speech, Obama also combined the principles of the *third position* in a way that was music to the listeners' ears: he passed the baton on to the future generations (even into the 22nd century!), to his and the audience's children, and in fact invited the listeners to use their judgment:

> America, we have come so far.
> We have seen so much.
> But there is so much more to do.
> So tonight, let us ask ourselves—
> if our children should live to see the next century;
> if my daughters should be so lucky to live as long as Ann Nixon Cooper,
> what change will they see?
> What progress will we have made?

Obama didn't miss an opportunity to use this ever-important principle in the last words of his inaugural address (January 20, 2009), as well:

> Let it be said by our children's children that, when we were tested, we refused to let this journey end, that we did not turn back nor did we falter; and with eyes fixed on the horizon and God's grace upon us, we carried forth that great gift of freedom and delivered it safely to future generations.

This part of his speech demonstrates the way to use the third position in order to have a great impact on how people think without creating a strong objection to the idea.

Here is what Obama suggested to his supporters who attended the 2008 Democratic National Convention, knowing his words would be televised, knowing his speech would get millions of hits online thus affecting the minds—and actions at the polls—of millions of potential voters:

> Yes, government must lead on energy independence,
> but each of us must do our part to make our homes and businesses more efficient.
> Yes, we must provide more ladders to success for young men who fall into lives of crime and despair.
> But we must also admit that programs alone can't replace parents;
> that government can't turn off the television and make a child do her homework;
> that fathers must take more responsibility for providing the love and guidance their children need.
> Individual responsibility and mutual responsibility—
> that's the essence of America's promise.

Obama's flexibility—like a ballet dancer, moving elegantly and shifting from *first position* to *second position* to *third position*—enables him to influence the minds and hearts of his listeners. You should do the same. Remember, this book is not about Obama's success. It's about *yours*.

As an individual who applies this thinking and stylistic flexibility, Obama joins the prestigious club of geniuses, who used the transition between perceptual positions to enhance their work processes.

Albert Einstein used the second and third positions to develop the Theory of Relativity. He imagined what it would be like to ride on the end of a light beam at 300,000 kilometers per second (or to be precise, 299,792,458 meters per second), while "another Einstein" observed him from the outside, from the third position. This was the basis for his Theory of Relativity, which resulted in a change in how the structure of the universe is perceived.

Walt Disney also used these techniques when he created his films of imagination. Disney would switch mental places with his audience. He would even put himself in the shoes of the figures he created and speak in their voices. In fact, the entire legendary service philosophy of Disneyland and Disneyworld theme parks, which places the customer or "the guest" at the center, is a result of thinking from different perceptual positions. For example, two peepholes are installed in the doors of Disney's hotel rooms: one peephole at standard height and the other significantly lower, so that children can look through and see who is in the corridor. You see, the third position adds magic to the Magic Kingdom.

The *fourth perceptual position*, which Obama uses often, is unlike the other three positions, because it is not experienced through the eyes of one person but represents the collective "us." It aims at the position everyone has in common, the agreement of the collective for the collective.

Obama applies the fourth position to inspire his audience to rise above the differences and see the overall picture shared by all.

Obama uses the fourth perceptual position well, and it is very dominant in his speeches. Thus, he establishes a close relationship (or "rapport," which we will discuss in Chapter 17) with the audience, and a mutual dependency between himself and the audience. In October 2008 he spoke of this, using "together" in a rhythmic litany:

> Now it falls to us.
> Together, we cannot fail.
> Together, we can overcome the broken policies and divided politics of the last eight years.
> Together, we can renew an economy that rewards work
> and rebuilds the middle class.
> Together, we can create millions of new jobs and deliver on the promise of health care
> you can afford and education that helps your kids compete.
> We can do this if we come together;
> if we have confidence in ourselves and each other;
> if we look beyond the darkness of the day
> to the bright light of hope that lies ahead.
> Together, we can change this country and change this world.

Obama's precise and persuasive use of the fourth position is made possible thanks to the other positions: the first position, through which he experiences events personally; the second position, through which he listens to others and experiences events through their eyes; and the third position, through which he observes the situation through the eyes of a fly on the wall. In fact, being familiar with the other three positions is what prepares Obama for the precise application of the fourth position. How?

When I know what matters to me and what I feel, and when I know what matters to you and what you feel, and when I understand what we must all do for our future—then I can state what our common interests are and what we can agree upon.

🔍 From Position to Position to Position

We now know there are four perceptual positions and that the effective secret of influence is based upon the flexibility and balance of their implementation.

Professor Dan Ariely, author of the bestseller *Predictably Irrational: The Hidden Forces That Shape Our Decisions,* emphasizes in his book the important of acknowledging that we all have biases and that we are trapped within our own viewpoints which partially blind us to the truth. Therefore, when it comes to confrontations or different approaches and viewpoints, we need a neutral, third point of view.

Do not be tempted to remain in the first position, which is natural for you, in which you see, hear, and feel the world only through your senses and from within the model of your outlook of the world, even though it is natural for you.

Leave this position and shift to the second position, where you see, hear, and feel the world through another person's eyes.

If you want to influence and change other people's attitudes and behavior, it is not important how you perceive the world. It is important how others perceive it.

Ask yourself how the person who hears you views the issues at hand, how he or she thinks, what he or she believes in, what matters to him or her, how he or she feels, and how your words will sound to him or her. That will assist you in delivering audience-centered communication.

Shift to the third position as well, where you can observe the events from the sidelines, see and hear everything from the outside in a neutral way. Though this does not happen naturally, though it is not necessarily easy to be an observer (or a fly on the wall), this is a position that will enable you to see things in a different light and enjoy new and creative modes of action.

Ask yourself: Do I understand the big picture? Can I discern the patterns and analyze the situation in a reasonable manner? Am I free from the pressure I feel when I experience the situation from within?

And, like Obama, use the fourth position to emphasize the common interests to inspire your audience to rise above the differences and see the overall picture—that which is shared by all of you.

The more you develop your ability to shift with flexibility among the various positions, the more you will maximize your capacity to persuade and influence others. Communicate like a ballerina and you will be a communication star.

Some people consider Obama a "magician," a born charismatic leader. But reality teaches us that Obama became a communication virtuoso and one of the finest speakers in the world today thanks to hard work and continuous practice during his entire adult life.

Our professional experience shows that though these secrets are basic and simple, many people do not use them, and that's the challenge we need to overcome to become better at communication.

To be an effective communicator, you should use some NLP (Neuro-Linguistic Programming) principles. Again, President Obama's speeches will help us to demonstrate how to do it the right way.

In the second part of the book, we will delve deeper into Obama's mind. We invite you to don your surgeon's robe and enter with us into Obama's head.

PART TWO
Obama's Brain Power

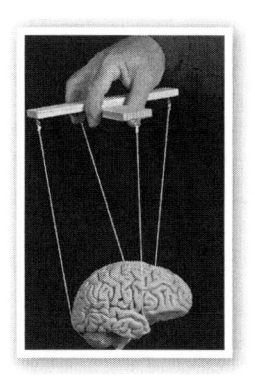

CHAPTER 5

IT'S ALL IN YOUR MIND — YOU ARE WHAT YOU THINK

> "I've missed more than nine thousand shots in my career. I've lost almost three hundred games. Twenty-six times, I've been trusted to take the game winning shot and missed. I've failed over and over and over again in my life. And that is why I succeed."
>
> —**Michael Jordan**

It has been said that Obama is the Michael Jordan of the communication game. So, after becoming familiar with Obama's street smarts, as well as the basic characteristics of his personality (which are evident in each and every one of his interactions with people), we will delve into his inner world, to examine not only what he does, but how he thinks. And like other secrets of his, which we reveal in this book, once you become acquainted with them, *you too can adopt a different way of thinking*.

After more than twenty years of work in which we trained Fortune 500 executives as well as presidents and CEOs of worldwide companies, we reached the conclusion that to achieve actual results, it is not enough to learn how to speak correctly. One must also learn to think effectively.

Perhaps you are already familiar with some of the information you have read in this book.

Perhaps you have even practiced some of the ideas, yet you still feel you are not getting it right but you would like to.

Why? The reason is simple. The capacity to speak and present well does not depend solely on the nonverbal communication that supports the words, but on the thought process that accompanies the words as well.

The thought process impacts our lives in many areas. If you want to learn to play basketball, you can purchase the tools of the game and watch videos of legendary NBA players such as Michael Jordan over and over again. You can watch how he moves, dribbles, and shoots the ball into the basket. Yet, it is unlikely you will turn into Michael Jordan, even if you meticulously mimic all his moves.

Why not? What makes the difference? Many people will say there are genetic differences that set you apart, and that is true. But there is another decisive factor that helps people excel in their field. It is what goes on in the minds of those experts and professionals while they are doing what they do so well.

The thoughts that went through Michael Jordan's head while he was playing—his mental preparation, the thoughts that accompanied him during the game, his emotional state of mind during the last minutes of the game, the things he said to himself in the last seconds when he knew the outcome of the game depended on his shot—all these made the difference.

After a professional analysis of Obama's speeches, we can say that technical improvement in the influence of speaking and communication skills is not enough. Only when it is combined with a fundamental change in thought patterns can significant improvement in the capacity to persuade and influence be obtained. Therefore, it is interesting to discover how Obama thinks when he is speaking and motivating people towards change.

> What is the vision before his eyes?
> How does he perceive his identity?
> What does he believe in?
> How does he perceive reality?
> What really matters to him?
> What are his guiding values?
> What are his true capabilities?
> What are his thinking strategies?
> And how do all these support his communication capacity and enhance it?

If you know how Obama thinks, you will be able to adopt his thought patterns and improve the effectiveness of your communication with others, whether it is interpersonal communication, communication with a large audience, a speech, or a TV or online appearance.

When we watch Obama speaking and witness the way he mesmerizes people and sweeps them towards change, with the right tools we can analyze his modus operandi, such as conveying messages through personal stories, metaphors, or phrase repetition.

However, this is not the way we are exposed to his inner world; his thoughts, beliefs, emotions, and internal dialogue.

We believe adopting Obama's style of success should include not only the tools he uses, but his manner of thought as well. It is vital to think like Obama in order to speak at a professional level such as his.

Honing these skills can allow one to procure a specific achievement or an achievement limited in volume, but it is not a sufficient requisite to achieve a significant, long-term goal. Only honing one's skills, combined with a significant change in thought patterns, can generate these achievements.

You could say Obama's overt tactics, the secrets that many people have analyzed in articles, books, and the media, are but the tip of the iceberg. It is only the external layer that is relatively easy to see. And, as we know, part of the iceberg that is hidden under water is much larger than the part that is visible.

Obama's thought patterns are part of his inner world, and they are conveyed externally in the words he says. When Obama speaks, his words come from deep within an authentic inner world. Therefore, they are persuasive, and they motivate people to take action and make changes.

What we see and hear on the surface is strongly connected to what's inside, and the speech is more convincing and effective because of it. The energy that is conveyed through the words and the body language of the speaker in this case is stronger and much more convincing, and here is where the difference lies.

To lead to a change and to influence others, one should first change his or her thought patterns.

NLP as a Tool to Attain Goals

When discussing a change in thought patterns, we need to mention NLP (Neuro-Linguistic Programming). This method, devised by Richard Bandler, a psychotherapist and computer expert, and John Grinder, a linguist, enables all individuals to improve their relationship with their neurological and linguistic systems and to harness them toward a desired result in a short period of time.

The method focuses on understanding the way in which the brain picks up messages through the senses and translates them into experiences. This is done by diagnosing language usage patterns in internal and external communication, understanding the relationship between these patterns and thoughts, emotions and behaviors, and teaching the brain to change patterns and act in new ways that will achieve the desired result.

The brain can be compared to a computer. Just as a computer can be programmed, so too can our brains be "programmed" or re-taught. This is what NLP is about, among other things. To understand learning and changing processes and to support them, NLP talks about "logical levels," which are thought levels in different layers that characterize every person individually. The logical levels are organized in the shape of a pyramid, from the most abstract, conceptual level to the most practical and concrete level. The highest level of the pyramid is the vision level. The identity level is next, and beliefs and values level is located below. The inner capabilities and more practical behavior levels are situated right below that, and finally, we have the tangible-environment level.

Here are the levels of the pyramid:

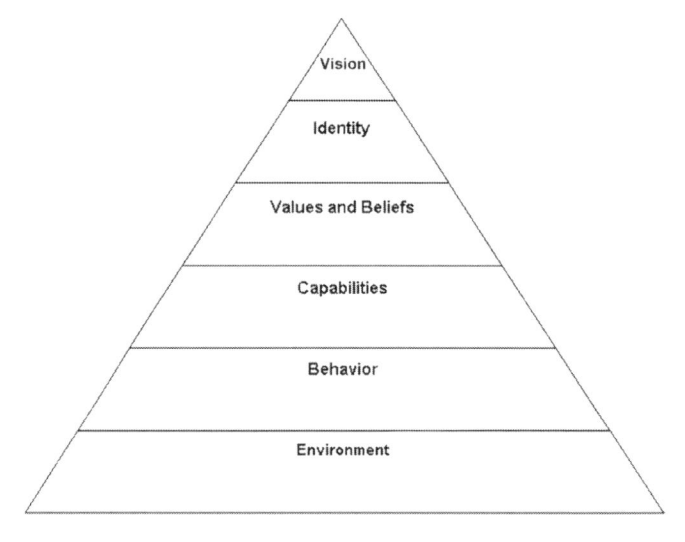

Similar to Maslow's hierarchy of needs, here, too, there is a connection among the diverse levels of the pyramid. The logical levels are connected to one another in a causative-logical relationship, and they mutually affect one another. They can support one another and act in harmony, but they can also contradict one another and act in an uncoordinated manner. A change in one logical level influences additional logical levels, and the more the change occurs on a higher logical level, the more far-reaching the ramifications are on the other logical levels. Confused? You won't be after reading a few more pages.

What can you say about someone who uses the word "difficult" in every other sentence he or she says? What can you say about someone who uses the word "risk" many times, as opposed to someone who often uses the word "opportunity?"

A lot can be learned about an individual's logical levels if you listen to the words he or she says and the language he or she uses. The words disclose an individual's inner world and his or her most profound layers of thought.

Social psychologist James Pennebaker, Head of the Department of Psychology at the University of Texas in Austin, found that the verbal way in which we express our thoughts discloses facets of our personality and character. His findings can be summarized with these five words:

You are what you say!

Next, we will see how Obama's logical levels–as disclosed in an analysis of dozens of his speeches and the first two books he wrote–work in harmony, enabling him to express himself in an optimal way when he speaks, and to persuade with power and a little magic.

We will also see how Obama influences his listeners' logical levels. He "programs" their minds in a manner that paves the way for change, and he does this by redesigning their logical levels and opening up the "obstructions" on the way to change.

Every adult who watches a magic show knows that behind each supposedly impossible trick there are secrets, and often the secrets are very simple. Let's reveal more secrets of the "wizard of communication," President Barack Obama.

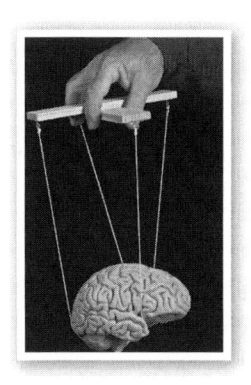

CHAPTER 6

A Wall or a Cathedral – Obama's Vision

There is a story, set in medieval times, that tells of a traveler who comes upon three stonemasons. He asks each in turn, "What are you doing?" The first answers, without hesitation, "I am cutting this stone." The second, who appears to be doing the identical job makes a gesture with his hand and says, "I am completing the wall." The third stonemason, who again seems to be doing the same job, slowly raises his eyes to the sky and says, "*I am building a Cathedral.*"

The third answer demonstrates the power of a vision. The last stonemason feels that he is a part of something bigger than himself.

Obama knows that a vision is like a magnet. It draws people toward it. The vision takes them from the past and commits them to the future.

To understand how Obama thinks, it's best to begin at the highest logical level on the pyramid: vision.

When Obama set out on his journey–when many weren't even aware of his existence, and many others didn't know how to pronounce his name–he was already speaking in terms of a vision.

Exactly one year before the polls opened, he said the following:

> I run to give my children and their children the same chances that someone, somewhere gave me…

and I run to keep the promise of the United States of America alive,
for all those who still hunger for opportunity,
and thirst for equality
and long to believe again.

—Spartanburg, South Carolina, November 3, 2007

Based on these words, it is easy to discern that Obama is a man of vision. He lives and acts for a higher purpose, a purpose that is greater than himself. He conveys to his listeners that he is not running for election for the respect and status of being president of the United States, but to perform the hard work the job entails. Everything he does, says, and strives for is derived from that vision—and herein lies his strength. He acts not only for himself, but also for everyone who hears him and for future generations.

A vision is one of the main characteristics of people who excel in different walks of life. A life with a vision, and striving to realize that vision, enhances an individual's ability to function and perform and to realize a greater part of his or her potential.

People need to be a part of something greater than themselves, beyond time and place. Obama calls this "a higher purpose" or "the spirit of service." To connect to these people, Obama unites them to a vision he believes everyone should have. And when he uses the various perceptual positions, combined with his vision, his words have as electrifying an effect. Here's an example of Obama's elegant prose that immediately grabs the attention of the audience ("Back to School" speech, September 2009):

> And this isn't just important for your own life and your own future.
>
> What you make of your education will decide nothing less than the future of this country.
>
> What you're learning in school today will determine whether we as a nation can meet our greatest challenges in the future.
>
> You'll need the knowledge and problem-solving skills you learn in science and math to cure diseases like cancer and AIDS, and to develop new energy technologies and protect our environment.

You'll need the insights and critical thinking skills you gain in history and social studies to fight poverty and homelessness, crime and discrimination, and make our nation more fair and more free.

You'll need the creativity and ingenuity you develop in all your classes to build new companies that will create new jobs and boost our economy.

We need every single one of you to develop your talents, skills, and intellect so you can help solve our most difficult problems.

If you don't do that—if you quit on school—you're not just quitting on yourself,

you're quitting on your country.

Read his words again to see how he combines different tools to create an impact: extensive use of the second-person plural (you); short paragraphs; repetition of expressions (you will need); creating a vision for students (and their parents), whereby the graduating students will join the circle of voters in 2012; and linking the personal vision to the national vision—solution of significant internal and global problems. Students who hear these messages may later relate Obama's words to their studies just as a worker laying bricks to build a cathedral!

The presidential inaugural speech provides an excellent opportunity to express a vision. It's easy for Obama because he thought in terms of *vision* from a very young age, from the moment he decided "to make something of himself." In his 2009 presidential inaugural speech he said:

As we consider the road that unfolds before us,
we remember with humble gratitude those brave Americans who,
at this very hour, patrol far-off deserts and distant mountains.
They have something to tell us,
just as the fallen heroes who lie in Arlington whisper through the ages.
We honor them not only because they are guardians of our liberty,
but because they embody the spirit of service;
a willingness to find meaning in something greater than themselves.
And yet, at this moment—a moment that will define a generation—
it is precisely this spirit that must inhabit us all.

Obama recognized that the American people had lost their way and vision, had lost the spirit that propels society forward to a better future. He identified his listeners' "obstruction" on the logical level of the vision and took steps to release it. Here is what he said just before the presidential election:

> That's what's been lost these last eight years—our sense of common purpose, of higher purpose.
> And that's what we need to restore right now.

And what is Obama's vision? What is the spirit that propels him forward and which he wants to convey to the audience? He answered this question in his inaugural speech in January 2009:

> The time has come to reaffirm our enduring spirit;
> to choose our better history;
> to carry forward that precious gift, that noble idea, passed on from generation to generation:
> the God-given promise that all are equal,
> all are free,
> and all deserve a chance to pursue their full measure of happiness…
> Let it be said by our children's children that, when we were tested,
> we refused to let this journey end,
> that we did not turn back nor did we falter;
> and with eyes fixed on the horizon and God's grace upon us,
> we carried forth that great gift of freedom
> and delivered it safely to future generations.

Obama acts and speaks from within a consolidated vision. Why is your vision so important that you want to persuade and influence? The reason is simple: because it's the way to influence your listeners to create their own personal vision! And once you've done that, you will have created a mutual attraction between you and them.

Obama plants in his listeners' ears his vision, thus influencing their highest logical level. He depicts his vision as a vision that is mutual to a nation, society, and country—a vision that propels everyone forward into the future, while overcoming difficulties and challenges. At the 2008 Democratic National Convention he expressed his vision explicitly:

It is that promise that has always set this country apart—
that through hard work and sacrifice,
each of us can pursue our individual dreams
but still come together
as one American family,
to ensure that the next generation
can pursue their dreams as well.

For Obama, the vision is what matters, and the audience has to embrace his vision in order to elect him and believe in him. Here is what he said in Virginia in 2008:

Together, we cannot fail.
Not now.
Not when we have a crisis to solve
and an economy to save.
Not when there are so many Americans
without jobs and without homes.
Not when there are families
who can't afford to see a doctor,
or send their child to college,
or pay their bills at the end of the month.
Not when there is a generation
that is counting on us
to give them the same opportunities
and the same chances
that we had for ourselves.

And here is what he said two years later, as president, on October 31, 2010, at the DNC "Moving America Forward" rally in Cleveland, Ohio:

Cleveland, the journey we began together
was never about just putting a president in the White House.
It was about building a movement for change that endures.
It was about realizing that in the United States of America,
if we are willing to fight for it,
if we're willing to work for it,
if we believe in it,
anything is possible.

When you speak with a sense of purpose, the words that come out of your mouth have a different energy, and that energy is passed on to your listeners.

Most people don't have a conscious, solidified vision. Some are not even aware of the possibility of creating a vision, and others simply fear the enormity of the task. Some cannot believe they were destined for greatness and are focused on the here and now. In some cases, the fear of creating a vision reflects the fear of failure, because when there is no vision or higher purpose, you can't fail in the attempt to attain them. Some believe they can't influence their destiny; therefore, the attempt to do so seems unnecessary.

But if you really want to influence and lead people, start at the highest logical level. Start with a vision. What is your vision?

Share Your Vision with Others

Ask yourself for whom or towards what you are striving. What is your higher purpose, a purpose higher than yourself, something beyond your routine reality?

Creating a vision will enhance not only your inner ability to persuade, but your external ability to persuade. It will move you to realize a large part of your potential and will provide more weight to what you say.

Sharing your vision will enhance other people's motivation, too. It will open a window to long-term collaboration. Since the dawn of man, people have wanted to be a part of something greater than themselves. It enhances their desire to act and fulfill themselves in a better way.

Like Obama, learn to turn your vision into a shared vision, a vision that others can believe in. Remember that you can convey messages with your words, but you can also shape the minds of your listeners and influence their logical levels. And that is communicating with power and a little magic.

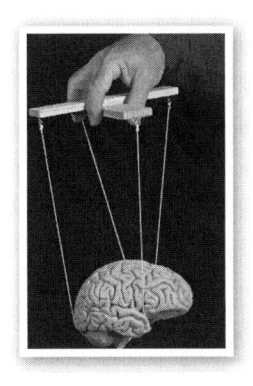

CHAPTER 7

WHO AM I – OBAMA'S IDENTITY

"We don't see things the way they are. We see things the way *we* are."

—**from the Jewish Talmud**

To understand how Obama thinks, we cannot remain at the level of the vision, which is the highest logical level on the pyramid of logical levels. Therefore, we will now move on to the second level, Obama's level of identity. In chapter one, we mentioned Mahatma Gandhi's words, according to which man is the message. Let's try to examine then, based on the message Obama conveys, who he is, what his personal identity is, and how he defines himself.

The way in which you define yourself influences your thoughts and the words you choose in every interpersonal interaction you create.

Therefore, special attention to Obama's words enables you to get to know the way in which Obama defines himself, his personal identity. Throughout the years, Obama has spoken in a manner that was compatible with his unique identity. In June 2008, he said to potential voters:

> For a young man of mixed race,
> without firm anchor in any particular community,
> without even a father's steadying hand,
> it is this essential American idea—
> that we are not constrained by the accident of birth

> but can make of our lives what we will—
> that has defined my life,
> just as it has defined the life of so many other Americans...

Obama has a complex and rich identity. He defines himself as an American who is both black and white. He regards himself as belonging to these two communities, but neither one defines him exclusively. Two great sources to get to know him "personally" are his two books. His early autobiography, *Dreams from my Father*, provides a once-in-a-lifetime opportunity to analyze his own words, without the involvement of advisors and speechwriters. And the second book he wrote himself, *The Audacity of Hope*, reveals his credo, as he wrote it.

In *Dreams from My Father*, he explicitly writes what he chose to believe in:

> My identity might begin with the fact of my race, but it didn't, couldn't, end there. At least that's what I would choose to believe

Analysis of Obama's messages indicates he is a man who designs his own destiny. He programmed, and keeps programming, his mind as a tool for his meteoric success. He is a proud American who defines himself in America's space of opportunities.

Obama believes he is not a victim of fate or arbitrary life circumstances. And this is also the identity he wishes to convey to his listeners.

One of his secrets of thought is the belief that being black is an identity to be proud of. He was raised on the perception that "black is beautiful," it is strong, and possesses a unique destiny.

He described this in *Dreams from My Father*:

> To be black was to be the beneficiary of a great inheritance, a special destiny, glorious burdens that only we were strong enough to bear. Burdens we were to carry with style. More than once, my mother would point out, "Harry Belafonte is the best-looking man on the planet."

Obama shaped his identity in just this way: a strong person with an undoubtedly unique destiny. He was the first African-American editor of the *Harvard Law Review*, and he wrote two books that became bestsellers. He was also the fifth African-American Senate member in history. Leading, being a leader, and breaking new ground comes naturally to Obama.

To understand his secrets of success, it is necessary to also understand the role of his biological father in his life, though he abandoned the family when Obama was two years old. It turns out that, while his father didn't raise him, Obama was influenced by his image, and the shaping of his identity was inspired by his father. The title of the first book he wrote, *Dreams from My Father,* emphatically testifies to the special impact his father had on his personal growth. And he also testifies to that himself in his book:

> And I realized, perhaps for the first time, how even in his absence, his strong image had given me some bulwark on which to grow up, an image to live up to, or disappoint.

Later on in the book, he expanded on his father's influence in shaping his character:

> All my life, I had carried a single image of my father, one that I had sometimes rebelled against but had never questioned, one that I had later tried to take as my own. The brilliant scholar, the generous friend, the upstanding leader— my father had been all those things

Obama, very aware of himself and the diverse logical levels, uses them to "program" the minds of listeners and lead them to realize the mutual vision. He uses the platform he was provided to redefine the identity of society in which he works.

He understands that changes in the political/national/financial reality require first a change in how society perceives its identity, and a shift from the perception of the victim to the perception of a hero who shapes his life. In his speech in Virginia, he expressed this in the messages he chose to convey:

> We are the United States of America.
> We are a nation that's faced down war and depression;
> great challenges and great threats.
> And at each and every moment,
> we have risen to meet these challenges—
> not as Democrats,
> not as Republicans,
> but as Americans.

With resolve.
With confidence.
With that fundamental belief that here in America,
our destiny is not written for us,
but by us.
That's who we are,
and that's the country we need to be right now.

Who are You?

To lead people and influence them, you should first identify yourself as a leader, as a groundbreaker, able to influence others. Know where you came from, and in this way you can shape your messages so that they are in sync with your personality.

Remember, too, that you can use the words you choose to reshape the identity of your listeners in such a way as to prepare the groundwork for the change you would like to lead.

"The value of identity of course is that so often with it comes purpose."

—**Richard R. Grant**

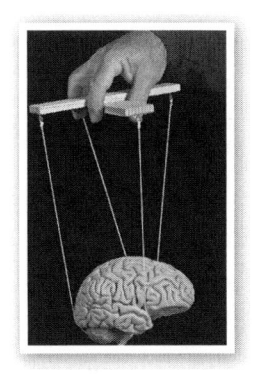

CHAPTER 8

YES, I CAN – OBAMA'S WINNING PERSONAL BELIEFS

"A failure is an event, not a person."

—**Zig Ziglar**

Let's delve deeper into Obama's mind. Now that you have an understanding of the importance of the vision and examining Obama's identity, we can continue the journey into the world of beliefs that shape Obama's world. And since he is the president of the United States, his beliefs and thoughts undoubtedly influence the entire world. The term "beliefs" in this context doesn't mean religious beliefs, but thought patterns, things Obama believes in, "laws" according to which he acts.

Early in his career, when he had no assistants, Obama wrote his speeches by himself. Today, he presumably doesn't write them on his own (though he once told Jon Favreau, his chief speechwriter at the White House, not to worry if he can't always find the right words, because he'll be able to fill in the blanks).

However, Obama makes sure his beliefs are explicitly expressed in his speeches–another way he influences his listeners. He aspires to persuade others to adopt these beliefs, so it will be easier to galvanize them to his vision and to the challenges along the way.

Consider how he talked about his beliefs while speaking at Kalamazoo Central High School Commencement, on June 7, 2010:

> First, understand that your success in life won't be determined just by what's given to you, or what happens to you, but by what you do with all that's given to you; what you do with all that happens to you;
> how hard you try;
> how far you push yourself;
> how high you're willing to reach.
> True excellence only comes with perseverance.
> This wasn't something I really understood when I was your age.
> My father, some of you know, left my family when I was two years old.
> I was raised by a single mom and my grandparents.
> And sometimes I had a tendency to goof off.
> As my mother put it, I had a tendency sometimes to act a bit casual about my future.
> Sometimes I was rebellious.
> Sometimes I partied a little too much.
> Oh, yes, yes, this is a cautionary tale…
> But after a few years, after I was living solely on my own and I realized that living solely for my own entertainment wasn't so entertaining anymore,
> that it wasn't particularly satisfying anymore,
> that I didn't seem to be making much of a ripple in the world,
> I started to change my tune.
> I realized that by refusing to apply myself,
> there was nothing I could point to that I was proud of that would last.

Many people are unaware that their every action (or their disinclination to take action) is a result of a belief or a thought pattern that developed throughout the years. To know how to lead people to change their behavior, one should understand what hides behind the behavior.

Beliefs are thought patterns that are not based on reason. There are empowering beliefs which provide a basis for support, change, and growth. Beliefs such as these propel us forward. And there are restricting beliefs which block and hinder growth and change. They prevent us from moving forward.

When we analyzed Obama's resume and hundreds of his speeches, we discovered several empowering beliefs that underline Obama's ability to speak and persuade, lead, and generate change.

1. The belief that people can shape their own destiny

One of Obama's basic beliefs, which has shaped his life and prepared him to be a leader, is the belief that people can shape their own destiny.

He learned from his mother to think in this way, and this belief became a cornerstone of his political doctrine. The belief that a person can shape his or her own destiny is not an innate belief. It's a belief we must teach ourselves to live by.

In his 2009 inaugural speech Obama talked about this:

> what free men and women can achieve when imagination is joined to common purpose, and necessity to courage.

It is amazing to discover that, in his youth, Obama challenged this belief and even dragged his mother into arguments about luck versus personal accountability, as he wrote in *Dreams from My Father*:

> "Remember what that's like? Effort? Damn it, Bar, you can't just sit around like some good-time Charlie, waiting for luck to see you through."
> "A good-time what?"
> "A good-time Charlie. A loafer."
>
> I looked at her sitting there, so earnest, so certain of her son's destiny. The idea that my survival depended on luck remained a heresy to her, she insisted on assigning responsibility somewhere—to herself, to Gramps and Toot, to me. I suddenly felt like puncturing that certainty of hers, letting her know that her experiment with me had failed. Instead of shouting, I laughed.
>
> "A good-time Charlie, huh? Well, why not? Maybe that's what I want out of life. I mean, look at Gramps. He didn't even go to college."

But when Obama matured, the belief that we all shape our own destiny became his main motto in life. This belief propels him to be accountable for his life and the lives of the people around him. This is the secret that helps Obama realize his full potential and makes him a leader who can shape the destiny of a nation; who can shape a new world.

When he ran for president, he said:

> You see, the challenges we face will not be solved with one meeting in one night. Change will not come if we wait for some other person or some other time.
> We are the ones we've been waiting for.
> We are the change that we seek.
> We are the hope of those boys who have little;
> who've been told that they cannot have what they dream;
> that they cannot be what they imagine.
>
> —Chicago, IL February 5, 2008

As far as Obama is concerned, the true test of any society and nation is whether they enable the historic events to shape them or whether they take an active part in shaping history. Are they reactive or proactive? Obama identifies with any individual, group, or nation that takes action to shape their future.

Thus, he teaches his audience to think. He shapes the logical level of the audience's beliefs when he releases the "obstruction" of the dependency on fate and restores accountability to the people. He teaches them their fate wasn't written for them but shaped by them. We saw this in his speech in Virginia, but it is worthwhile reading it again in the context of Obama's empowering beliefs:

> With that fundamental belief that here in America,
> our destiny is not written for us,
> but by us.
> That's who we are,
> and that's the country we need to be right now.

Obama believes the individual shapes his own destiny, and this is also the basis for another one of his beliefs:

2. The belief that shaping one's destiny requires hard work and accountability

Shaping the destiny and reality of the individual and of society requires not only belief but hard work, effort, and determination. We tend to believe meteoric success occurs overnight. However, it often takes many years of hard work and persistence to become an overnight star. Obama's star didn't rise overnight. He too tasted the bitter tang of political losses.

He failed in his 2000 political campaign when he tried to get elected to the House of Representatives. In fact, that is where he began his intense journey of learning how to be an effective politician. Instead of talking in a Harvard-elitist manner, he realized he must speak to the people at eye level. Thus, he learned to speak with different people in different ways. This flexibility became one of his secrets.

When he started out, his diction was too good at times, and so he was perceived as an elitist, and worse—artificial. He was also perceived as "not black enough," because his mother was white, and he didn't grow up in the church areas where he addressed the congregations. Some people who heard him described him as distant and detached; at other times, he chose to use words and phrasings that didn't suit the audience to whom he was speaking. And there are many examples of interviews and appearances in the media where he didn't speak eloquently, displayed hesitancy, and used too many *um…* sounds.

But none of this stopped him. He knew that Michael Jordan, in his youth, was thrown off of his school basketball team. And Obama truly believed he could do anything. So he searched for the secrets of success. He searched for examples of successful people to inspire an audience and motivate them into action. He searched, and he found them.

Every Sunday, one can hear moving sermons at many churches. Obama began listening attentively to the preachers at the African-American churches he visited. He studied the preachers' musical rhythm and saw how the congregation reacted to them. He observed with his own eyes the magic that took place, and he said to himself that he could do that, too.

And Obama did in fact realize what he believed in—that a person can shape his own future, but he must take into account that this requires hard work and persistence.

Therefore, for a long while, he sought opportunities to speak in public. And he practiced; and practiced; and practiced.

President Ronald Reagan said leadership is 80 percent effective communication. Obama understood this when he set out on his professional path, and rehearsed his speeches many times. He even practiced the way he would get on a platform, on his own or with his wife Michelle. He learned that "all the world is a stage," and one must practice becoming a pro.

In Malcolm Gladwell's book, *Outliers: The Story of Success*, a study is described which discovered that most successful people need twenty years of preparation or ten thousand hours of practice before they conquer the peak. Examples are Bill Gates, Mozart, and many others who are considered geniuses. It turns out that their success is backed by years of hard work and persistence.

Obama didn't say to himself, "Ten thousand hours of practice? I'd better forget about it." He understood that every day in life and every hour of work were opportunities to practice, to learn, and to grow. And he acted accordingly. Obama is another proof of the accuracy of Malcolm Gladwell's study.

Where did Obama draw his strength from to practice more and more? From his system of beliefs, especially his belief that, with hard work, one can achieve anything. This is also the personal example he saw growing up in his grandparents' home.

Obama learned from presidents like Ronald Reagan, and corporate leaders, such as Ken Blanchard and Jack Welch, to thread personal stories in his speeches in order to connect to the listeners' hearts. He used this skill every time he wanted to shape other people's beliefs through his own. Here's what he said to the attendants of the 2008 Democratic National Convention:

> When I hear a woman talk about the difficulties of starting her own business, I think about my grandmother, who worked her way up from the secretarial pool to middle-management, despite years of being passed over for promotions because she was a woman.
> She's the one who taught me about hard work.
> She's the one who put off buying a new car or a new dress for herself so that I could have a better life.
> She poured everything she had into me.
> And although she can no longer travel,
> I know that she's watching tonight,
> and that tonight is her night as well.

Obama believes one must fight to bring about change. Anything can be achieved if one is willing to make an effort. But one must fight and dream. Obama adopted this basic belief of Walt Disney who said, "If you can dream it, you can do it."

He believes in being personally accountable, as well. He asks his listeners to be accountable for their areas of responsibility, such as child education. In *The Audacity of Hope,* he states this very clearly:

> Half of all teenagers can't understand basic fractions, half of all nine-year olds can't perform basic multiplication or division…I don't believe government alone can turn these statistics around. Parents have the primary responsibility for instilling an ethic of hard work and educational achievement in their children.

Obama believes the future can be shaped with hard work, but it cannot be done alone. And this leads us to another of his beliefs:

3. The belief in his ability and the ability of others to generate change together

There is not one individual who was exposed to Obama's election campaign who does not remember the message, "Yes, we can." This message stems from Obama's basic belief that anything is possible.

In a speech in New Hampshire in January 2008, a speech that is considered one of his finest, Obama reiterated this belief several times:

> For when we have faced down impossible odds; when we've been told that we're not ready, or that we shouldn't try, or that we can't, generations of Americans have responded with a simple creed that sums up the spirit of a people. Yes, we can. It was a creed written into the founding documents that declared the destiny of a nation. Yes, we can. It was whispered by slaves and abolitionists as they blazed a trail toward freedom through the darkest of nights. Yes, we can. It was sung by immigrants, as they struck out from distant shores and pioneers who pushed westward against an unforgiving wilderness. Yes, we can. It was the call of workers who organized; women who reached for the ballot; a president who chose the moon as our new frontier; and a King who took us to the mountaintop and pointed the way to the Promised Land. Yes, we can, to justice and equality. Yes, we can, to opportunity and prosperity. Yes, we can heal this nation. Yes, we can repair this world. Yes, we, can.
>
> —Nashua, New Hampshire, January 8, 2008

We have seen that Obama has a strong belief in his ability and in society's ability to bring about change. As someone who understands that true change begins on the streets, with the people who make up society, Obama makes sure to introduce this empowering thought pattern deep into the logical level of his listeners' beliefs and values. Not only I can, but you can, too. We can.

He did this as early as 2004, when he wasn't even a presidential candidate, in the keynote speech at the Democratic National Convention, and continued to do so a week before the presidential election. This is what he said in Ohio in October 2008:

> I ask you to believe—not just in my ability to bring about change,
> but in yours. I know this change is possible.
> Because I have seen it over the last twenty-one months.
> Because in this campaign,
> I have had the privilege to witness what is best in America.

You can truly see how Obama "programs" the mind of his listeners. He invites the people in his audience to believe, not only in his capability as a leader, but in their own capabilities and in the future they can build together. Here is a message he repeated many times in similar ways:

> I ask you to believe—to believe in yourselves, in each other,
> and in the future we can build together.

He incorporates the message "together, we can" in his speeches and, thus, compliments each of his listeners and creates a Pygmalion effect which turns anticipation into reality.

In the 2008 Democratic National Convention, he stirred up the audience by saying:

> America, we are better than these last eight years. We are a better country than this.

The belief in shaping the future, combined with hard work, determination, and joint effort, leads us to the fourth belief that underlines Obama's behavior:

4. The belief in better days

Obama believes tomorrow will be better, that the future will bring good tidings, hope, welcomed change, no matter how difficult today is.

As early as *Dreams from My Father*, he described these thoughts fifteen years before becoming president.

> The audacity of hope! I still remember my grandmother, singing in the house, "There's a bright side somewhere…don't rest till you find it…"

> That's right!

> The audacity of hope! Times when we couldn't pay the bills. Times when it looked like I wasn't ever going to amount to anything…at the age of fifteen, busted for grand larceny auto theft…and, yet, and still, my momma and daddy would break into a song…

> Thank you, Jesus…And it made no sense to me, this singing! Why were they thanking Him for all their troubles? I'd ask myself. But see, I was only looking at the horizontal dimension of their lives!...I didn't understand that they were talking about the vertical dimension! About their relationship to God! I didn't understand that they were thanking Him in advance for all that they dared to hope for in me!

Obama emphatically expressed this belief in the message underlying one word, "hope." This message was conveyed in a special poster designed for him during the 2008 presidential election.

The four basic beliefs we discussed propel Obama towards another belief, a belief on which the majority of his speeches are based:

5. The belief in the power of words to bring about change

A well-known Jewish saying determines that "Death and life are in the *power* of the tongue." Indeed, on the one hand, one wrong word or devastating sentence uttered to a child, such as "you'll never be able to…" can have an adverse effect on his or her entire life. On the other hand, words can have a positive and constructive impact.

Therefore, Obama's beliefs that pertain directly to his speech and influence capabilities are especially interesting. There is a reason Obama goes into detail in every speech and examines the influence of each word and paragraph. He believes in the power of the right words to bring about change. He believes words are not an ornament or lip service. Words create reality; they influence and change. Indeed, when Obama speaks, he influences people.

In *Dreams from My Father* he refers to the impact of words:

> I knew the score, had helped plan the script. Only, when I sat down to prepare a few notes for what I might say, something had happened. In my mind, it somehow became more than just a two-minute speech…I started to remember… the power of my father's words to transform. If I could just find the right words, I had thought to myself. With the right words everything could change.

The belief in the power of words is what generates in Obama the intensity, the energy, and the passion that comes forth in what he says. He chooses the right words with forethought–extensive forethought.

Yes, you too can use words to make a change. Personal changes to begin with, then changes in your close environment, your community, your country, and even the entire world.

One of the reasons people admire great speakers such as Barack Obama, Ronald Reagan, Bill Clinton, John F. Kennedy, Indira Gandhi, Angela Merkel, Benazir Bhutto, Winston Churchill, Shimon Peres, Mahatma Gandhi, Martin Luther King, Jr., Nelson Mandela, and Tony Blair is the fear they themselves experience when speaking before a group, even more so in front of a large audience. People feel these speakers do something they will never be able to do. This feeling stems from restrictive belief, and this is what leads us to two more of Obama's beliefs, which are the exact opposite of this restricting belief:

6. The belief that self-confidence is the secret of success

Obama believes self-confidence is the secret of success. His grandfather used to tell him to learn from his biological father that the secret of any man's success is self-confidence.

Obama expressed this belief many times in his speeches, just as he did in the following brief message he conveyed at a speech in October 2008:

> And above all confidence—
> confidence in America,
> confidence in our economy,
> and confidence in ourselves.

Obama uses self-confidence to control his emotions. *In Dreams from My Father*, he wrote:

> That you didn't let anyone sneak up behind you to see emotions—like hurt or fear—you didn't want them to see.

Obama also believes another trait is required that should be combined with self-confidence:

7. The belief that's it's always best to be the strongest

Obama believes an individual must be strong. The strongest. It is interesting that some interpret Obama's desire to bridge gaps, to speak with enemies and colleagues, and to listen to them instead of applying strength—as a weakness. However, if you analyze Obama's overt and hidden thought process, you will understand he was raised on the notion that it is always better to be strong.

He tells a story about Lolo, his Indonesian stepfather, and put this very simply in *Dreams from My Father*:

> "Better to be strong," he said, finally, rising to his feet. "If you can't be strong, be clever and make peace with someone who's strong. But always better to be strong yourself. Always."

This belief and the previous belief that self-confidence is the secret of success can explain the strength, the determination, and the power Obama emanates when he speaks. Thanks to these beliefs, Obama is considered a man who controls his emotions, and only very rarely does he manifest his feelings.

During his 2008 presidential election campaign, he was even afforded the nickname "No Drama Obama." Obama always seems calm, someone who doesn't allow the tough questions or crises to get to him, at least outwardly. This is an example of his self-control, and his strength stems from his beliefs.

Your Brain Power

We examined seven of Obama's main empowering beliefs that are directly related to his capacity to communicate with power:

1. You can shape your own destiny.
2. Shaping your destiny will require hard work and accountability.
3. It takes teamwork to succeed.
4. The result will be positive, because the future will be better.
5. The words you choose have the power to bring about change in yourself and in others.
6. Self-confidence is the secret of success.
7. You must be stronger than others.

These empowering beliefs can be your beliefs too, if you so choose. These seven beliefs, together with Obama's vision and identity, are part of his inner program for success. If you want to make a big change in your life, learn from Obama. The secret is to examine your beliefs, get rid of the restricting beliefs, and adopt, instead, empowering beliefs.

Yes, you can. Anyone can. It all begins and ends with the way you think.

As Zig Ziglar said, "You are the only person on Earth who can use your ability."

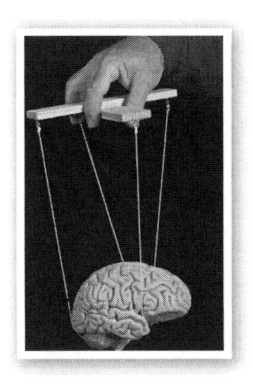

CHAPTER 9

WHAT REALLY MATTERS – OBAMA'S VALUES

"Let your tongue speak what your heart thinks"

—**Davy Crockett**

One of Obama's powerful communication secrets is the fact that he speaks about subjects which comply with his core values as a person, and the values of the USA, as he perceives them. Speaking in a manner which complies with values is perceived as authentic, and thus, it is easier to bring to the speeches the personal feelings that undoubtedly influence the listeners' feelings.

Right after Obama found out he had won the presidential election, he spoke of the importance of the values of democracy, freedom, equality, opportunities, and hope. Obama gave great weight to values. The values of the American nation are, in his view, its true source of strength. In his inaugural speech, he mentioned this to three hundred million Americans and a billion viewers who watched him worldwide:

> Recall that earlier generations faced down fascism and communism not just with missiles and tanks, but with sturdy alliances and enduring convictions. They understood that our power alone cannot protect us, nor does it entitle us to do as we please. Instead, they knew that our power grows through its prudent use; our security emanates from the justness of our cause, the force of our example, the tempering qualities of humility and restraint.

Obama speaks in the language of values. He says, in *The Audacity of Hope*, that he is aware of what is important to him and what is important to others. Values motivate him, and he motivates others with them. Obama believes people use the language of values to map their world and what really matters to them.

And what really matters to Obama? Equality, decency, integrity, democracy, freedom, equal opportunity, hard work, family, hope, and more. He considers these values the source of the entire nation's strength, the common denominator that unites people. He said this in his speech in Berlin in the summer of 2008:

> What has always united us—
> what has always driven our people;
> what drew my father to America's shores—
> is a set of ideals that speak to aspirations shared by all people:
> that we can live free from fear and free from want;
> that we can speak our minds and assemble with whomever we choose and worship as we please.

Obama believes that we must be willing to pay a price for the values we deem important. If we are not willing to pay the price, we had best ask ourselves if, indeed, we believe in these values. Here are some examples of the way in which he uses values to influence the world.

Equality

In February 2008, Obama gave a speech in Virginia where he talked about the importance of equality:

> We are the party of Jefferson,
> who wrote the words that we are still trying to heed—
> that all of us are created equal—
> that all of us deserve the chance to pursue our happiness.

Obama considers equal opportunity a supreme value. His mother instilled this value in him when he was a child, as he described in his book *The Audacity of Hope*:

> Whenever the opportunity presented itself, she would drill into me the values that she saw there: tolerance, equality, standing up for the disadvantaged.

Obama believes that all men and women were created equal; therefore, they are all entitled to an opportunity to realize their happiness. This is what he considers the essence of America, and this is the simple, undisputed truth.

Honesty and decency

In ancient Rome, statues were typical status symbols and they represented wealth, importance, and even immortality. The sculptors used stone and wax and were granted compensation and admiration. The wax was used to repair flaws in the stone and concealed these flaws until the sun, wind or time exposed them.

But the great craftsmen refused to use wax. They proudly hung on the doors of their workshops the sign "Sine Cera"—without wax. The sculptors who worked without wax guaranteed the real thing. These sculptors were sincere.

Obama grew up in a home where values in general, and honesty and decency in particular, were the center of education. He described this in detail in *Dreams from My Father*:

> It was those sorts of issues, I realize now, less tangible than school transcripts or medical services that became the focus of her lessons with me. "If you want to grow into a human being," she would say to me, "you're going to need some values…"
> Straight talk—if you didn't like the shirt I bought you for your birthday, you should have just said so, instead of keeping it wadded up at the bottom of your closet. Independent judgment—just because the other children tease the poor boy about his haircut doesn't mean you have to do it too.

Not only from his mother did Obama learn about the importance of honesty and decency. His grandparents, too, were role models in this regard. He wrote something he heard from his grandmother:

> "Your grandfather and I just figured we should treat people decently, Bar. That's all."

Here is what he said, as president, on May 22, 2011, at the AIPAC Policy Conference:

> I know that stating these principles -- on the issues of territory and security -- generated some controversy over the past few days. I wasn't surprised.

> I know very well that the easy thing to do, particularly for a president preparing for re-election, is to avoid any controversy.
>
> I don't need Rahm to tell me that. Don't need Axelrod to tell me that. But I said to Prime Minister Netanyahu, I believe that the current situation in the Middle East does not allow for procrastination. I also believe that real friends talk openly and honestly with one another.

Therefore, when you want to understand what is behind Obama's words and messages, it is important to keep in mind that the basis is equality and honesty. If your messages are sincere, you can influence with much more power.

To get a "yes"—be sincere!

In addition to sincerity, we can discuss integrity, which we see as personal honesty, decency, and uncompromising loyalty to being complete. A relationship of any kind, either with an individual or an audience of listeners, must be based on integrity. The word "integrity" is related to the word "integer," which means a whole natural number. When you are a person of integrity, it means you are a whole person. However, this does not mean you must be perfect.

Leaders don't have to be perfect, either. But whoever follows a leader would want the leader to admit his faults and mistakes, correct them immediately, and learn from them. When you communicate with people, remember to maintain your personal brand as a sincere person of integrity.

Determination, sacrifice and hard work

Barak Obama was raised on hard work, determination, and perseverance. His parents demanded he make the best of himself at every stage in life. Even his father, who was virtually absent from his life, managed to leave his mark in the short time he visited Obama. Obama wrote in his book *Dreams from My father*:

> "If the boy has done his work for tomorrow, he can begin on his next day's assignments. Or the assignments he will have when he returns from the holidays." He turned to me. "I tell you, Barry, you do not work as hard as you should. Go now, before I get angry at you."

When his mother told him stories about children from schools in the south–children who had to study from books that were passed on to them from rich white children's schools yet they went on to become doctors, lawyers, and scientists–he felt reprimanded for his lack of desire to wake up in the mornings and go to school.

These values, instilled in Obama at an early age, values of hard work, determination, and perseverance, are what made the difference between a routine, meaningless life and the extraordinary achievements he reached. He studied, worked hard, and paved the way from the bottom up.

In his speeches in front of students, he tends to tell them what he also wrote in his book about the years when he lived with his mother in Indonesia. She made sure he completed his schooling through an American correspondence course. At one point, she even doubled her efforts—she entered his room four times a week at 4:30 a.m., woke him up, made him eat breakfast, and taught him English for three hours, before he went to school and she went to work.

His mother was undoubtedly the model of a strong, determined woman, who lived her life with the promise of something great and important and didn't fear the challenges that could be expected on the way.

His father too was, for him, a symbol of determination and personal strength, despite his absence. He said as much in *Dreams from My father*:

> She had only one ally in all this, and that was the distant authority of my father. Increasingly, she would remind me of his story, how he had grown up poor, in a poor country, in a poor continent; how his life had been hard, as hard as anything that Lolo might have known. He hadn't cut corners, though, or played all the angles. He was diligent and honest. No matter what it cost him. He had led his life according to principles that demanded a different kind of toughness, principles that promised a higher form of power. I would follow his example, my mother decided. I had no choice. It was in the genes…

Determination is what Obama expects of himself and others. Determination is what transforms all his speeches into something at which he cannot fail, an opportunity that must be taken advantage of.

The Value of Education

One of Obama's main values is education, a value related closely to the value of equal opportunity. Obama believes every country and family must make education a priority on the scale of values. He says of himself and his wife that, without the education they received, they wouldn't have achieved the accomplishments they did. And this is exactly the opportunity he wants to provide every child in America.

In the 2008 Democratic National Convention he said:

> Michelle and I are only here tonight because we were given a chance at an education. And I will not settle for an America where some kids don't have that chance…

In Virginia he promised voters that this value would be central if he is elected:

> And if I'm president, we'll give every child, everywhere, the skills and the knowledge they need to compete with any worker, anywhere in the world.
> I will not allow countries to out-teach us today so they can out-compete us tomorrow.
> It is time to provide every American with a world-class education.
> That means investing in early-childhood education.

Obama's mother is also responsible for instilling in him the value of education. When he was very young, this is where she focused her efforts. Obama calls on every parent to do the same: to place education on the top of their ladder of values and to be responsible for their children.

As president, he promoted the "Race to the Top" program to challenge schools all around the US. Race to the Top is an education program designed to spur reforms in state and local district K-12 education. It was announced by President Barack Obama and Secretary of Education Arne Duncan on July 24, 2009.

But that's not all. Obama's many speeches to school children and students show that he "walks his talks." He lives by his values. You will not find many presidents and prime ministers around the world who speak so often about education.

All of these values are part of Obama's "inner program." They provide him with the kindling for the fire and enthusiasm in his speeches.

🔍 What is Important to You?

Stop and reflect: what are the issues that matter to you?

What are the values you deem important to promote?

To what extent do the things you say comply with your values as a human being?

Remember, speech that complies with values is perceived as authentic and evokes emotion.

Now that we have examined Obama's vision, identity, beliefs, and values, let's move on to the next phase in the pyramid of logical levels.

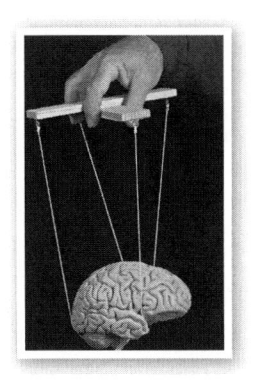

CHAPTER 10

AWAKENING THE COMMUNICATOR WITHIN – FULFILLING INNER CAPABILITIES AND STRATEGIES

Obama's inner capabilities and strategies in terms of influencing people through words are very interesting. They are the next phase in the logical levels pyramid. How does Obama think? What does he see in his mind's eye? What does he hear? What does he say to himself?

Obama undoubtedly was not born with a teleprompter in front of his eyes. On a *60 Minutes* program that depicted Obama's personal story, his campaign team said that at the beginning of the presidential election campaign, he wasn't convincing enough and was monotonous, academic, and hesitant.

"I'll learn how to be an excellent candidate," Obama said. And he did learn. This is his strategy—relying on his learning skills. This is the way he speaks to himself before speaking to others.

Obama has high-learning capabilities, and he galvanizes them for every new area he enters. He is perceived as courageous because he is not afraid to leave his comfort zone and reach new and challenging arenas. He is aware of the power and strength that stem from the willingness to learn new things; therefore, he is not fazed by the fact that he didn't develop his career in the corridors of Washington. He says to himself: *So what if I am not a "natural" candidate for the presidency? I will learn to be.*

Obama's Secrets

Obama has extensive capabilities and skills that make him an effective speaker. He has an extraordinary listening capability and empathy that allows him to gauge the other person's motives.

He has the capacity to simplify complex messages, to mediate, to move, to discern between what's important and what's not, and, of course, enormous willpower to succeed and generate the desired change.

Obama believes in his capabilities. In *Dreams from My Father*, he writes about the moments that led up to the speech he gave as a community organizer when he first started out. It's a segment we already saw, but now, pay special attention to the last sentence:

> I knew the score, had helped plan the script. Only, when I sat down to prepare a few notes for what I might say, something had happened. In my mind, it somehow became more than just a two-minute speech, more than a way to prove my political orthodoxy. I started to remember…the power of my father's words to transform. If I could just find the right words, I had thought to myself. With the right words everything could change…I was still in that trancelike state, when I mounted the stage. For I don't know how long…

Obama describes a near ecstatic moment when he got on stage, when he was aware of the power of his words and believed the right words could change everything.

When Obama uttered the words he chose to say, he believed at that moment in the power of those words and their energy. He also believed in his ability to touch people and in his own voice. He wrote:

> Somebody suggested that I open the thing; I quickly agreed. I figured I was ready and could reach people where it counted. I thought my voice wouldn't fail me.

His purpose is to galvanize people into action. He believes that if he addresses people directly, in a genuine and sincere manner, and presents the issues as he knows how, people's natural instinct will draw them closer to him. He wrote in *The Audacity of Hope*:

> If I could reach those voters directly, frame the issues as I felt them, explain the choices in as truthful a fashion as I knew how, then the people's instincts for fair play and common sense would bring them around.

Here we can see his inner monologue saying, *I'm ready; I can do this job.*

In *Dreams from My Father,* he writes that everything he says and does is not only for himself but for others, as well. He sees himself as a messenger or trustee of all the people who are crying out for change. The struggle he is conducting, the change he wants to make, the gospel he is trying to spread—all these do not affect only him, but all the people on whose behalf he is working; the people he met along the way and listened to; his family members and anyone who ever opened up his or her heart to him.

Obama sees in his mind's eye the people who need him and all his partners to the path. These sights motivate him into action and strengthen him like a prayer. They prove to him that he is not alone in his struggle and that many people rely on his way and the things he chooses to say.

He also hears an inner voice that reminds him of stories of peoples' lives, historic stories, stories of freedom and hope.

All these motivate him to act for change and to influence others. Thus, he motivates himself to motivate others. These are Obama's inner capabilities and thought strategies.

And they fit the logical levels we analyzed before—the vision, the identity, the beliefs, and values—and form another layer in Obama's secrets.

There are two other logical levels in NLP—behavior and environment. We won't discuss these levels now because, later on, we will specify what Obama does and how he behaves to better influence and persuade his listeners, including the way in which he builds his speeches, prepares them, gets ready for them, and conveys them to his audience.

Obama lives with an inner conviction, and his logical levels comply with one another, support one another, result from one another, and fit together harmoniously. Thus, when there is a congruence in terms of a person's logical levels, he or she is truly him or herself, the person feels comfortable with him or herself, consistent in his or her opinions and thoughts, lives as he or she wants to live and is in his or her natural surroundings; as a result, people grasp that person's external and internal being as sincere and genuine.

Obama's vision is supported by his identity, and his identity is supported by his beliefs and values. His inner strategies, combined with his capabilities and skills, support the logical levels above them, and are supported by Obama's actions and by his environment.

Obama speaks and communicates with power because he believes in his words and lives with them in harmony. When Obama conveys his vision—a vision of passing on the wonderful gift of freedom, equal opportunity, and the pursuit of happiness one generation after another—he sounds authentic and persuasive. He, of all people, knows how important this gift is. He, of all people, profoundly understands the meaning of equal opportunity. He, of all people, knows the importance of equal opportunity, as an individual who was born and raised in tough circumstances, both black and white, without a father most of those years, and a harsh financial situation.

Obama's beliefs and values support his identity and vision and enrich them. His belief that people can shape their own destiny supports his identity as a man who shapes his destiny; his belief that through hard work, determination, and effort one can achieve everything one wants, is in fact the story of his life.

As a person who believes in his ability and the ability of others to make a change, and as a man full of hope for better days, he directly supports his identity as a fair, groundbreaking leader, and thus instills his vision for a better future and for passing the gift on to the future generations.

The values that are important to Obama develop his identity and his vision. Equality, decency, integrity, freedom, opportunities, hope, and hard work—all these are well packed in the gift he seeks to grant future generations. His many capabilities—listening, empathy, learning, mediation, and the ability to simplify complex issues (as we will demonstrate further on)—support his beliefs and values and develop them.

When Obama is on stage, he is entirely aware of the power of his words to generate change. When he says the words with passion and energy, reserved for people who believe in what they say; when he thinks about the people who depend on him, envisions what moves him, and reminds himself that he is not alone in the struggle; and when he tells himself that he can touch the hearts of people and make a change through words—when all these occur at the same time, Obama succeeds at communicating, influencing, and leading—big time.

Obama, like a well-oiled machine, acts in a harmonious and well coordinated fashion. All of his logical levels support one another, develop one another, and comply with one another. This creates profound inner persuasion that enables external persuasion and motivates people.

As we wrote before, Obama is your role model. You can adopt his thinking patterns and adapt them to your vision, your values, and your needs.

Using The New Tools

How do you talk to yourself?

What motivates you?

What images do you envision when you address the issues that matter to you?

What sounds do you hear?

For whom are you acting?

Who really needs you and the ideas you are promoting?

How do you motivate yourself to motivate others?

Now that you have gained a bit of insight into the way in which Obama sees the world and into his thought process, you have the tools to develop an awareness of your thoughts, and a backdrop to use these thoughts to empower your messages.

Consider:

To what extent is the way you live and speak based on inner conviction?

To what extent does your vision comply with your identity, beliefs, and values?

To what extent do your actions support all of these?

Persuading others depends on the answer to the question "to what extent are you convinced of your ideas and do you live with them in harmony?"

If you know *your* answer, you will have the enthusiasm in your communication.

The source of the word *enthusiasm* is the Greek *enthousiasmos,* which comes from the adjective *entheos,* "having the god within."

As we tell our leadership and communication skills seminar participants, "Cash can buy, but it takes enthusiasm to sell."

Do you have it?

Now that we have an understanding of the special engine in Obama's head, we can remove the surgeon's robe and examine more overt aspects of his strategies: the secrets of his speeches and the engineering of his winning messages.

PART THREE
Engineering Winning Messages

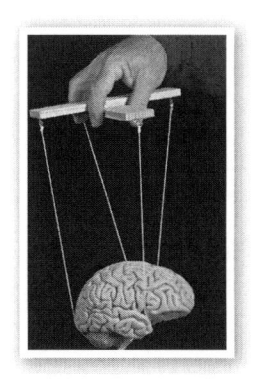

CHAPTER 11

THE CORE MESSAGES – HOW TO USE AND INSTILL OPTIMISTIC MESSAGES

"I wasn't a great communicator, but I communicated great things"

—Ronald Reagan

The time has come to reveal the strategy with which Obama shapes and prepares effective speeches. What does he do before he speaks in front of an audience in such a successful manner? To adopt Obama's communication secrets that afforded him the reputation as one of the finest speakers of the early 21st century, we should get to know them well. We call it "Engineering Winning Messages."

So put on your sweatshirts and your running shoes because we are embarking on a fascinating marathon through Obama's world of power words.

To prepare for speeches and media appearances, Obama consciously uses what Stephen Covey, author of *The 7 Habits of Highly Effective People*, calls "begin from the end." That's a habit of highly effective communicators, too!

First Obama sets a clear goal for himself.

His goal is never formulated in the style of "I am going to talk about…" This is how people who speak from the first perceptual position formulate their speeches. Obama's goal is formulated from the second perceptual position, i.e., from the audience's point of view.

He asks himself, "What will the listeners feel during my speech and at the end?" "What action will they take following my speech?"

Obama is like a laser-guided missile: first he marks his target, and then he crafts his speech and formulates his messages accordingly.

After marking the target, Obama selects the core messages of his speech. His messages are generally positive, they provoke a sense of hope, and motivate to action—his are messages that many can identify with. He tends to speak of mutual accountability, promise, change, and realizing dreams and equal opportunities. He speaks of hard work and the effort required to realize the American promise and to generate the change.

This is the refrain in many of his speeches. The words Obama selects are pleasant, inspiring, and agreeable to the ear, so much so that Will I.AM produced the song "Yes, We Can." He set Obama's words to music and turned them into a motivational song suitable for people of every color, race, gender, and age. The song became a beacon of hope during the 2008 election campaign; an anthem for a new era.

Musical Choices

The words Obama says are often written like a song. When you read them you can clearly see the art of crafting a speech is present in every one. Musical motifs and creative thinking are apparent in each line of each paragraph and in each and every word.

It is easy to see when Obama starts sequential sentences or sequential paragraphs with the same word. You can see the rhythm of the words, the contrasts between the beginning of the sentence and its end, and other poetic characteristics. Here is an example from a speech Obama gave in October 2008:

> We can do this if we come together;
> if we have confidence in ourselves and each other;
> if we look beyond the darkness of the day
> to the bright light of hope that lies ahead.
> Together, we can change this country and change this world.

Obama speaks like a skilled composer writing a musical piece, or like a poet writing a brilliant poem. He lights a flame at the onset of the speech and keeps it burning until the end. He focuses on several central and optimistic messages, which he repeats again and again in different variations.

It is interesting to discover that Jon Favreau, Obama's chief speechwriter, is in fact a pianist with a musical sense for language. Some of Obama's other advisors call him Mozart. He considers how the words work together, how they sound together, how their rhythm sounds.

Obama worked closely with Favreau throughout the election campaign, and he still does as president. Since President Obama speaks frequently as president, he meets Favreau or his staff almost every day. In Obama's inaugural speech, we can see that his speechwriter is indeed well versed in the world of music. Obama said:

Starting today, we must pick ourselves up, dust ourselves off, and begin again the work of remaking America.

These words are taken from a song written by Dorothy Fields, music by Jerome Kern, and sung by Fred Astaire and Ginger Rogers in the 1936 musical *Swing Time*. Here's an excerpt from that song:

> Nothing's impossible I have found,
> For when my chin is on the ground,
> I pick myself up,
> Dust myself off,
> Start all over again…

The Message of a Better Future

Obama follows in the footsteps of great leaders who focused on optimistic content and painted a picture of a better future, even when times were rough. Leaders have always used stories about a positive future to motivate people. Obama knows this secret. He learned it from the multitude of great leaders who preceded him.

Effective leaders always know that the key to leadership is to be effective in conveying a story. To this day, the stories of great spiritual leaders who promise a better future—Jesus, Moses, Confucius, Muhammad, and Buddha to name a few—continue to shape the beliefs and behaviors of billions of people.

Obama's Secrets

The American dream of freedom and the pursuit of happiness, as set forth in the Declaration of Independence by Thomas Jefferson, John Adams, and Benjamin Franklin, remains to this day unique in its power to motivate and inspire all men and women.

Obama keeps weaving the dream. He sensitively sketches for his listeners the future vision of the USA which, at present, is wounded and bleeding. He promises his listeners a better tomorrow, when it will be possible to realize the American promise of individual freedom, and the fulfillment of an individual's dreams, while maintaining unity of the nation and of society. Tomorrow will be better in terms of the economy, education, medicine, politics, and so forth.

Why is it so important to use positive messages? Because speaking of a positive future influences not only the audience, but the speaker as well. Just like a winning game plan helps athletes excel, so too does a story about a positive future help to empower the person telling it. To communicate effectively, you need your own energy, belief, and enthusiasm. It is hard to have it while speaking about negative issues.

People follow leaders who offer positive messages. Leaders such as Roosevelt, Churchill, and Reagan used this secret well. A study of the presidential election campaigns in the USA between 1900 and 1984 shows American voters chose the candidate who conveyed a more optimistic message in eighteen out of twenty-two campaigns.

People long for a positive future. Notice how nice it is to hear these words by Obama, and how he is perceived as so full of power, when he promises a positive vision such as the following, by his listeners at the 2008 Democratic National Convention:

> It is that American spirit—
> that American promise—
> that pushes us forward, even when the path is uncertain;
> that binds us together in spite of our differences;
> that makes us fix our eye not on what is seen,
> but what is unseen,
> that better place around the bend.
> That promise is our greatest inheritance.
> It's a promise I make to my daughters when I tuck them in at night,
> and a promise that you make to yours—
> a promise that has led immigrants to cross oceans

and pioneers to travel west;
a promise that led workers to picket lines,
and women to reach for the ballot.

President Reagan, who was both a movie star and governor of California prior to his presidency, painted a picture of national renewal at every opportunity. The voters were captivated by Reagan and handed him a landslide victory. The optimistic content of Reagan's words was so convincing that it was hard for even his opponents not to be convinced. Reagan said:

> It is time to reawaken this industrial giant, to get government back within its means, and to lighten our punitive tax burden…When action is required to preserve our national security, we will act. We will maintain sufficient strength to prevail if need be, knowing that if we do so, we have the best chance of never having to use that strength.

Years later (January 11, 1989), in his farewell speech from the Oval Office at the White House, Reagan said:

> I won a nickname, "The Great Communicator." But I never thought it was my style or the words I used that made a difference: it was the content. I wasn't a great communicator, but I communicated great things…

It's worthwhile remembering this message from a man who in the 1980s was considered The Great Communicator. It is clear that Obama learned from the people that succeeded before him.

A central message that Obama repeats in his speeches is a message of change and hope for better days. In May 2008 he said:

> You know, there is a spirit that brought us here tonight—
> a spirit of change, and hope, and possibility…

This message is repeated in many speeches. The reason is simple: repetition helps commit an idea to one's memory. Repetition during a speech or a presentation, and undoubtedly during an election campaign, "glues" the messages to the listeners' minds. When something is easier to remember, the mind believes it more.

A message of change fits in of course with the slogan that accompanied Obama throughout his presidential election campaign: "Change we can believe in." Obama speaks of hunger for new ideas, new leadership, and new politics. He plants in the audience the belief that change is possible, and invites audience members to believe in their shared ability to make a change. This is what he said in Ohio in 2008:

> It won't be easy, Ohio.
> It won't be quick.
> But you and I know that it is time to come together and change this country….
> I ask you to believe—
> not just in my ability to bring about change,
> but in yours.
> I know this change is possible…

"Hope" was another key word in Obama's speeches. He chose it back in 2006 as part of the title of his second book, *The Audacity of Hope*, and it was repeated in many of his speeches.

At the 2004 Democratic National Convention, when Obama first won over the audience and became an overnight star, the word hope was repeated as a motto in his speech at the convention:

> Do we participate in a politics of cynicism or a politics of hope? …
> I'm talking about something more substantial…
> the hope of immigrants setting out for distant shores;
> the hope of a young naval lieutenant bravely patrolling the Mekong Delta;
> the hope of a mill worker's son who dares to defy the odds;
> the hope of a skinny kid with a funny name
> who believes that America has a place for him, too.
> The audacity of hope!

The hope for better days became a cornerstone in virtually all of Obama's addresses, from his first ones, right up to his 2008 victory speech.

However, it is important to note that the hope which Obama proposes is not the hope that things will come easy or without effort. It is a hope that demands hard work. This relates, of course, to his basic beliefs and mainly to the belief that one can attain anything if one is prepared to work hard. In his speech in Iowa in 2007, which became one of his first key speeches, he expressed this concept clearly:

> There has been a lot of talk in this campaign about the politics of hope. But the politics of hope doesn't mean hoping that things come easy. It's a politics of believing in things unseen; of believing in what this country might be; and of standing up for that belief and fighting for it when it's hard.
>
> —November 7, 2007, speech on the "American Dream," Bettendorf, Iowa

Here again, we should emphasize an important issue concerning communication: it's not what you say, it's what people hear, see, and feel.

There are always three speeches for every one you actually give. The one you practiced, the one you give, and the one people hear. Look again at the last sample. Obama said hundreds of times in his speeches, "It won't be easy and it won't be quick." Yet, many citizens of the US expected him, as president, to deliver easy, quick solutions for the economic crisis in the USA.

You should use positive messages when you communicate, but unless you are a politician, make sure you do not over-promise. It is almost always better to under-promise and over-deliver, rather than the reverse.

Another central message in Obama's speeches is the message of the American promise: a promise related to fulfillment of the individual's dreams and also accountability among men.

This is what Obama said at the 2008 Democratic National Convention:

> That's the promise of America—
> the idea that we are responsible for ourselves,
> but that we also rise or fall as one nation;
> the fundamental belief
> that I am my brother's keeper;
> I am my sister's keeper.

In his 2008 victory speech he said:

> Let us remember that if this financial crisis taught us anything,
> it's that we cannot have a thriving Wall Street while Main Street suffers—
> in this country, we rise or fall as one nation; as one people.

See how he effectively uses the word "street" in two different ways, and how all these connect to his basic belief that the future can be shaped through hard, mutual work.

Obama often uses the word "promise," as well. In his speech at the 2008 Democratic National Convention, he used this magic word over twenty times. When Obama promises his audience better days, he makes the audience feel better because he links them to the hope embodied in the fulfillment of the promise.

Obama adds to his positive messages a sense of urgency and vital mission and, thus, extends a call to action. At the 2008 Democratic National Convention he said:

> This moment—this election—is our chance to keep, in the 21st century, the American promise alive.

As early as November 2007, a year before he was elected, he gave a speech in which he stressed that this is a rare moment:

> I'm running for president because I believe we find ourselves in a moment of great challenge and great promise—a moment that comes along once in a generation.

Another message is one of equal opportunities that Obama repeats in various forms, especially in the context of his personal story. He lets his listeners understand that if he has succeeded, despite the less-than-ideal starting point in his life, they can, too. This is evident, as he opened with his personal story about his childhood in two important speeches he gave at the 2004 and 2008 Democratic National Conventions.

Through his personal story, Obama managed to instill in his listeners' minds, at the onset of his speeches, his important message about equal opportunities.

When Obama told his personal story at the two conventions, he lingered on the details that emphasize the equality he is seeking to achieve. For example, the fact that his parents believed a funny name is not an obstacle to success in tolerant America, or that in generous America you don't have to be rich or famous to realize your potential. Obama presented a concept to his listeners: nowhere else in the world would his story have been possible. Thus, he emphasized another optimistic message: the true opportunity that only America offers, its openness, and the belief that, in America, if you dream it, you can do it.

Positive Words

When we examine the key words in Obama's speeches, in addition to the words "change," "promise," and "hope" that were already mentioned, we discover a long list of positive words:

> Choice; faith; belief; dream; love; progress; strength; courage; confidence; believe; purpose; opportunity; freedom; possibilities; energy; passion; safe; secure; chance; peace; spirit; success; can.

Obama's words calm us, reinforce his vision, and inspire us. Some words emerge from the realm of emotion, some come from the arena of relationships, and others seem to be taken from a romantic movie.

To achieve effective influence, Obama repeats these optimistic words several times during every speech or in a series of different speeches. But even when the optimistic words come up only once or a few times, they play an important role in the speech, and their location within it generally indicates how significant they are.

But most interesting is the use Obama makes of the phrase "hard work," which he repeats often. This phrase, together with the word "belief," creates a new combined message. Though there is a belief that change is possible, it is only attained through hard work and effort. And, as of September 2011, we can see that, indeed, a lot of hard work is still ahead of him.

If you want to speak and communicate with power, you should use and instill optimistic messages.

What is Your Tune?

Whenever you speak in front of people, like Obama, you too can choose the core messages, which you deem important, to convey to your listeners.

It's best they be optimistic and hope-filled messages.

Repeat these optimistic messages in various ways, while focusing on positive key words to express them. Repeating key words, especially with abstract generalities that listeners can interpret freely, is an effective tool to persuade and motivate people.

Open words such as *change*, *hope*, or *promise*, as Obama chooses, present listeners with the opportunity to fill them with subjective content. Also, repeating these words helps them to penetrate deep into the listeners' subconscious. Repeating words makes listeners remember and internalize, just as a student remembers and internalizes a lesson as he or she goes over it many times while preparing for an exam.

Churchill suggested planning every speech like a symphony. According to him, a speech may have three parts, but it will always have one dominant tune. So if you want to make the "victory sign" gesture ("V") like Churchill during your next speech, ask yourself:

What is the tune I want everyone to hum after I speak?

What is the bottom line of my speech?

What do I want everyone to remember at the end?

What is the headline of my speech?

Truth be told, most people tend not to listen attentively to each and every word you say. Therefore, positive messages that evoke hope, inspiration, and belief in a better future, expressed often, better penetrate the mind which tends to censor and distort. Listeners are more likely to be exposed to your important messages and take them in if you repeat them several times. Repetition is also beneficial in that, when someone misses the messages the first time, they will get an opportunity to hear them again (see also chapter 26).

Think positively, and don't be a pessimist. Remember, a pessimist says that O is the last letter in the word ZERO. An optimist says it is the first letter in the word OPPORTUNITY.

Yes, you can speak powerfully if you use positive messages and think positively.

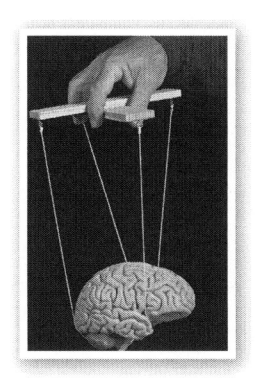

CHAPTER 12

THE WINNING TOPICS – HOW TO SPEAK ABOUT WHAT MOTIVATES PEOPLE

How would you feel if you were a student and a proposal was brought before you to reduce tuition? How would you feel if you were unemployed and someone discussed creating new jobs? How would you feel, deep down inside, if you were promised medical insurance for which you cannot pay for yourself?

What topics should you use in order to win?

Obama addresses issues that make people take action; concrete issues; specific; issues that matter to everyday, ordinary people who listen to him.

On December 4, 2010, at the announcement of a U.S.-Korea Free Trade Agreement, Obama spoke about what mattered most to his people:

> Today, I want to speak briefly about two issues that matter most to me and matter most to the American people—creating jobs and economic growth on which our country's prosperity depends.

He addresses people's most basic needs. He discusses creating instant relief in tangible areas, such as food, work places, homes for the homeless, worthy education for every child, reducing gas prices, reducing taxes, and investing in roads and medical insurance for every citizen. This is the way in which he seeks to motivate people. Here is a sample of what he said in Philadelphia in 2008, where he used the motif of the older generation making sacrifices for the younger, which is relevant to every society, culture, and nation:

> We can do this.
> We've done it before.
> Some of us had grandparents or parents who said
> "Maybe I can't go to college but my child can;"
> "Maybe I can't have my own business but my child can;"
> "I may have to rent,
> but maybe my children will have a home they can call their own."
> "I may not have a lot of money,
> but maybe my child will run for Senate."
> "I might live in a small village,
> but maybe someday my son can be president of the United States of America."

The samples from life that Obama uses in his speeches are basic and familiar: the choice between maintaining a job or treating a sick relative; the unemployed or the youth who want to study but cannot finance their schooling.

In *Dreams from My Father,* Obama said he learned in his youth how to motivate and lead people:

> If you want to organize people, you need to steer away from the peripheral stuff and go toward people's centers. The stuff that makes them tick. Otherwise, you'll never form the relationship you need to get them involved.

Therefore, he pours concrete content, taken directly from people's daily lives, into his general, optimistic messages about change, hope, and the American promise.

Thus, his change is not vague; it is a tangible change pertaining to the issues that hurt and challenge people the most—medical insurance for every person, assistance to small businesses, putting an end to insurance companies' discrimination.

During his first term in the White House, Obama sought to implement reform in the U.S. health system, in which many citizens do not have medical insurance. Here is what he said on this matter in Philadelphia in 2008:

> Change means finally fixing our health care system.
> Under my plan, if you have health insurance,

> the only thing that will change is that you'll pay lower premiums.
> If you don't have insurance,
> you'll be able to get the same kind of health insurance
> that members of congress get for themselves.

"The American promise" is a phrase Obama instills with real content from daily life: to keep our water clean and our toys safe; to invest in new schools, new roads, science and technology; and to make medical insurance accessible to every American.

Obama provides the phrase "opening a window of opportunity" a specific meaning: providing jobs to the unemployed, providing homes to the homeless, and preventing violence among youths.

"Realizing dreams" is transformed by Obama from a vague fantasy into providing people with their most basic needs. Even the idea of "equal opportunity" is concretely applied to the issue of equal pay for men and women:

> And now is the time to keep the promise of equal pay for an equal day's work, because I want my daughters to have exactly the same opportunities as your sons.

Obama successfully conveys to the entire audience the sense that he is focusing on matters that are truly important to him. In his 2009 inaugural speech, he expressed this well:

> The question we ask today is not whether our government is too big or too small, but whether it works—whether it helps families find jobs at a decent wage, care they can afford, a retirement that is dignified. Where the answer is yes, we intend to move forward. Where the answer is no, programs will end.

Obama knows anyone can be persuaded, if you talk about what interests him or her.

This strategy is a way of life for him, and he has been using it for many years, despite the difficulties in implementing it. In *Dreams from My Father,* he spoke of himself in this context:

> Once I found an issue enough people cared about, I could take them into action. With enough actions, I could start to build power.

And how did he identify so precisely what the issues are that motivate people? As we saw in the beginning of the book, Obama lives the streets. He lives real life, not the interpretation of real life. He listens to people and puts himself in their shoes. He exchanges roles with people until he is able to understand what motivates them. All these attributes enable him to identify, with great precision, the central issues that activate people. Thus, he can motivate them into action and motivate them to choose him as the person to implement the desired change.

Remember: people don't want a quarter-inch drill; they want a quarter-inch hole.

What Ails Them?

Before your next speech, presentation, or sales pitch, ask yourself: What are the issues that activate the people I will meet? What motivates them? What matters to them?

What kind of "quarter-inch holes" do they want?

Remember that if you want to activate people, you should talk about the issues that interest them personally—their problems. You should investigate and understand these questions. What really interests them? What ails them? What do they want to change? What problems do they want me to solve?

When you speak to people, remember to pour concrete and specific content into the general messages you choose to convey. If you only speak about the big, important issues, it won't change the situation. The person you are speaking to will continue to think about the daily problems he or she wakes up with in the morning and to which he or she returns after a day's work.

But if you focus your message on solving these problems, and consider what pain-relief medicine you can provide them, they will listen to you!

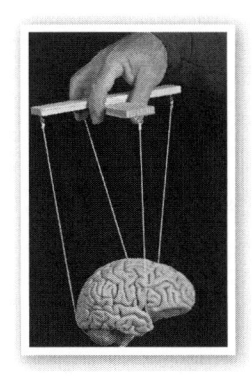

CHAPTER 13

TRUE, IT'S DIFFICULT – HOW TO HANDLE POTENTIAL OBJECTIONS

This chapter will add real magic to your communication skills. After Obama chooses his core optimistic messages and the issues that motivate people, he uses one of the most effective tactics for persuading, influencing, and motivating people: he notes the hardships that can be expected along the way before realizing the end goals.

Thus, he responds to every one of his listeners' inner needs, the hardships they can expect to be addressed. Obama speaks of the difficulties explicitly, as we can see in the statements he made in Virginia in 2008:

> Make no mistake:
> the change we need won't come easy or without cost.
> We will all need to tighten our belts,
> we will all need to sacrifice
> and we will all need to pull our weight…

Many people expect young politicians or a new CEO in their organization to work miracles and generate change in the bat of an eye. They expect the new leader to be a magician who will change reality and turn the impossible into the possible within just a few weeks.

Obama, who entered the White House in the face of global challenges that existed at a scale sufficient for ten presidents, never promised to solve all of the problems at once.

He does not profess that the path to realizing the vision is easy or short. Nor does he profess to be the perfect candidate or immune to criticism.

But he makes sure to bring to the surface, in an honest manner, the difficulties expected on the road to realizing the goal and the personal criticism directed towards him. He also outlines a way to handle these difficulties and gives a decisive answer to any raised objections.

His inaugural speech provided him another opportunity to raise these difficulties:

> Today I say to you that the challenges we face are real.
> They are serious and they are many.
> They will not be met easily or in a short span of time.
> But know this, America—they will be met.
> On this day, we gather because we have chosen hope over fear,
> unity of purpose over conflict and discord.

Obama implements the principle about which Winston Churchill once spoke: "Courage is going from failure to failure without losing enthusiasm."

He acts according to the famous theory of the highly gifted screenwriter Robert McKee. According to this theory, in every good story and every good screenplay, there is an element of tension, conflict, or contradiction: transition from a problem to a solution; from darkness to light; from uncertainty to certainty.

This is the energy from which life is made, and this is the energy that mesmerizes people and rivets them to a good story or good screenplay. When Obama talks about the difficulties that can be expected and the objections of his own accord, he conveys authenticity, leadership, and power. Thus, he also establishes trust between the audience and himself - a relationship that forms the basis for his capacity to persuade. In an address on November 3, 2007, he made the following bold statement:

> I don't pretend to be a perfect man,
> and I will not be a perfect president.
> But I am in this race because I believe
> that if we want to break from the failures of the past

> and finally make progress as a country,
> we can't keep telling different people what we think they want to hear—
> we have to tell every American what they need to know.
> We have to be honest about the challenges we face.
>
> —"A Change We Can Believe In," Spartanburg, SC, November 3, 2007

And he said it again with some humor:

> During the course of this campaign,
> we've all learned what my wife reminds me of all the time—
> that I am not a perfect man.
> And I will not be a perfect president
>
> —Evansville, Indiana, April 22, 2008

Obama doesn't simply discuss the difficulties. He shows his audience, step by step, how to handle the difficulties as they occur. He does not rely on the luck, or on the wisdom of his listeners. Instead, he guides his listeners and repeats again and again the message on how to deal with the expected difficulties according to his winning method. Hardship or crisis is, in his eyes, a test one cannot fail. He is instilled with the belief and confidence in his shared ability with others to handle any hardship together, to learn from it and win.

At first, he discusses the hardship or objections and makes them part of the dialogue, part of the speech. He doesn't round corners, nor does he paint a pretty picture. He provides a sense that he is depicting the situation as it is. Alongside the recognition of the expected hardship, he plants in the audience hope and optimism that the hardship can be conquered, if it is confronted correctly. This is what he said in Philadelphia in 2008:

> It's a test we cannot fail.
> Not now.
> Not when we have a crisis to solve and an economy to save…
> We can do this. We've done it before…

In January 2010, the global media summed up Obama's first year in the White House. These analyses were always joined by studies on the decline in his popularity, a phenomenon that always happens after you discover that the person you thought was a magician is merely a leader. However, Obama never promised to solve all the crises within one year.

In November 2010, right after the Republicans and the "Tea Party" movement's success in the elections to Congress, President Obama spoke at a press conference:

> And yesterday's vote confirmed what I've heard from folks all across America:
> People are frustrated—they're deeply frustrated—
> with the pace of our economic recovery
> and the opportunities that they hope for their children and their grandchildren.
> They want jobs to come back faster,
> they want paychecks to go further,
> and they want the ability to give their children
> the same chances and opportunities as they've had in life.

Here is another example of the way in which Obama actively handles objection. In October 2009, he awoke one morning and was informed that he was to be the recipient of the Nobel Peace Prize. Several hours later, he referred to the surprising win in the White House Rose Garden. Since he knew this win would arouse criticism, he handled it with this statement:

> I do not view it as recognition of my own accomplishments, but rather as an affirmation of American leadership on behalf of aspirations held by people in all nations.

> To be honest, I do not feel that I deserve to be in the company of so many of the transformative figures who've been honored by this prize—men and women who've inspired me and inspired the entire world through their courageous pursuit of peace.

> But I also know that this prize reflects the kind of world that those men and women, and all Americans, want to build—a world that gives life to the promise of our founding documents. And I know that throughout history, the Nobel Peace Prize has not just been used to honor specific achievement; it's also been used as a means to give momentum to a set of causes. And that is why I will accept this award as a call to action—a call for all nations to confront the common challenges of the 21st century.

Doctorate for Handling Objections

In May 2009, Obama was invited to speak at the University of Arizona, right after it decided not to grant him an honorary degree. With or without the degree, Obama is certainly deserving of one in mass communication and engineering messages. With great humor, he referred in his speech to the fact he didn't receive an honorary degree:

> Now, in all seriousness, I come here not to dispute the suggestion that I haven't yet achieved enough in my life.
>
> First of all, Michelle concurs with that assessment.
>
> She has a long list of things that I have not yet done, waiting for me when I get home.

Obama knows how to bring to light the expected difficulties and the objections his competitors and opponents raise about him, including personal criticism directed at him. In the same breath, he rejects the objections and criticism and removes them from the agenda.

As early as February 2007, when he announced his presidential candidacy in Springfield, Illinois, he admitted he hadn't devoted much time to learning the ways of Washington, but he added that he stayed there long enough to know these ways must change.

If you want to handle objections well, it's best you know what's going on behind the scenes of Obama's technique. Obama handles objections with a method that became popular in modern medicine.

He has a secret that can be called "injecting the audience with a vaccine." He injects his audience with a low dose of the virus of the disease, so that the audience can develop the healing mechanism and immunization to that disease.

Thus he "immunizes" his audience not only against the concrete objection he refers to, but future objections or rumors that will come up (mutations of the disease). And the audience, who is already immune, will now be fit to handle future objections and fight them off on its own, even if they are bigger or more virulent.

Thus, for example, Obama raised in his main speech in the 2004 Democratic National Convention the sensitive issues of his problematic name, his lack of political experience in Washington, and the fact that he is the son of a black father and white mother.

He wasn't afraid to tell the truth. Moreover, his team created a website (www.fightthesmears.com), designed to combat the rumors. He revealed on the website every rumor about himself and gave his version. Thus, Obama succeeded in turning what could have been a disadvantage into an advantage of credibility.

He addressed the claims of his political rivals in the same way. At the 2008 Democratic National Convention, he used this immunization technique:

> I know there are those who dismiss such beliefs as happy talk.
> They claim that our insistence on something larger,
> something firmer and more honest in our public life
> is just a Trojan Horse for higher taxes
> and the abandonment of traditional values.
> And that's to be expected.
> Because if you don't have any fresh ideas,
> then you use stale tactics to scare the voters.
> If you don't have a record to run on,
> then you paint your opponent as someone people should run from.

In May 2008, using the same technique, he warded off additional expected tactics used by his rivals:

> We will face our share of difficult and uncertain days in the journey ahead.
> The other side knows they have embraced yesterday's policies
> and so they will also embrace yesterday's tactics to try and change the subject.
> They will play on our fears and our doubts and our divisions
> to distract us from what matters to you and your future.
> Well they can take the low road if they want,
> but it will not lead this country to a better place.
> And it will not work in this election.
> It won't work because you won't let it.
> Not this time. Not this year.

While communicating, Obama uses what many professional salespeople do to handle objections before a customer raises them. They say it up front. For example, if you have the most expensive product in your category, you know that your potential customer will ask you, "why is it so expensive?" Instead of waiting to handle it later, you bring it up as part of your presentation, to your advantage. You may say, "our product gives you much more value and benefits than product x, and your investment will be 20 percent higher. Does that make sense?"

This technique uses the concept of "elephant in the room." The expression, "there's an elephant in the room," describes a truth we ignore, even though it stands out and is well known. The elephant may be a question, problem, solution, or controversy, that is ignored out of shame or because the issue is considered taboo: race; ethnic origin; or sexual preference.

When Obama explicitly addresses the elephant in the room, he puts things on the table. You cannot ignore things, once they've been said. It's part of Obama's worldview, where facts must be said clearly and directly.

In May 2004, he used this technique when he said he was "a thin man with a funny name." The moment *he* said it himself, his opponents could no longer laugh at him or refer to his unique name again. When you use this tactic, you are, in effect, voicing objections that are in the minds of the listeners.

Therefore, before your next speech, media appearance, or sales pitch, consider these questions: What are the most important questions your listeners have? What would they like to know? What are they afraid of? What objections are they likely to raise? Then state the issues explicitly. Put them on the table.

For example, if you are leading a change, and you know many do not understand why it is necessary, say, "perhaps some of you are wondering why it is so important to make this change at this time. Well…"

Bear in mind, though, that this technique should be performed in measure. You do not want to have too many elephants. Use it twice at most in one speech, so it will be especially effective.

Learning to Confront Difficulties

You can learn about Obama's views on confronting difficulties from his speech to American students in September 2009. Here is what he said at the beginning of the school year on bringing the difficulties to the surface and confronting them:

> But the truth is, being successful is hard.
> You won't love every subject you study.
> You won't click with every teacher.
> Not every homework assignment will seem completely relevant to your life, right this minute.
> And you won't necessarily succeed at everything the first time you try.
> That's OK.
> Some of the most successful people in the world are
> the ones who've had the most failures.
> JK Rowling's first Harry Potter book was rejected twelve times
> before it was finally published.
> Michael Jordan was cut from his high school basketball team,
> and he lost hundreds of games and missed thousands of shots during his career.
> But he once said, "I have failed over and over and over again in my life.
> And that is why I succeed."

Obama, who set a goal for himself to change the level of education in the USA, teaches millions of students to learn from their failures and not let those failures define them as human beings:

> These people succeeded because they understand that you can't let your failures define you—you have to let them teach you.
> You have to let them show you what to do differently next time.
> If you get in trouble, that doesn't mean you're a troublemaker,
> it means you need to try harder to behave.
> If you get a bad grade, that doesn't mean you're stupid,
> it just means you need to spend more time studying.

And here is how he reveals to students his strategy on the importance of repetition, practicing, and learning:

> No one's born being good at things,
> you become good at things through hard work.
> You're not a varsity athlete the first time you play a new sport.
> You don't hit every note the first time you sing a song.
> You've got to practice.
> It's the same with your schoolwork.
> You might have to do a math problem a few times before you get it right,
> or read something a few times before you understand it,
> or do a few drafts of a paper before it's good enough to hand in.

So far, we have seen how Obama addresses a difficulty or objection and makes them part of the dialogue. In the next phase, he teaches his audience how to triumph over the difficulties and not vice versa. He invites the audience to adopt his style of confronting difficulties and crises. It could be called a **five-step success strategy.**

1. Difficulties, challenges, and failures cannot be avoided. One can only learn from them, grow, and improve. Obama was elected to the Illinois Senate three times between 1996 and 2004. But he never got elected to a seat on the American House of Representatives.

In 2000, he lost a campaign which resulted in heavy financial losses. Bobby Rush won that campaign with double the number of votes of Obama.

But Obama doesn't let failure stop him. In 2004 he ran again, this time for the United States Senate, and was elected in November with results the likes of which had not been seen in the history of Illinois.

He won 70 percent of the votes. Obama said in this regard:

> Making your mark on the world is hard.
> If it were easy, everybody would do it.
> But it's not.
> It takes patience,
> it takes commitment,
> and it comes with plenty of failure along the way.
> The real test is not whether you avoid this failure,
> because you won't.
> It's whether you let it harden or shame you into inaction,
> or whether you learn from it,
> whether you choose to persevere.

And here is what he said in his remarks on the Middle East and North Africa on May 19, 2011:

> It will not be easy.
> There's no straight line to progress,
> and hardship always accompanies a season of hope.

2. A challenge or difficulty is a test one cannot fail. You must succeed. There is no turning back, no giving up. Obama shared this message with the attendees of the 2008 Democratic National Convention:

> America, we cannot turn back.
> Not with so much work to be done.
> Not with so many children to educate,
> and so many veterans to care for.
> Not with an economy to fix and cities to rebuild and farms to save.
> Not with so many families to protect and so many lives to mend.
> America, we cannot turn back.
> We cannot walk alone.
> At this moment, in this election,
> we must pledge once more to march into the future.

3. Difficulties must be handled, by combining forces between all parties involved and using all means. Obama's third step on the way to handling difficulties is based on his inner belief that together we can handle big challenges. He expressed this notion in a speech in October 2008:

> Together, we cannot fail.
> Not now.
> Not when we have a crisis to solve and an economy to save…

The emphasis is on handling crises *together*, while leaning on the combined mutual strength of the nation. See how many times he uses the word "together" in another speech in October 2008:

> Together, we cannot fail.
> Together, we can overcome the broken policies
> and divided politics of the last eight years.
> Together, we can renew an economy that rewards work
> and rebuilds the middle class.
> Together, we can create millions of new jobs,
> and deliver on the promise of health care
> you can afford and education that helps your kids compete…
> Together, we can change this country and change this world.

4. One must take a proactive approach. He or she must initiate, fight, be accountable, and live with the knowledge that our fate is in our hands. Based on Obama's approach, when you encounter a difficulty, there is no room for fear or alarm. In that same speech in October 2008, he depicts the fourth step:

> Now is not the time for fear.
> Now is not the time for panic.
> Now is the time for resolve and steady leadership.
> We can meet this moment.
> We can come together to restore confidence in the American economy.
> We can renew that fundamental belief—that in America,
> our destiny is not written for us,
> but by us.

Obama underlines that every solution must be measured by common sense and the actual results.

And he went on to say:

> This is not a time for ideology—
> it's a time for common sense and a politics of pragmatism.
> The test of an idea must not be whether it is liberal or conservative—
> the test should be whether it works for the American people.
> That's what we should all be focused on in the days and weeks ahead.

5. To handle the present, it is important to look back to the past to draw strength, and to the future with the belief that change is indeed possible. Obama conveyed in that same speech in Londonderry, NH (October 15, 2008) the same messages we saw earlier, but they are especially relevant in this context:

> I know these are difficult times.
> I know folks are worried.
> But I believe that we can steer ourselves out of this crisis…
> This is a nation that has faced down war and depression;
> great challenges and great threats.
> And at each and every moment,
> we have risen to meet these challenges…
> The American story has never been about things coming easy
> it's been about rising to the moment when the moment is hard;

> That's why we remember that some of the most famous words ever spoken by an American came from a president who took office in a time of turmoil—"The only thing we have to fear is fear itself."

Obama astutely applied these strategies himself to handle difficulties that arose in the midst of an election campaign, which occurred after some embarrassing video segments of Jeremiah Wright from Trinity United Church of Christ were made public. Obama had been identified with the pastor in the past.

Barack Obama remained level-headed, reasonable, and practical. He asked his staff to set aside time for him to make a speech on race, a speech he indeed made in Philadelphia in March 2008, and which became one of his most inspiring speeches. In this speech, Obama addressed the embarrassing issue of his own accord and persuaded many potential voters that the words of the pastor should not overshadow his candidacy.

This is an excellent example of the way in which Obama applies what he preaches. He doesn't give up, nor does he back down in the face of surprise and extreme awkwardness. Nor does he blame his staff for not anticipating the move; rather, he joins forces with them in an attempt to turn things around.

This is a fine example of the way in which Obama operates. Despite the huge challenge before him, he does not lose his cool. He initiates a fiery speech, based on the practical attitude that if he speaks, he has a good chance of persuading his listeners.

Note to the reader: Our book was published in September 2011. It will be interesting to see—very soon—how President Obama will use his "five steps to handle difficulties" system in his run for a second term in office, in the 2012 elections.

Now, let's see how to make complex messages catchy and make them stick in your target audience's mind.

Difficulties as Opportunities

One of the most effective persuasion tactics is to directly address the objections and the anticipated difficulties. Ask yourself: What will your opponents say about your ideas? How will they attack them? What difficulties await you and others on the way to realizing the messages?

Don't wait for others to raise the expected objections and difficulties; handle them yourself.

"Immunize" your audience in advance. Guide your listeners on how to handle the expected difficulties and repeat the message again and again.

Remember, hardship or crisis is a test, a test you cannot fail. Have belief and confidence in yourself and in your audience's mutual ability to handle the difficulty together and triumph. You can adopt Obama's five steps to handle difficulties:

1. Difficulties, challenges, and failures cannot be avoided; you can only learn from them, grow and improve.

2. A challenge or difficulty is a test you cannot fail. You must succeed. There is no way of backing down or giving up.

3. Difficulties must be handled by combining forces with all the parties involved and by using all the means.

4. Adopt a proactive approach, initiate, fight, take responsibility, and live with the knowledge that your fate is in your hands.

5. To handle the present, it is important to look back at the past for strength and look forward to the future with a belief that change is possible.

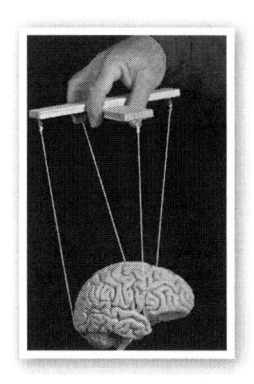

CHAPTER 14

It's simple — How to make complex messages clear and catchy

"Great leaders are almost always great simplifiers, who can cut through argument, debate, and doubt to offer a solution everybody can understand."

—**General Colin Powell**

We saw how Obama creates communicative messages based on three basic principles: optimistic messages; concrete issues that motivate listeners by providing them "a pill for their headache;" and handling objections and difficulties in advance by "injecting a vaccine."

Now, we'll move on to a secret that's easy to explain, but not always easy to apply: the secret of simplicity.

Montesquieu, the French philosopher, said over two hundred years before Obama was born, "What speakers lack in depth, they make up for in length." Ninth American president William Henry Harrison applied this insight to the fullest: his inaugural speech was the longest inaugural speech in history of U.S. presidents and included 8,445 words. In 1841, he spoke for almost two hours, in freezing cold and without a coat. Following the speech, he caught a cold, the cold turned into pneumonia, and he died a month later. So remember the acronym KISS: "keep it simple, stupid!" if you want to stay alive after a speech…

George Washington, on the other hand, the first and only US president who won the support of 100 percent of the electorate, made his inaugural speech the shortest in history: only 135 words. What speech would you prefer to hear?

It's worth mentioning Calvin Coolidge as well, the thirtieth president of the United States, who began his term in 1923. He is remembered as a man of few words. Once, a young lady sat beside him at dinner, and told him she had made a bet with a friend that she would get three words out of him during the evening. The president answered, "You lose!"

Obama has the capacity to simplify complex issues and convey clear, brief, and catchy messages. This capability is manifested in virtually every area in which he is involved: clear and concise wording of complex ideas, light structuring of paragraphs which directly address sensitive issues using the "elephant in the room" method we read about, and creating catchy key phrases.

Here's a short example from the 2008 Democratic National Convention:

> The change we need doesn't come from Washington.
> Change comes to Washington.

Obama uses secrets that have been known for many generations. He knows that to make a short and effective speech, one should prepare, practice, and focus. And he indeed managed to translate the complex issues he talked about into simple, brief, and clear messages. He takes a complex issue such as the economy, and manages to simplify and condense it down to the basic level of understanding of every person in the audience, even a ten-year-old child. Instead of going into complex descriptions of the US economy in the midst of a crisis, he simply describes the Americans who are experiencing the crisis:

> Tonight, more Americans are out of work
> and more are working harder for less.
> More of you have lost your homes
> and even more are watching your home values plummet.
> More of you have cars you can't afford to drive,
> credit card bills you can't afford to pay,
> and tuition that's beyond your reach…

He promises people what matters to them most: that their wallets won't suffer. This is what he said in his October 2008 speech:

> No matter what Senator McCain may claim, here are the facts—
> if you make under $250,000,
> you will not see your taxes increase by a single dime—
> not your income taxes,
> not your payroll taxes,
> not your capital gains taxes.
> Nothing.
> Because the last thing we should do in this economy is raise taxes on the middle-class.

Even if you don't listen to Obama attentively, you can understand very well what he's talking about. With his art of being concise, Obama is always loyal to his method; that is, one should focus on central issues that motivate people. Thus, he effectively makes every topic concise.

On December 17, 2010, just before signing the Middle-Class Tax Cuts Bill, President Obama gave a simple message to the American people:

> We are here with some good news for the American people this holiday season. By a wide bipartisan margin, both Houses of Congress have now passed a package of tax relief that will protect the middle class,
> that will grow our economy,
> and will create jobs for the American people.

He did not include details that were not necessary to his listeners, instead he focused on the core, on what mattered to people, fascinated them and motivated them into action. Here's a short, simple example, where he applies this skill:

> We can't afford four more years of our addiction to oil from dictators.
>
> —Democratic Nomination Victory Speech
> June 3, 2008, Saint Paul, Minnesota

As part of his simplicity, Obama is not afraid to be direct. As we saw, at the basis of this tactic is his most central value: he believes it is important there be full equivalence and congruence between what one thinks and what one says, and there should not be a gap between the two. This is the exact opposite of the expression, "saying one thing and thinking another." The direct speech, which Obama uses often, helps him be better understood and more persuasive.

He manages not only to simplify complex topics and speak directly, but to create catchy and memorable slogans that will most likely remain long after he is gone.

These slogans that adorn his speeches have become his trademark, like an artist's signature. These catchy key phrases are repeated in Obama's speeches until they ultimately become winning slogans whose true power is in their simplicity.

You too should think before key presentations how to simplify your message and shorten it. Add a short catch phrase and win!

Keep It Simple

Dr. Danny Oppenheimer of Princeton University found that people tend to buy more stocks of companies that have a catchy name, a name that's easy to pronounce. He published the findings of a study he conducted with Adam Alter in May 2006. This study is mentioned in Dan Ariely's book *Predictably Irrational*.

Oppenheimer also discovered in his studies that the use of long words to impress an audience has the opposite effect: the audience thinks *you* are less intelligent if *they* don't understand what you are saying.

This is why Obama adopted simplicity. Here are some examples of simple, catchy slogans from Obama's speeches:

> I am my sister's keeper. I am my brother's keeper.
> You invest in America, America will invest in you, and together, we will move this country forward.
> That's the change we can offer in 2008—not change as a slogan, but change we can believe in.
> Our destiny is not written for us, but by us.
> This victory alone is not the change we seek—it is only the chance for us to make that change.
> Now is our chance to turn the page. Now is our chance to write a new chapter. We will win this election, and then you and I—together—will change this country and change this world.
> The greatest risk we can take is to try the same old politics with the same old players and expect a different result.
> Opportunity doesn't come easy.
> One man cannot make a movement.

You've got an obligation to yourselves, and America has an obligation to you, to make sure you're getting the best education possible.

You can't change direction with a new driver who follows the same old map.

The Genius of Simplicity

"Everything should be as simple as it is, but not simpler."

—Albert Einstein

Obama's art of simplicity is manifested in the way he structures his speeches. He does this in the same simple way he conveys messages. His speeches are built of short paragraphs, and every paragraph stands alone and expresses a certain idea. Obama builds his speeches like a TV series. You can watch the entire series if you want, but you can also watch a single episode and still understand it as if it stood alone. This structure makes all of Obama's speeches light and flowing. He enables listeners to listen to part of the speech and still remain on top of things; even someone who walks in at the middle, for example, will understand what he's talking about, because the speech isn't structured like a building, floor above floor, but like a train, compartment next to compartment.

Even the language Obama uses is basic, easy to understand English. *The New York Times* reported in October 2009 that, according to experts, Obama's English is easier to understand because he pronounces the words clearly and speaks relatively slowly. He also uses an expansive vocabulary, which addresses all layers of the population.

As a Scrabble fan, Obama knows many extraordinary words. But the game of communication is different. Simple words and short words are his secrets. When you read his autobiography, *Dreams from My Father*, you will find out that 72 percent of the 101,000 words in the book, have only one syllable, and about 20 percent of the words have two syllables. This is a technique that many memorable writers use in their work, including greats like Ernest Hemingway.

Obama's speech style is virtually musical, which makes it easy to pick up what he's saying. We found that in Japan they use recorded and transcribed speeches of Obama to teach English, because his English is easy to understand. It seems the Japanese, who often find it hard to understand speakers whose mother tongue is English, feel comfortable with Obama's friendly language.

There is another simple advantage: most people's attention spans are short - only a few minutes' duration. So instead of writing a speech that *demands* concentration, Obama focuses on conveying short and simple ideas, teeming with peaks.

In Obama's speeches, you can almost always find a strong opening and end. He creates a clear outline for every speech, captures the listeners' attention, moves them, and then motivates them into action.

You should know how to use different opening techniques when you speak. A strong opening can be a personal story, a question, or directly addressing the audience - something one cannot remain indifferent to. In November 2009, Obama met with the prime minister of Thailand during a convention at the Shangri-La hotel in Singapore. He began his speech like a news flash. The conclusion came right after the beginning of his words:

> We have just concluded the first ever meeting between a United States president and the leaders of all ten Asian countries.

Six months earlier, in May, he also opened with the "news-flash method" when he discussed employment in the USA:

> Good morning, everybody. This morning we learned that our economy lost another 539,000 jobs in the month of April. And while it's somewhat encouraging that this number is lower than it's been in each of the past six months, it's still a sobering toll.

Power Open

Plan your opening statement so that you begin your communication with power. Plan the words so the audience connects to you quickly and knows you have something special in store. This is something the audience wants to hear. If you have news to convey, start with that. The listeners' attention and concentration are much higher at the beginning of your speech. Start with a "bang."

If you have dramatic news, start with that. On May 1, 2011, President Obama started with a "bang":

> Good evening. Tonight, I can report to the American people and to the world that the United States has conducted an operation that killed Osama

bin Laden, the leader of al Qaeda, and a terrorist who's responsible for the murder of thousands of innocent men, women, and children.

Even if you're not the president of the United States, begin with the news that is most important to your audience.

Here are a few more techniques that will allow you to open strongly: a personal story; an anecdote from the past; connecting to the news or a relevant issue that most of the audience is familiar with; a quote from a famous personality relevant to the message; rhetorical questions that create interest and intrigue; using a dramatic prop to attract immediate attention; and mentioning something that happened on this date in the past and connecting it with the message.

The Importance of the End

A powerful ending is an important factor in any speech or presentation. The end is what the audience remembers most–it is the last thing they hear. This is your opportunity to hammer home everything you have said up to this point simply by rousing the emotions of the audience.

Obama understands this technique and takes advantage of it at the end of his speeches. Simply by raising his level of energy, the pace of his words, and the tone of his voice, he motivates the audience to take action. In Virginia in 2008, for example, his speech concluded with a powerful emotional hammer:

> If you want the next four years looking like the last eight,
> then I am not your candidate.
> But if you want real change—
> if you want an economy that rewards work,
> and that works for Main Street and Wall Street;
> if you want tax relief for the middle class and millions of new jobs;
> if you want health care you can afford
> and education that helps your kids compete;
> then I ask you to knock on some doors,
> make some calls,
> talk to your neighbors,
> and give me your vote.
> And if you stand with me in thirteen days,

Obama's Secrets

> I promise you—we will win Virginia,
> we will win this election,
> and then, you and I—together—
> will change this country
> and change this world.

And at the end of his speech at the Democratic National Convention's "Moving America Forward" rally in Cleveland, Ohio (October 31, 2010), he utilizes this technique by sending out a call to action (note also his repetitious use of the phrase "I need you," and how he identifies what the pay-off will be if his listeners take action):

> So, Cleveland, *I need you* to keep on fighting. *I need you* to keep on believing. *I need you* to knock on some doors. *I need you* to talk to your neighbors. *I need you* to talk to your friends. *I need you* to go early and vote. Because if you are willing to step up to the plate…We will restore our economy. We will rebuild our middle class. And we will reclaim the American dream for future generations.

The end of your speech is your last chance. It's your final opportunity to repeat your messages, your slogans, and your refrain. Obama's calls for action, whether they are general or specific, are almost always direct, clear, and unambiguous. And he delivers them in a way that rouses the emotions of the audience and makes them *want* to respond.

Another option for the end of your speech is to offer your audience a surprise. Think *The Sixth Sense* (written and directed by M. Night Shyamalan), where the plot of the film hinges entirely on the surprise at the end. (If you don't know what that surprise is, don't worry, we won't spoil it for you.)

In his June 2009 speech at the annual conference of the American Medical Association (Chicago, Illinois), Obama seized every opportunity to market the health reform plan he proposed during his presidential election campaign–a promise realized in March of the following year. A health convention is as good a place as any at which to utilize the technique of a surprise ending, and Obama did not fail to recognize this. He said:

> You know, the other day, a friend of mine, Congressman Earl Blumenauer, handed me a magazine with a special issue titled, "The Crisis in American Medicine." One article notes "soaring charges." Another warns about the "volume of utilization of services." Another asks if we can find a "better way than

fee-for-service for paying for medical care." It speaks to many of the challenges we face today. The thing is, this special issue was published by *Harper's Magazine* in October of 1960—before I was born.

You too can surprise your audience by ending a presentation with an unexpected twist. Surprises and twists are one of the six ingredients to making your ideas stick in the minds of your target audience, according to *Made to Stick: Why Some Ideas Survive and Others Die*, by Chip Heath and Dan Heath.

There is a story about legendary British Prime Minister Winston Churchill that offers a valuable lesson. In 1940, Churchill was invited to speak to the congregation of a church. He asked, "How much time do I have," to which the pastor replied, "Why do you care?" "Because," he responded, "if I have an hour, I can go up there and speak right now. If I have ten minutes, I need six hours to prepare. If I have only three minutes, I won't speak, because I need three days." This story identifies that Churchill understood that making things simple and brief is one of the most challenging feats in the arena of public speaking.

It's not Easy to be Simple.

The secret of simplicity is important, even though it's not easy to apply. When you speak before an audience or persuade others, remember to simplify complex issues and convey clear, brief, and catchy messages.

Use simple language that everyone can understand. Forego details that are not vital to your listeners, and focus on what matters to them, what fascinates them, and what motivates them. Formulate your ideas clearly and concisely, and don't be afraid to speak directly about sensitive issues.

Consider how to create catchy key words and slogans that will illustrate your messages with simplicity, so the listeners can internalize them.

The best way to make an effective speech is to create a powerful opening, add a strong ending, and make sure these two parts are close to one another.

Between these two parts, you can express ideas in light and flowing paragraphs that stand alone. Formulate your words using the TV series method—episode by episode, so the listeners can leave the room, come back in, and still be on top of things.

In the next chapter we will reveal a very simple secret that makes all of Obama's media appearances a success.

Remember: to be simple, you should prepare, practice, and focus.

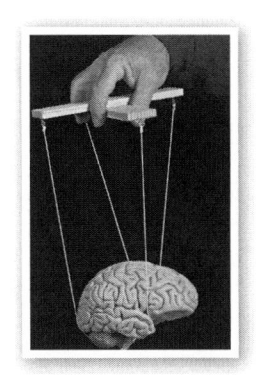

CHAPTER 15

YOU CAN BE A STAR – HOW TO SPEAK ON STAGE WITH CONFIDENCE, LIKE OBAMA

"I'm convinced that about half of what separates the successful entrepreneurs from the non-successful ones is pure perseverance."

—**Steve Jobs**

One of Obama's secrets of successful communication is perhaps the most simple to apply. We will reveal the secret in this chapter.

The secret is so obvious that we debated whether or not to include it as a chapter. Later, as befits people who live in the Facebook and Twitter age, we contemplated shortening it to only one hundred, forty characters. But even that was too much. Because to describe such a basic secret, directly related to Obama's success on stage, three words will suffice: "rehearse and practice."

Why then does this chapter appear in all its glory? The reason is simple: After work of over twenty years on four continents, preparing CEOs and many executives for media, "financial road shows," and speeches, we have no doubt this is many people's Achilles' heel.

People expect magic, and they often simply can't find the time to prepare. But it can't be avoided. To speak powerfully takes what every Olympic champion in any sport does: practice physically and psychologically, for a length of time, not at the last minute. And, of course, obtain feedback.

Therefore, we feel this chapter is of the utmost importance for anyone who wants to succeed. We hope that, after you read this chapter, you will internalize its basic message and start practicing, just like Obama, even when you reach the height of your career, to remain on top.

Even legendary Steve Jobs, considered one of the best presenters in the world, uses personal coaches and prepares for months for every important presentation. So, if you use an IPAD, IPhone, or other cool gadgets, why not take Jobs' advice, and practice like him and like President Obama?

Almost every communication expert will agree that Obama's speech at the 2004 Democratic National Convention is the speech that paved his way to the White House four years later.

In a speech that lasted sixteen minutes and twenty-five seconds, the fuse was lit that activated the engine of the first African-American to become president of the United States. Obama electrified the room. You could hear a fly buzz in the silence that followed as soon as he began to speak. That day, a star was born in the Democratic Party.

We studied how Obama reached such a high level of performance and overwhelming success with that speech. What made him convey such polished messages? What helped him get on stage with confidence and power? The answer is the secret Obama takes with him to every speech he makes since then and to this day.

It seems the inspirational speech Obama made in 2004 was a result of practice, practice, and more practice. Obama did what they often do with Broadway shows: they are performed off Broadway, sometimes off-off Broadway, meaning they are performed in front of smaller audiences before larger ones.

Before Obama spoke at the 2004 Democratic National Convention, he had practiced his speech many times and in different forums. As we mentioned, Obama absorbed the value of studying when he was a child. He adopted the basic belief that one must make an effort to succeed. For years, he learned that new messages can be tried out on an "experimental" audience. He practiced various formulations of the same message on different audiences and, no less important, he listened to the feedback he got. He was aware of the body language of the audience that listened to him when he tried new messages. He was aware of the audience's reactions. And he learned to routinely polish messages.

All this enabled him also to practice another skill: combining personal stories to move the audience and motivate it into action. The constant practicing enabled Obama to reach an extremely eloquent and energetic level of speech. Practicing enabled him to become the Obama we know today. As president, a team of speechwriters assists him. But when he first started out, he had to write most of his speeches himself. As a man who loves words, a jurist by education, and one focused on the goal, Obama honed his ability to write speeches and invested a lot of time therein.

The experience he accumulated enables him, today, to give precise instructions as to the structure of the diverse speeches he must convey, and to add ideas of his own when he goes over the draft and "lives the words" during the speech itself.

As soon as Obama was invited to make the keynote speech at the 2004 Democratic National Convention, he took advantage of every waking moment to plan the speech and to practice. He invested hundreds of hours to become prepared. He knew he wouldn't get a second chance to make a first impression, and he wanted his first impression to be a powerful one. Obama also remembered his political loss in the 2000 elections to Bobby Rush, and he wanted to take advantage of the opportunity that fell into his lap.

Most US citizens didn't know his name at that time, but Obama was not unknown to the many activists in the Democratic Party. They knew he had a stage presence, because they heard him in different forums. They were familiar with his performance as an Illinois senator, and knew he was running for the US Senate. They knew he could excite the participants at the convention and expectations of him were high.

Obama decided to transcend their level of expectation.

They say he even wrote ideas for this speech in the men's room or while traveling to meetings. He recited the speech to himself. He memorized the messages. He practiced. He asked for feedback and used it to improve the messages. He programmed his brain to believe he could do it. He believed he was the perfect person to deliver the speech. And moments before the speech itself, he did something simple: he read the speech back stage out loud (not a quiet reading of the speech to himself), to get up there "raring to go."

Obama provided his listeners a full-course meal. He caused the audience to swallow his messages and believe in him. He planted in this speech the basis for the slogan that later accompanied him throughout his presidential campaign: Yes, we can.

The Audience is not Naked

To reduce the anxiety of public speaking, some books suggested many years ago to imagine the audience is naked. But there are much better methods.

The first is to prepare well and watch video recordings of yourself successfully conveying messages. Multiple repetitions, combined with watching the videos, are a formula Obama uses too, even when he is very busy.

The second is related to the audience. Imagine the audience listening, taking an interest, clapping and enthusiastic. Because if this is the image you draw for yourself in your mind, this is also the image you will actually see when you get on stage.

Obama once said he loves writing at night, when he's alone. It is then his concentration level is high, and his ideas flow. He says he also wrote his two books in the wee hours of the morning.

And here's another one of Obama's secrets worth knowing, especially in the digital era: Obama prefers writing ideas that come to him on a piece of paper, not typing them on a computer.

Only later does he shift the ideas to an electronic document, so he can play with the words, move paragraphs, delete, add, and undoubtedly, send the documents to other people to add ideas and comments.

It turns out that, even in the computer age, there is an advantage to writing ideas on a piece of paper. Why? Because writing on paper is a creative action that better activates the "right brain," the creative side. And this is also the part which you want to function best when you are seeking ideas.

On the other hand, typing on a computer will inadvertently activate the "left brain," the critical side that hinders the flow of ideas and the creative process that is so important at this stage.

There is a huge benefit to using this secret of Obama's: in this way a separation is created between the first phase, designed mainly to enable you to think in a more associative manner and come up with ideas, and the second phase, which includes a judgmental and critical process and which is easier to perform on the computer.

> ### 🔍 Left Brain / Right Brain
>
> Researchers have confirmed that, though both the left and right hemispheres of the brain can perform most mental tasks to some degree, their abilities to do so differ - some mental tasks are better handled by the right hemisphere, and some by the left (though, according to Jean Mercer, author of *Child Development: Myths and Misunderstandings*, both hemispheres do communicate with each other during most tasks). Thus, throughout our book we use the term 'left brain' when we talk about the mind's analytical processes and we use the term 'right brain' to indicate holistic or subconscious processes (as opposed to using these terms to point to the physical hemispheres).

If you can imagine yourself succeeding like Obama, you should use this secret. It's true that the busier we become, the less free time we have to prepare and practice. But you should find the time to practice and watch your recordings so you can see what others see and what they hear.

The more Obama's career progressed, the more his writing, especially his speech writing, went from being personal work to group work. This, too, is an aspect of professionalism: to know when and how to work as part of a team.

Obama learned the importance of speeches from presidents such as Reagan and Clinton. In fact, the presidents of the United States almost always had speech writers. George Washington used several speechwriters. Lincoln, considered the greatest speaker of the 19th century, also used speechwriters. President Kennedy was not ashamed to say he sought the help of Ted Sorensen, his legendary speechwriter.

The speechwriter carries decisive weight as to the content of the speech itself, but ultimately, every successful speech is liable to be ruined by a bad speaker.

Before the 2008 Democratic National Convention, when Obama was very busy with his presidential election campaign, he didn't have much time to prepare. The first draft, written for him by Jon Favreau, was ready less than two weeks before the speech was scheduled. Obama closed himself up in a hotel room in Chicago with Favreau and strategic advisor David Axelrod, and they worked on this speech together, as a team.

Obama knows how to make the best of teamwork, knowing that at the end of the day he will be the one making the speech. Therefore, the speech should be written in a way in which its words sound authentic, as if he chose them himself. Therefore, he makes sure his values, beliefs, and vision are always incorporated in the speech.

We saw that Obama comes on stage prepared, because he begins the process of writing his speech long before the scheduled date of the speech. This enables him to come up with ideas over a period of time, sleep on them, and hope to wake up in the morning with new ideas, and of course, to practice many times, not at the last minute.

The combination of practice with feedback is a winning formula that Obama takes pains to apply, because he knows it works. He's not the first person in the White House to do so; there is a significant positive correlation between American presidents who were considered communication magicians and the secret of preparation.

During his eight years as president, Ronald Reagan said almost four million words in 2,500 speeches and appearances. Despite his vast experience, Reagan used to practice and rehearse every evening for a week before the main speech was slated. He was taught to practice and did so despite years of experience as an actor and as governor of California. He would often practice for a full day in front of a video camera, in addition to his rehearsals. He knew that on TV every facial expression is visible, and if you are unaware, this can work against you.

President Clinton is a communication star, as well, and he also used to prepare for his speeches and obtain feedback on how well his messages worked in order to improve them later on.

Clinton was considered charismatic from birth and a great speaker; however, he wasn't born with a microphone in hand. In his autobiography *My Life*, he wrote that he had failed at his attempts to lecture as a high school student. He also wrote about a speech he had given at the Democratic Convention in Atlanta, Georgia (July 1988) when he had still been governor of Arkansas, and admitted, "Those were thirty-two minutes of total disaster."

In the early 1990s, Swedish psychologist Anders Ericsson conducted a study at the Berlin Academy of Music. He divided the young violinists who studied there into three groups. The elite group was comprised of the stars considered having potential to be global solo artists. The second group was comprised of talented violinists, who didn't have the potential to be global solo artists, and the third group was comprised of the youths defined as lacking real potential (though it is worthwhile bearing in mind that all the students accepted into this Academy excel). Ericsson asked the students, "Since you began playing the violin, how many hours have you played?" It turned out that most began playing at around five years old and, in the early years, played two to three hours a week on average. The difference began at around the age of eight. At nine years old, the stars played six hours a week on average; at age twelve they played eight hours a week; at fourteen they played sixteen hours; and towards the end of their studies, they played thirty hours or more. By the age of twenty they had accumulated ten thousand hours of playing the violin.

In contrast, the members of the second group accumulated only eight thousand hours of playing the violin by the age of twenty, and the violinists in the third group accumulated half the hours accumulated by the members of the second group. Of all the violinists, there were no "natural born" violinists who excelled without practicing and without putting in ten thousand hours by the age of twenty.

This study joins a series of studies that found that true expertise is a result of hard work over a period of ten years or ten thousand hours.

There is a story which tells of an actor who walked along the streets of Manhattan early on in his career and asked a passerby, "Excuse me, how do I get to Carnegie Hall?" The passerby answered, "Practice, practice, practice."

The Winning Formula

"The tongue is the only tool that gets sharper with use."

—Washington Irving

Apply Obama's winning formula and combine practice and rehearsals with feedback. To speak powerfully, you have to practice physically and psychologically over a period of time and obtain feedback. Practice new messages on an experimental audience. Memorize your messages. Listen to the feedback. Repeat the words out loud back stage to get on stage "raring to go." Use teamwork. Remember, only with continuous and consistent practice over time will you be able to speak in front of an audience in an energetic and eloquent way

President Barack Obama, who has been speaking virtually every day for the last decade, accumulated vast experience that allowed him to control his natural instrument: his baritone voice. He proves in his actions that it sometimes takes twenty years to become an overnight star.

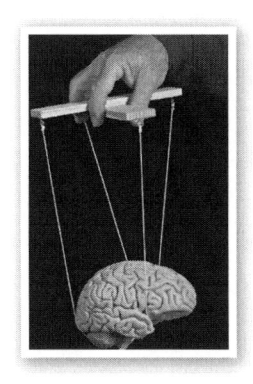

CHAPTER 16

Uhh, Uhhmm... – The secret of quiet charisma

What do the following sentences have in common?

- I *really* do think Obama is an excellent speaker.

- *The truth is,* Obama practices a lot before important speeches.

- *I just want to say,* Obama made mistakes when he first started out and learned lessons from them.

- *In principle,* there is no big difference between Obama and Clinton.

- *Um…* we want Obama to make changes but, *like,* changes that won't hurt us.

In all of these sentences, there are words or expressions that contribute nothing to the message. Bottom line—empty words that create superfluous noise and damage the message.

Obama practices and keeps practicing to convey messages devoid of noise. When we analyze the way in which he gives winning speeches, it is important to understand that some of his expertise is self-control and the ability to remain silent during pauses between the words.

Obama's Secrets

Let's become familiar with one of the most superfluous aspects of interpersonal communication: empty words known as clutch words, because they are like the clutch you press down on when changing gears in a gearshift vehicle. When speaking before an audience, you should know to shift to the next gear without pressing the clutch. While driving, you are forced to coordinate between the hand that shifts gears and the left foot that presses down on the clutch and the right foot that comes off the gas pedal; when you speak before an audience, you should know how to create coordination between the brain and the mouth, while shifting "gears."

If you do not consciously control this, you are liable, like many others, to integrate superfluous words in your speech, such as *the truth is, you know, really, only, in fact, in principle, it's just that, over all, for sure, like,* and other superfluous words that may be habitual to you.

One of Obama's secrets of success is the fact that he tries avoiding these superfluous words and the use of superfluous and worthless sounds. A superfluous sound, even if it is made up of one letter, says a lot about the speaker, even before he starts speaking.

A long "uh…" conveys lack of professionalism. Many speakers naturally add insignificant sounds before their words, such as *err, ah, um*, and more. These superfluous sounds are known as *unwords*, because they have no meaning. Also, poor use of the word "and," when spoken continuously, adds nothing.

Why does this happen to us? It happens, among other reasons, because we are nervous, and with some people it happens every time they have to think of the next word they are about to say. To prevent this from occurring, we should learn to say nothing while we think of what to say instead of using *unwords*. Instead of making sounds, such as "um…" or saying words such as "like"–just stay quiet.

But, uh…it's like…like it's not…it's not easy to get rid of, um…you know, the superfluous sounds.

We can learn from Obama how to improve the situation. Obama has few "uhs…" in his sentences, thanks to the use of teleprompters and his constant practice, which enable him to control messages. Obama generally uses two teleprompters, one on his right and one on his left. The teleprompter helps him avoid adding superfluous sounds because, at the end of each paragraph or whenever there's a comma or new sentence, he turns his head and shifts to the other teleprompter with ease. Every time he shifts from the right teleprompter to the left and vice versa, he pauses between words and doesn't add superfluous sounds. But Obama is not perfect. In his appearances without a teleprompter, at press conferences for example, he tends to use *unwords* and superfluous sounds such as "uh…" Due to his control of the material, his enthusiasm and desire to sound natural, when he speaks without a teleprompter, he tends to add superfluous sounds, to speak with passion and skip the pauses, which would undoubtedly be inserted were it a formal speech. Therefore, he practices and learns lessons from media appearances, in which he added superfluous words and sounds.

The use of superfluous sounds detracts from your image as an eloquent, professional speaker, and it has another disadvantage: it prevents your listeners from processing in their brains the messages they feel, hear, and see in their mind's eye. Therefore, you should create intentional pauses, brief recesses between the words. You should stop and not create a sequence of superfluous words that prevent the brain from taking in and internalizing the messages. The brain needs a break every so often to process your words.

Obama Learned Obama-ese

As we saw, Obama is the master of learning from feedback. After he was elected, he obtained feedback that, in his first press conference, there was a dramatic difference between the first part, where he conveyed his message with the help of a teleprompter, and the second part, where he answered journalists' questions. As long as he was reading off the teleprompter, he spoke classic "Obama-ese." But as soon as he began speaking without an aid, especially given the stressful questions, he inserted superfluous sounds and conveyed a hesitant message.

Obama worked on this skill, practiced, and by the time he gave his fifth press conference in the White House, there was a dramatic improvement. He answered most of the questions with the same degree of professionalism, without superfluous sounds, even though he didn't read from a prepared text.

Almost everyone uses clutch words. It happens mostly when you don't prepare enough and when you don't control the messages. It also happens when you are asked a question and you don't want to begin answering before you have given the question some thought. However, you do not want to give the impression that you have nothing to say.

There's a difference between the type of superfluous words women and men inadvertently insert. A study conducted in the USA found there's no difference between men and women when using the sounds "um" and "uh." However, with *unwords*, such as *like, you know*, women use these much more than men. The study, conducted at the University of Oklahoma in

2004 among students ranging between nineteen and twenty-four years of age, analyzed one hundred and fifty spontaneous speeches by students. It seems young women use the expression "you know" twice as much as young men, and with the word "like," the gap is even greater; the women used it five times more than the equivalent men's group.

Here are four practical tips to reduce the number of times it happens to you:

1. Do what Obama does: practice, rehearse, and say your messages out loud. The more you control the material, the less you will have to think while actually speaking. Control of the material helps continuous speech.

2. Practice speaking without superfluous sounds in your conversations throughout the day. Make sure you say nothing when you are thinking about what to say.

3. Record yourself and listen to the recording (even without watching). Focus on the words and sounds and pinpoint your vocal weaknesses. Learn lessons and reduce the use of the superfluous words next time.

4. Ask for feedback from people who listen to you. Ask them in particular to tell you what superfluous sounds and words you tend to use.

Good luck!

🔍 Obama's 10 Secrets for Preparing Speeches

To sum up the third part of the book, here are Obama's ten secrets for preparing speeches. Use them to speak powerfully.

1. **Obama consolidates the purpose of the speech or the communication with an audience.**

He asks himself, "How do I want my audience to feel when it hears my words?" "What actions do I deem important that the audience take after hearing what I have to say?" While he prepares his speeches, he performs like a laser-guided missile. He marks the target, and only then does he build the speech or determine the messages accordingly.

2. **Obama chooses the core messages he deems important to convey in his speech.** He focuses in each speech on a small number of central, optimistic messages. He focuses on messages that evoke hope and motivate people into action, messages that anyone can identify with.

3. **Obama chooses the key words of the speech.** These key words represent, in short, the positive messages he's saying, and he repeats them over and over, throughout the speech, to cause the message to stick in the minds of his listeners.

4. **Obama selects concrete topics to address in his speech**. Through these topics, he conveys his messages. He speaks about specific issues that matter to people on a day-to-day basis. These are generally widespread problems that can be solved, concrete issues that can be handled, and human needs that are important to provide for.

5. **Obama voices the hardships expected on the way and the objections that are liable to arise.** He can do this because he puts himself in the other person's shoes, and thus, he also responds to his listerners' inner needs. In the same breath, he shares with his listeners some ways to handle the difficulties, according to his method, and guides them to ward off the objections in a proactive way.

6. **Obama simplifies complex messages and makes them brief**, simple, and catchy. He summarizes every issue efficiently, foregoes details that are not vital to the listener, and focuses on the central core of the issue. At this point, he even dares to say things directly and creates catchy and memorable slogans.

7. **Obama creates a concise speech, the principles of which are a strong opening and ending, spoken in simple language.** The speech is made of short paragraphs and a complete and consolidated idea in each paragraph or each series of sequential paragraphs. Thus, he enables his listeners to be attentive only part of the time and still remain on top of things.

8. **Every speech also reflects his world of values, beliefs, and messages,** as well as ideas of skilled speechwriters and diverse advisors hired for specific events. He makes sure that his speechwriters craft the messages based on his values.

9. **Obama practices his speech or parts of it several times before diverse audiences.** He reads the speech out loud and focuses on the message and the nonverbal communication. Despite his busy schedule, he regards practicing and improving to reach the proper level of refinement as of the utmost importance. He aspires to control the content so that, even if he uses the teleprompter or speaker's notes, it will still sound as if he's speaking without aids.

10. **Obama watches recordings of his speeches, learns lessons, and obtains feedback from his advisors.** He does this with all of his media appearances. As a man who is always attentive to his surroundings, he knows that the effectiveness of communication is based on the effect on the target audience and not on the speaker's gut feeling. Obama is an eternal student who applies the lessons he learns almost immediately.

Obama's magic formula is: there is no real magic. One should practice and improve all the time. However, Obama and magicians do have something in common: audiences of all ages are fascinated by them!

Now that we know the secrets of Barack Obama's strategy for engineering winning messages, we will reveal Obama's special code that attracts people to him. We will see how Obama "dances the tango with his audience," no matter how large the audience is, and how he creates an intimate relationship.

PART FOUR
Intimate Communication

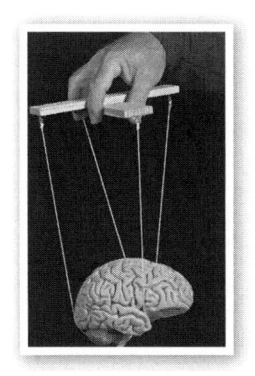

CHAPTER 17

A LOVE STORY – HOW TO CREATE AN INTIMATE RELATIONSHIP WHEN YOU COMMUNICATE

"The meeting of two personalities is like the contact of two chemical substances; if there is any reaction, both are transformed."

—**Carl Gustav Jung**

Welcome to Obama's secrets of love. We will now reveal how Obama gets his audience to like him and even fall in love with him. You will see the way he makes instant connections with people, creates a sort of relationship, and inspires them. As always with Obama, there is a method based on experience and scientific studies.

༄

The professional speakers in the world can be divided into different styles of speaker. Some focus on sales, some focus on humor, some inspire and motivate, and more. Every lecture style dictates both the content and the manner in which the speaker conveys his or her messages to the listeners.

Obama uses tools that are typical of "motivational speakers" who inspire and motivate, speakers who provide the audience with life insights–professional or personal– and arouse in audience members energy and an emotional experience that motivates them to change a facet of their attitude or behavior. And Obama does indeed motivate his audience into action.

As we will see, Obama consistently nurtures an intimate relationship with every audience, a relationship that involves trust, closeness, and mutual respect. You could even say Obama has a love affair with the audience. If you want to communicate effectively, you will want to know—and use—these simple techniques that Obama uses.

At the 2004 Democratic National Convention, Obama was explicitly invited to instill energy and motivation among the Democratic Party representatives. John Kerry, whom the Democratic Party members elected to run for president, is the man who invited Obama. Several months after this convention, Kerry lost the election to the Republican candidate, incumbent President George W. Bush, by a small margin.

Obama's 2004 speech, which was analyzed from every possible angle, had an explicit motivational style, including repetition of words at the beginning of sentences, use of the infinitive "to feel," and other exhilarating words, such as "energy," "passion," and "hope":

> America, tonight,
> if you feel the same energy that I do,
> if you feel the same passion that I do,
> if you feel the same hopefulness that I do,
> if we do what we must do…
> a brighter day will come

Obama produced the goods that John Kerry had anticipated with Obama's speech, and Kerry—who announced in January 2007 that he would not run again for president—rewarded Obama for his assistance. In January 2008, he announced his support of Obama as Democratic presidential candidate, a source of support that was very important to Obama, who still had to triumph over Hillary Clinton within the Democratic Party.

Selecting the right messages and expressing them with simplicity is important—but they are not enough to influence people. To generate a real change in thinking and to motivate people into action, you have to know how to serve up the messages and how to create the right atmosphere so that they are internalized. Obama knows this. He creates an intimate relationship with every audience comprised of trust, respect, and mutual understanding. He pours his messages into this relationship, so he can be sure they will be absorbed in fertile soil. His aim is to win over the audience's heart, and to motivate listeners into action.

How does he succeed at creating an intimate relationship with an audience of thousands of people? Obama has an extraordinary ability to establish *rapport* with every individual and every audience—a human chemistry, which is the basis of a relationship that entails *trust* and *mutual respect*.

The origin of the word "rapport" comes from French. It means establishing a close and harmonious relationship. When we refer to people as having rapport, we mean they are "transmitting on the same wavelength," that they are "in sync;" that they "click."

With Love and Respect

Seth Godin, an international marketing guru, creative speaker, and author of many best-selling books, claims there are two elements that are shared by all excellent speakers:

1. Respect from the audience.

2. Love for the audience.

Obama surely implements this, but at times, the opposite occurs: he exhibits respect towards the audience and, in return, he gets love from them.

In November 2009, a press conference took place in Tokyo, after Obama met the Japanese Prime Minister Yukio Hatoyama. As a man who knows that the setting is important, too, Obama chose Japan as the first country on his trip to Southeast Asia.

> It is a great honor to be making my first trip to Japan, as President of the United States. I have fond memories of visiting Japan in my youth. I've been looking forward to this trip for some time. I'm only sorry that Michelle and the girls could not join us. The girls have been studying Japan in school, and so they have a great interest in Japanese culture. And, hopefully, I'll be able to bring them next time.

Obama emphasizes why he chose Japan as the first stop on his trip to Asia:

> Japan is my first stop as President in Asia. I began my trip here in Tokyo because the alliance between the United States and Japan is a foundation for security and prosperity, not just for our two countries, but for the Asia Pacific region.

Two days later, after his meeting with Indonesian President Susilo Bambang Yudhoyono at the Shangri-la hotel in Singapore, Obama repeated his custom. He immediately mentioned his personal past in Indonesia and went on to congratulate President Yudhoyono and wish the country and the newly re-elected president well.

As a person who, during the presidential election campaign, often addressed the importance of rebuilding the relationship between America and *Ummah*, the Muslim world, Obama sees in Indonesia a role model:

> As many of you know, I have some historic ties to Indonesia, but I am also extraordinarily impressed with the progress that Indonesia has made in developing its democracy. I want to congratulate the President for his recent re-election, and he now has his government in place.
>
> Indonesia is not only regionally important, but as a member of the G20, as one of the world's largest democracies, as one of the world's largest Islamic nations, it has enormous influence and really is, I think, a potential model for the kind of development strategies, democracy strategies, as well as interfaith strategies that are going to be so important moving forward.

And when German Chancellor Angela Merkel visited Washington in November 2009, he wished her well too:

> But the main reason she's here is that a great honor has been bestowed upon her. She is going to be the first German chancellor in fifty years to address Congress—the first chancellor ever to address a joint session of Congress. And it is, I think, a very appropriate honor that's been bestowed on Chancellor Merkel.

The secret of rapport between people is so essential to the success of relationships, in general, and effective communication in particular, that we decided to grant it a place of honor in a book that reveals Obama's secrets of communication and influence.

When you have rapport with someone, you have a sense of utter faith and mutual respect. You feel comfortable with that person, and you know he or she understands you, no matter how different you are. When people have a good rapport, they tend to treat one another with more understanding, tolerance, and patience, which enables them to bridge gaps and cooperate. Of course, nothing is black and white. There are different levels of rapport as there are varying shades of gray. But rapport can only exist when there is reciprocity.

To influence someone, you should first be willing to be influenced by him or her. You don't have to like someone, or agree with him or her, to establish rapport. You can agree with someone, with or without rapport, and you can also disagree with someone, and have a great rapport. You can create rapport quickly, but you can lose it with the same speed. And remember, you can create rapport slowly and lose it quickly.

True, rapport is based on the instinctive sense of trust and integrity, regardless of the content. In a world where there are different types of people, with different opinions, from different backgrounds, rapport is a powerful tool with which to appreciate diversity and work together despite that diversity, on the basis of mutual respect. True rapport enables every individual to express him or herself freely and know the other will respect him or her.

The NLP approach, of which Obama uses many tools consciously or subconsciously, was developed in the 1970s. Its original developers, Richard Bandler and John Grinder, studied therapists who brought about rapid and profound changes in their patients. The common denominator that stood out among these excellent therapists—psychiatrist Milton Erickson, psychiatrist and family therapist Virginia Satir and founder of the Gestalt theory Fritz Perls—was their unique ability to create an effective rapport with their patients, and accordingly, achieve especially effective and quick results.

The secret underlying the process of creating rapport lies in entering the other person's world and becoming like him or her. The following sentence sums up nicely why rapport is so effective and important:

I like you, because you are like me.

Can you see now why your Facebook friends want you to *like* them?

People like other people and can relate to them if they feel there is a similarity between them. The similarity can come to light in different areas, such as a similar name, use of similar words, similar background, similar body gestures, similar appearance, similar values, similar problems, similar beliefs, and more.

Here's an example of the way in which Obama applies the similarity effect.

In 2009, Obama hosted ambassadors from various countries at the White House and created rapport with them:

One of the nice things about America is there are many global aspects represented in our cities and towns. I think we have immigrants who came to our shores from every country represented here this evening. In fact, you could even say my hometown of Chicago alone can prove it.

Who's the Boss?

Obama was interviewed for *Rolling Stone* magazine and talked about his love for music. He praised Bruce Springsteen for his authenticity and stressed that he considers it an important trait.

In that same interview, Obama exhibited his knowledge about other musicians and knew the names of songs they wrote and albums they produced. He stated that he listens to diverse music and gave examples. Among others, the readers discovered that Obama likes Stevie Wonder and Elton John.

Obama is young at heart, and he knows that music is a universal language, especially among youths and "Generation Z." And in this interview, he conveyed to them that he is like them. That's "rapport." When Obama embraced Bruce Springsteen at a special concert in Cleveland, Ohio, just before the day of the presidential election, he conveyed to his supporters, "I am like you." The images of Barack Obama, his wife Michelle, and their daughters Malia and Sasha with Bruce Springsteen "The Boss," excited many of the star's fans from a wide range of ages, and the aura of both men merged in the minds of the fans.

The ability to consciously create rapport will enable you to be effective in every interpersonal communication: managing a business, marketing and sales, negotiating, coaching people and, of course, in your relationship with your spouse, children, parents, friends, and more. You can use the secret of rapport in all your conversations.

But Obama is faced with a much greater challenge. He implements the skill of creating rapport on stage, before a crowd of thousands, in an asymmetric situation, where the audience can listen to him, but he cannot hear most of the audience's reactions.

Also, he stands far away from the audience, preventing him from studying the listeners' body language or other elements of nonverbal communication, such as breathing rate or body gestures.

How is it possible then, under these conditions, to become similar to an audience of thousands? How can one create a relationship of trust and mutual understanding when only one party speaks most of the time? How can one person create an intimate relationship and evoke emotions with such a large group of people? How can you do the same when you present your ideas to large groups?

In our study, we discovered that Obama develops genuine interest in his listeners, displays curiosity about them, and is prepared to see the world from their points of view. He joins them on their terms, as someone who walks at their pace. He in fact creatively applies basic tools of rapport, such as making eye contact, using one's name, addressing someone directly, adapting body language and speech, adapting language and style, and adapting content.

Intent on Creating Rapport

Obama directs his entire being into creating trust, respect, and mutual listening with the audience before him. And he talks about this directly with the audience. If rapport is a type of language, Obama speaks it like a mother tongue. Obviously, he wants to win over his audience and their trust, so he can later motivate them into action. Here is an example we saw in Chapter 2, from his 2008 victory speech. This time we will see how it is geared towards creating rapport:

> There will be setbacks and false starts.
> There are many who won't agree with every decision or policy I make as President, and we know that government can't solve every problem.
> But I will always be honest with you about the challenges we face.
> I will listen to you, especially when we disagree.
> And above all, I will ask you to join in the work of remaking this nation…

Creating Eye Contact

One of the essential elements in establishing rapport is creating eye contact with the person with whom you are communicating (though maintaining eye contact must be to a degree that suits the other person as well). But how does one create eye contact with a large audience? How do you create eye contact when you have to read a speech that was written in advance?

Using a teleprompter enables Obama to give speeches without losing eye contact with the audience. Reading this invisible screen, located at eye level, creates the effect of eye contact with the audience while maintaining the continuity of the speech.

Obama makes sure to use two teleprompters on either side of him, so he can turn his gaze from side to side, enabling him to create eye contact with large groups of people and maintain mobility and dynamics while he speaks.

Obama is in command of the messages prepared for him and, as we will see further on, he doesn't read his speech from the prompter, he just uses it as a reference. And he doesn't take his eyes off the audience.

If you want to establish rapport in every conversation, make sure to create direct eye contact. However, keep in mind there are cultural differences between people. In some countries and cultures, making direct eye contact is unacceptable, and conversing without making eye contact is preferred. If you meet an individual from another culture, and you are not knowledgeable of its customs, inquire in advance about this issue.

A Dangerous Tool

During seminars and workshops for executives in which we demonstrate Obama's secrets and train participants to hone their communication skills, we run into the disparaging comment, "Oh well, all he does is read off a teleprompter."

But whoever has tried working with this tool knows it's not easy to use. If you don't have command over the content and especially if you don't control the emotions you want to evoke in the audience, you will be perceived as phony, and there will be no rapport. In some cases, the teleprompter can be a communication impediment.

Obama learned to use the teleprompter as a tool that reminds him of the messages, but the messages come from within him, and he is focused on the audience—proof of his command of this medium.

From familiarity with Obama's thought patterns, it isn't the teleprompter that makes the difference; it's his true and honest desire to create eye contact with the audience because of his love of man, his inquisitiveness, and his desire to learn about the other person's motives.

Make It Personal

> "Remember that a man's name is to him the sweetest and most important sound in the English language."
>
> —Dale Carnegie, author of *How to Win Friends and Influence People.*

Most people feel better when they are called by their first name. This increases their sense of self-worth and reinforces the sense of closeness and intimacy with the other person.

When making a person's acquaintance, this is easy to do. When you present an idea before a small group of people, it is also easy to call some of the participants by name. But how do you call an audience of tens of thousands by name?

Obama gets around this obstacle. He manages to characterize people in the audience by using "group" names, as their identifying mark. Thus he can speak before a very large audience and create the sense of a personal face-to-face conversation between two people who know one another. He provides diverse groups in the population the sense that he is talking to them personally and understands them. If there are diverse groups in the audience, Obama mentions many of them. Just like in the following example from a speech in May 2008:

> You are Democrats who are tired of being divided;
> Republicans who no longer recognize the party that runs Washington;
> Independents who are hungry for change.
> You are the young people who've been inspired for the very first time
> and those not-so-young folks who've been inspired for the first time in a long time.
> You are veterans and church-goers;
> sportsmen and students; farmers and factory workers;
> teachers and business owners who have varied backgrounds
> and different traditions,
> but the same simple dreams for your children's future.

Obama doesn't speak to an anonymous audience. He speaks to the workers, the soldiers, the students, the teachers, the women and men, the families, the neighbors, the Democrats, the Republicans, the Americans, and others. When Obama speaks in a specific city he refers to it by name, as if it were a good friend.

He refers to the nation as "America" and speaks to it as if it were a living and breathing entity that one can have a face-to-face conversation with. America is no more than each and every person in the audience:

> *America*, we have come so far. We have seen so much.

Let's see how he spoke as president on a personal level to all the students in the USA at the beginning of the 2009 school year. He began the conversation as if he were talking to a friend:

> Hello everyone—how's everybody doing today? I'm here with students at Wakefield High School in Arlington, Virginia. And we've got students tuning in from all across America, kindergarten through twelfth grade. I'm glad you all could join us today.

If it is possible to specifically thank people in the audience, Obama states their names explicitly. He knows that by mentioning even a few names of people in the audience, the entire audience feels much closer.

Using a first name is not common in Japanese society, but Obama managed to create a change here, too. In November 2009, he met with Japanese Prime Minister Yukio Hatoyama. At the press conference following their meeting, Prime Minister Hatoyama said they reached such a close relationship that they call each other by their first names. That's international relations' rapport!

Adapting Body Language and Speech

TV rapport demands that the person be creative and get into the mind of the viewers of the program he is on. Obama knows to use the medium of television very well. In February 2008, he entered Ellen DeGeneres' studio. He danced and shimmied with the host to the sound of the music, boxed with a punching bag he found on site, and only then did he walk over to his designated chair.

As we will see in the last part of the book, Obama knows that the main communication channel between people is nonverbal and is manifested through body language. Creating effective rapport with an individual or group of people is based, among others, on the mirror principle: creating a physical mirror image with the person in front of us by mimicking his body language with mirroring or cross-over mirroring.

Mirroring entails adapting one's body language to the other person. This is an opportunity to join someone without saying a word, for example, by mimicking and mirroring his body language, voice, or speech rhythm. For instance, when two close girlfriends sit at a restaurant, one folds her arms, and the other does a similar gesture. This is rapport, and they aren't even aware of it. When there is natural chemistry between people, the rapport takes place without one's awareness of it.

Cross-over mirroring entails adapting the other person's body language to our behavior on some level. Adapting our speech rate to the other person's breathing pace is an example.

If you want to influence others, invest in establishing rapport. Make the other person feel there is an inexplicable connection between you, by adapting yourself to the other person's body language. If he or she is sitting with legs crossed, do the same. You can also breathe at his or her pace and speak at his or her pace or in the same tone.

The influence will take place on a subconscious level. Rapport can be created by adapting your voice to the person with whom you are communicating, rapid or slow speech, voice high or low, weak or strong, and using the local, customary jargon.

One of the important aspects of creating rapport is to do it in such a way that the other person doesn't feel he or she is being mimicked. As long as the mirroring of the other person's gestures is not done simultaneously, but delayed by a few seconds, it is likely the mirroring won't be consciously sensed. Therefore, it is best the mirroring not be blunt or too precise.

Obama understands the importance of physical and direct contact. We need do no more than observe him during his visit to George Mason University, where five thousand students greeted him like a rock star, with cheers and applause. He went into the crowd, touched, shook hands, flattered, and gave himself over to the people.

In fact, even then, at the onset of his campaign, you could see something different about the relationship Obama created with an audience, with warmth, closeness, and a type of intimacy.

Undoubtedly a Love Story

On *60 Minutes* it was dubbed "Obamania." But the craze is nothing more than an intimate relationship that Obama creates and nurtures with the audience in many ways.

Even when he's on stage, physically remote from the audience, he communicates with them in a nonverbal manner. When the audience applauds, he stops the speech, pauses, and joins the applause with a smile or beaming look. Thus, he indicates to the audience that he is with them. He is one of them!

When he addresses serious issues or topics that pain the audience, he chooses a serious and determined tone of voice and dons a concerned expression. At times, he merely says nothing to give the people in the audience a chance to express their feelings.

Obama knows how to touch people, literally. A series of studies that were conducted in the past two decades prove that handshaking or any other fleeting touch can convey a wide range of emotions and often much quicker than words. Scientists at the University of California at Berkley studied physical touch in diverse situations and proved how a fleeting touch can lead to an instant change in people's behavior and thought.

Adaptation on Every Level

You can establish rapport by adapting and mirroring on every logical level. In terms of the environment, you can meet people's expectations as to a dress code and personal appearance.

In terms of behavior, you can mirror the other person's gestures, but maintain your personal identity and integrity, just like a musical duet. You can adapt your breathing rate, body positions, gestures, tone of voice, speed of speech, volume of speech, and its rhythm.

At times, you will be able to achieve good rapport just by verifying there is no lack of obvious compliance between you and the other person. You can adopt a similar position but not identical and even adapt a certain aspect of your body language to another aspect of the other person's body language, for example, adapting a small movement of your hand to the other person's breathing.

Adapting the Language and Style

Obama speaks to the entire audience with three main senses: visual; auditory; and kinesthetic (sensations). This range of senses enables all people to find their preferred sensory style in his speeches.

The NLP approach is based on the understanding that we all create inner maps of reality, according to which we act. Every external stimulus enters through neurological paths and representational systems that filter it and create the inner representation.

The brain has five sensory representational systems: visual (through images); auditory (through voices and sounds); kinesthetic (feelings in the body and emotions); olfactory (through smell); and taste. Every person has a dominant sense or preferred representational system that develops to a larger extent during his or her lifetime.

This dominant sense obtains preferred representation in the internal maps and is also manifested in a person's thought process and language. But many people are unaware of the sensory representational system and the differences between them, and assume everyone processes information in the same way.

Based on studies, the visual people, those for whom the sense of sight is dominant, comprise 45 percent of the population (though in seminars, lectures, and workshops we conducted all over the world, we found that the rate of people who think they are visual is significantly larger). These are people for whom seeing is important; they think in pictures and images and they often use words related to the visual sense, such as "imagine," "focus," "observe," "look," "show," and "color" and sentences such as "it seems to me" and "to see the full picture." At the Democratic National Convention, Obama talked to the visual people in their language:

> Because *in the faces* of those young veterans who come back from Iraq and Afghanistan, *I see* my grandfather, who signed up after Pearl Harbor, marched in Patton's Army, and was rewarded by a grateful nation with the chance to go to college on the GI Bill.

The kinesthetic people, with the dominant sense of touch, comprise 40 percent of the population. They prefer the sense of touch and refer to feelings, sensations, and physical actions. The words that characterize them are related to feelings and touch.

They tend to say such things as, "that does not feel right," "I get that," and "get a hold of yourself."

Obama speaks a lot about feelings, sensations and actions:

> People don't expect government to solve all their problems.
> But they *sense deep in their bones* that with…

The auditory people, with the dominant sense of hearing, comprise 13 percent of the population. Their memory is auditory, and they often use words such as "say" and "sounds like" and sentences, such as "sounds good" and "that sounds familiar." Obama doesn't shortchange them, either. He relates in his speeches what he hears, listens to, or says:

> When *I listen to another worker tell me that* his factory has shut down, I remember…

There's a definite advantage to the number of visual and kinesthetic people, and this is important to remember because, although the majority of our communication is vocal—in speeches and meetings—most people are not auditory.

Therefore, *it is best to speak so that people see and sense the messages and not only hear them.* Obama overlooks no one in the audience. He speaks to everyone. He shows and conveys emotions and sensations. As a person who knows the secrets of the human mind, he creates a relationship with every audience and speaks in everyone's language, creating trust and closeness with a wide range of people. He speaks in words that characterize all the central senses, and any person can find in his words the language he prefers.

Obama doesn't ignore the sense of smell, either. Here's how he reacted to a question in September 2008 in Lebanon, Virginia, that referred to McCain's economic reform:

> "You can put lipstick on a pig," he said, as the crowd cheered. "It's still a pig." "You can wrap an old fish in a piece of paper called *change*. It's still gonna stink."

Speak in Their Language

For Obama, adapting language is manifested in other areas as well. He knew for example that the Hispanic immigrant community carries great weight during the elections. So he spoke in their language and incorporated in his speeches words in Spanish at every election assembly where the Hispanic community was present. This touched them, and many of them said "Si."

Using the target population's language is classic rapport. Obama could learn this from his model president, John F. Kennedy, who in June 1963 gave a speech in West Berlin and just before getting up to speak decided to strengthen his speech and say, "I am a

Berliner" in German. On his speech cards he wrote to himself the phonetic pronunciation in English that the translator dictated to him, and in the moment of truth, he said with precision, "ich bin ein Berliner." It was short, quick, and surprising. And the result was that the German audience, in the cold war era, was excited. The statement went down in history and is considered to be one of the most famous and memorable of all time.

On March 20, 2011, Obama talked to the people of Brazil in Rio de Janeiro:

> Alo! Cidade! Maravilhoso!
> Boa tarde, todo o povo brasileiro.
> Since the moment we arrived, the people of this nation
> have graciously shown my family the warmth and generosity of the Brazilian spirit.
> Obrigado. Thank you.

An easy way to establish rapport in every conversation, to influence and lead to change, is to use words and expressions that the other person uses.

You can also be similar to people in terms of their language by repeating expressions that are important to them or that characterize them or their culture and the country they are from.

The use of familiar words "ignites" within other people a sense of comfort, something pleasant and familiar, and makes them more open to listening and accepting new things.

When you repeat key words that characterize other people's thought style, you are showing them that you respect their way of thinking.

Another important advantage of this method is that communication of this type directly penetrates the "right brain" of the listeners and bypasses the critically-thinking "left brain." The other person simply "clicks" with the speaker, without knowing exactly why.

Adapting the Content

Three months after entering the White House, Obama hosted outstanding teachers in the Rose Garden to select "The Teachers of the Year." He easily connected to this special population and created rapport with them by acknowledging the importance of teachers who don't always get the respect they deserve:

> I'm a big fan of teachers because every single day in classrooms all across America, you are making a difference.
> You don't always get the recognition that you deserve.
> We don't always value the teaching profession like we should.

Later in the speech, Obama created a common denominator when he addressed what motivates teachers, and incorporated in his speech vast inspiration and vision in terms of this profession.

> My sister, Maya, is a teacher…We know how hard teachers work. And I know what all of you do by staying past that last bell; staying up late grading those papers; putting together lesson plans; spending your own money on books and supplies; and going beyond the call of duty. You do it because you know that's what will make a difference, because you believe that there's no such thing as a child that can't learn;

Creating rapport with teachers isn't easy. But Obama, like a flexible ballet dancer, knows how to adapt his content to his audience. Here is the flexibility he demonstrates when he speaks to young children. At the same speech at the "Back to School" event in September 2009, he created an amazing rapport with the students, knowing the parents and teachers would also be exposed to his messages:

> I know that for many of you, today is the first day of school. And for those of you in kindergarten, or starting middle or high school, it's your first day in a new school, so it's understandable if you're a little nervous. I imagine there are some seniors out there who are feeling pretty good right now, with just one more year to go. And no matter what grade you're in, some of you are probably wishing it were still summer, and you could've stayed in bed just a little longer this morning.

And he continues with a personal story that creates closeness:

> I know that feeling. When I was young, my family lived in Indonesia for a few years, and my mother didn't have the money to send me where all the American kids went to school. So she decided to teach me extra lessons herself, Monday through Friday—at 4:30 in the morning.

> Now I wasn't too happy about getting up that early. A lot of times, I'd fall asleep right there at the kitchen table. But whenever I'd complain, my mother would just give me one of those looks and say, "This is no picnic for me either, buster."

Rapport can also be created directly, when addressing issues that are relevant to and of interest to the other person.

When Obama addresses the topics that motivate people, topics from daily life that matter to them the most such as health, employment, and education, he gives them a deep sense of understanding, acceptance, and acknowledgment. He does this thanks to his connection to the *person in the street* and the *listening* he adapted for himself. This acknowledgment of content, the most basic needs of people, creates intimacy and trust in Obama's relationship with the people. This was manifested in Virginia in 2008:

> Now, more than ever, this campaign has to be about the problems facing the American people—because this is a moment of great uncertainty for America.
>
> The economic crisis we face is the worst since the Great Depression. Businesses large and small are finding it impossible to get loans, which means they can't buy new equipment, or hire new workers, or even make payroll for the workers they have…

Addressing difficulties and expected challenges are also perceived as an act of integrity and creates trust and mutual respect. When the person speaking before you or speaking to you understands what really matters to you and what the expected difficulties are along the way, when the person understands what you are dealing with in your daily life and knows your most profound needs and desires, all this makes you feel relaxed and more confident and enables you to open up to new ideas.

Obama knows his audience's world of beliefs and values. Thus, he paves the way to the audience's heart and the desired change. To create good rapport, you don't have to agree with the other person, just respect what matters to him or her, take a sincere interest in that person's identity and share that person's beliefs and values. That is *intimate communication* at its best.

Cross-Cultural Rapport

On November 10, 2010, President Obama spoke at the University of Indonesia in Jakarta, Indonesia.

Obama's Secrets

He opened his remarks by creating rapport with the audience:

> *Terima kasih. Terima kasih*, thank you so much, thank you, everybody. *Selamat pagi…Assalamualaikum dan salam sejahtera.*
> Thank you for this wonderful welcome.

Obama knows that people like to like people like themselves.

When Obama spoke in Cairo in June 2009, he made a point of creating rapport with the Muslim world. As early as the end of the first paragraph of his speech, he chose to incorporate a greeting in Arabic, "*Salaam Aleikum*," and, as befitting a man who does his homework, he mentioned "The Holy Koran," as devout Muslims call it, five times during that same speech. The speech was over six thousand words long and this was designed to give respect to the Arab nation in an attempt to create a bridge between the Arab world and the American nation. As a result of using the right messages in this way, Obama was applauded forty-one times during his speech in Cairo.

The Muslim nation is important to Obama, according to the vision he believes in—to create a better world; therefore, he creates rapport at every opportunity by demonstrating respect and by understanding the fine details. In honor of the Ramadan fast, Obama gave a speech that was broadcast online in August 2009. To create rapport, he said a greeting in Arabic at the end of the first sentence and, during the speech, he also incorporated words in Arabic. Here is the first part:

> On behalf of the American people—including Muslim communities in all fifty states—I want to extend best wishes to Muslims in America and around the world. *Ramadan Kareem*.
>
> Ramadan is the month in which Muslims believe the Koran was revealed to the Prophet Muhammad, beginning with a simple word—*iqra*. It is therefore a time when Muslims reflect upon the wisdom and guidance that comes with faith, and the responsibility that human beings have to one another, and to God.
>
> Like many people of different faiths who have known Ramadan through our communities and families, I know this to be a festive time—a time when families gather, friends host *iftars*, and meals are shared. But I also know that Ramadan is a time of intense devotion and reflection—a time when Muslims

fast during the day and perform *tarawih* prayers at night, reciting and listening to the entire Koran over the course of the month.

Obama, extremely skilled at creating rapport, wants to show there is a similarity between the religions, and so, later in his speech, says that the fast is mutual to everyone, even to his own religion, Christianity.

On October 13, 2009, he hosted the Latin Festival at the White House. He launched the evening in Spanish with "Buenas Noches," showed his command of Latin music and took the festival and Latin music in a direction he loves. He emphasized that the spirit of diversity is a uniting factor. Here is what he said at that lively event to create rapport:

> Like our own Latino community, Latin music is not easy to define. Styles like Cuban salsa, Mexican norteño, Puerto Rican reggaeton and Dominican bachata are as vibrant and unique as the places they come from.
>
> But although Latin music takes many forms, this spirit of diversity also unifies us.

On April 6, 2009, Obama spoke before the Turkish parliament in Ankara. In the opening of his speech, he incorporated expressions of respect for the Turkish people:

> This is my first trip overseas as President of the United States. I've been to the G20 summit in London, the NATO summit in Strasbourg, and the European Union summit in Prague. Some people have asked me if I chose to continue my travels to Ankara and Istanbul to send a message to the world. And my answer is simple: *Evet*—yes.

Yes, that is how you create rapport. Later, he was applauded when he celebrated the excellent Turkish basketball players in the US:

> The ties among our people have deepened, as well, and more and more Americans of Turkish origin live and work and succeed within our borders. And, as a basketball fan, I've even noticed that Hedo Turkoglu and Mehmet Okur have got some pretty good basketball games.

Rapport, as you can see, is a result of attention to fine detail. Later in the speech, Obama said:

> There's an old Turkish proverb, "You cannot put out fire with flames." America knows this. Turkey knows this. There's some who must be met by force, they will not compromise. But force alone cannot solve our problems, and it is no alternative to extremism. The future must belong to those who create, not those who destroy. That is the future we must work for, and we must work for it together.

Obama takes advantage of every international encounter to establish rapport and dialogue. On November 8, 2010, Obama spoke to the joint session of the Indian Parliament in New Delhi, India. Obama knows to use history to bond with his listeners:

> For me and Michelle, this visit has, therefore, held special meaning. See, throughout my life, including my work as a young man on behalf of the urban poor, I've always found inspiration in the life of Gandhi and his simple and profound lesson to be the change we seek in the world. And just as he summoned Indians to seek their destiny, he influenced champions of equality in my own country, including a young preacher named Martin Luther King. After making his pilgrimage to India a half-century ago, Dr. King called Gandhi's philosophy of nonviolent resistance "the only logical and moral approach" in the struggle for justice and progress.

The listeners applauded him thirty-four times during his speech there. That's the respect and love you get when you use intimate communication.

On December 8, 2010, right after meeting with President Komorowski of Poland, he said:

> This year, we mark the 30th anniversary of Solidarity. And all those around the world remember how inspired we were by the brave Poles who sought their freedom, including a young—or younger—President Komorowski, who, himself, was imprisoned. And we continue to draw inspiration from the tremendous strides that Poland has made. We continue to deeply appreciate the strong friendship between our two countries.

On November 16, 2009, he met with China's future leaders at the Museum of Science and Technology in Shanghai, China. In this encounter Obama placed an emphasis on dialogue and responding to questions from the audience and said to participants:

> I am very sorry that my Chinese is not as good as your English,
> but I am looking forward to this chance to have a dialogue.

He added in his opening statement many samples of relationships that developed between the two countries throughout the years, to reinforce the existing relationship. And like Turkey, in China, too, Obama knows the name of the Chinese professional basketball player in the US:

> The second highest number of foreign students in the United States comes from China, and we've seen a 50 percent increase in the study of Chinese among our own students. There are nearly two hundred "friendship cities" drawing our communities together. American and Chinese scientists cooperate on new research and discovery. And of course, Yao Ming is just one signal of our shared love of basketball—I'm only sorry that I won't be able to see a Shanghai Sharks game while I'm visiting.

The next time you want to speak and communicate with power, add some love and build rapport. Then you will be able to dance with your audience.

How to Create Trust

To create real change in thought and motivate people into action, it's not enough to choose the right messages—one must also know how to serve them up.

If you want to influence, convince, persuade, and motivate, build rapport. Create a relationship based on trust, respect, and mutual understanding with your listeners. The secret lies in entering the other person's world and becoming like that person. It can work well if you do it with sincerity, if you develop a genuine interest in the people listening to you, and if you show an interest in them and are willing to see the world from their point of view.

Good rapport is created by combining several actions at the same time: intention to create rapport; creating eye contact; addressing the people you want to influence by name; adapting body language and speech; and adapting your language, style, and content to that of the listener.

Next time you speak before an audience, make sure you are fully intent on creating rapport. Remember that eye contact is significant in creating rapport.

Address people by their names, and if it's a large audience, mention some of the participants specifically. If groups of people in your audience have a common trait, mention them out loud.

Make sure to create the sense of a face-to-face conversation between two people who know each other.

In a personal conversation, adapt your body language and speech to those of the other person. If you haven't identified the sense your conversation partner prefers, talk to him or her with the three main senses—sight, sound, and touch.

Emphasize sight in particular, the preferred "language" of most people, which automatically activates the right brain.

Use the language of the people listening to you; repeat expressions that are important to them and that characterize them or their culture.

Use certain words a person tends to use, which "ignite" a warm, pleasant, and familiar feeling and which make him or her more open to listening, more receptive.

Thus, you obtain what Daniel Goleman, author of *Emotional Intelligence*, calls "the hidden biological dance," which occurs as a type of underground element in every interaction.

When you repeat key words that characterize the thought style of your audience, you show them that you respect their way of thinking. Moreover, you subconsciously convey to them that you are alike.

Address issues that motivate people. These are largely the issues that matter to them the most. Your knowledge of the content and most basic needs of people creates intimacy and trust in your relationship with them. These tips will help you in a wide range of opportunities in life, when you want to influence, persuade, and sell.

Many people in the world of marketing, in general, and the world of sales, in particular, make mistakes in using rapport on two counts:

First, they use it sparingly and often only when beginning a conversation or a meeting. But rapport is a relationship one has to build, maintain, and develop throughout the meeting, conversation, or presentation, and even afterwards. A relationship is something you should work at. Always.

Second, many use rapport artificially, merely as a tactic. But if you want to build true rapport, you should mean it, from your heart. You must focus on the other person: his or her needs and what makes him or her unique. Get used to thinking in terms of the second perceptual position, then go on to the third and fourth positions, the power of which we already examined. When you do all this methodically and consistently, you will magnetize people towards you and your ideas.

The world is built upon a simple formula of mutuality: if you love people, people will love you back. People like people who like people. And communication is a love story.

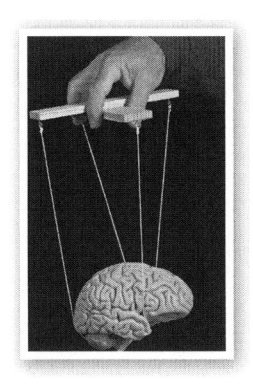

CHAPTER 18

Dance with them – How to connect and stimulate action by using the "Pacing and Leading" technique

> "It was like he was dancing at the podium. His feet were moving to the rhythm of the speech."
>
> — **Stephanie Cutter**

When you have an intimate romantic relationship with someone, do you like to dance with him or her? If so, let's see how Obama dances with his audience, right after he creates the intimate relationship. The *dancing* in communication is called *"pacing and leading."*

The skill of pacing and leading is an NLP tool with which to establish rapport. This is a necessary stage in influencing others, while at the same time communicating with them. After joining the other person, you can influence him and lead him to a new position. But you can only lead a person effectively if he or she is willing to be led. And people are willing to be led after they are "paced." Obama knows the secrets of this skill and applies it successfully. At the 2008 Democratic National Convention he said to the audience:

> Tonight, more Americans are out of work
> and more are working harder for less.
> More of you have lost your homes

and even more are watching your home values plummet.
More of you have cars you can't afford to drive,
credit card bills you can't afford to pay,
and tuition that's beyond your reach.

Pacing can be in the form of acknowledging the other person's situation or his or her feelings, needs, thoughts, or emotions. Obama paces his audience in all these ways, as he did in his speech in Virginia:

We've lost more than 750,000 jobs this year.
Wages are lower than they've been in a decade,
at a time when the cost of health care and college have never been higher.
It's getting harder and harder to make the mortgage,
or fill up your gas tank,
or even keep the electricity on at the end of the month.
At this rate, the question isn't just "are you better off than you were four years ago?"
it's "are you better off than you were four weeks ago?"
So I know these are difficult times.
I know folks are worried.
But I believe that we can steer ourselves out of this crisis
because I believe in this country.
Because I believe in you.
I believe in the American people…

Obama, as we can see from this example, begins with acknowledging his listeners' situation and joins them. Only after that does he lead them to the desired direction. He asks them, "Are you better off than you were four weeks ago?"

He adopts and adapts, with great wisdom, the legendary quote that Ronald Reagan used, "Are you better off than you were four years ago?"

An efficient way to join and pace other people is by putting yourself in their shoes while using the second perceptual position, to see what the other people see, what they hear, and what they feel. Obama joins his audience on all levels. He acknowledges the objective problems the audience is facing and knows their feelings, thoughts, and emotions. He acknowledges their special needs and he even acknowledges the concerns and specific difficulties of a specific audience in a specific town. Thus, when he speaks to the people of Ohio, he addresses specific problems that the residents in Ohio

Dance With Them – How To Connect And Stimulate Action By Using The "Pacing And Leading" Technique

are confronting and, at the end of the paragraph below, he also tells them that they are his number one concern:

> We know that it's time to create the good-paying jobs of tomorrow.
> Ohio is hurting.
> 12,000 jobs have been lost this year.
> You've got 7.4 percent unemployment.
> Wages are flat-lining.
> But it doesn't have to be this way.
> That's why I'm going to stop giving tax breaks
> to companies that ship jobs overseas,
> and start rebuilding the middle class
> by helping companies create jobs here in Ohio.
> I will be a president who puts you first, Ohio…

Even in his inaugural address, Obama applies the skill of pacing and leading:

> Our nation is at war, against a far-reaching network of violence and hatred. Our economy is badly weakened, a consequence of greed and irresponsibility on the part of some, but also our collective failure to make hard choices and prepare the nation for a new age. Homes have been lost; jobs shed; businesses shuttered. Our health care is too costly; our schools fail too many; and each day brings further evidence that the ways we use energy strengthen our adversaries and threaten our planet.
>
> These are the indicators of crisis, subject to data and statistics. Less measurable but no less profound is a sapping of confidence across our land—a nagging fear that America's decline is inevitable, and that the next generation must lower its sights.
>
> Today I say to you that the challenges we face are real. They are serious and they are many. They will not be met easily or in a short span of time. But know this, America—they will be met.

Obama describes in detail and with precision, one after the other, facts that are not in dispute that depict the audience's situation and the difficulties they are confronting. He adds to that thoughts and emotions the audience may be feeling.

He persuades his audience to agree with him, to nod an inner nod, given the precise description of the situation. Why is this format of speech so effective? Why can you use it whenever you want to persuade and lead to change?

It seems that once people agree and approve (with an inner "yes"), a positive conditioning occurs in the brain. In a situation such as this, the objections of the conscious brain weaken, and there's a tendency to agree and become open to new ideas. This is a technique also used during a counter-interrogation in court and during therapeutic relaxation. Obama uses this technique very well.

Pacing and leading are effective in particular because when people feel they are understood, they are calm and more relaxed, and are open to hear and accept new things.

So, next time you dance with a partner and want to take the lead, first follow her or his steps. Then take the lead.

Tap Into the Concerns

Only after Obama joins his audience and gains their trust does he lead them to a new place. His main goal is to motivate the audience into action. But first he leads them to a belief in the ability to bring about change, and only after he motivates them to action. In Virginia he said this explicitly:

> This is one of those moments. I realize *you're* cynical and fed up with politics. I understand that *you're* disappointed and even angry with your leaders. *You* have every right to be.
> But despite all of this, I ask of *you* what's been asked of the American people in times of trial and turmoil throughout our history.
> I ask *you* to believe—to believe in *yourselves*, in each other, and in the future we can build together.

The use of pacing and leading propels Obama towards his goal. During the election campaign, he knew he could get people to feel the importance of change in the air. But he also knew he must make people act and have others join his camp. Otherwise, he wouldn't win the election. So, he used a direct request for action, generally at the end of the speech. In his 2008 speech in Philadelphia, he called on the people to undertake actions and implement measures that would generate change:

> And if you keep standing with me, if you keep fighting with me, if you keep making those calls, and knocking on those doors, and making sure everyone you know gets out to the polls on November 4th—if you do these things, then I promise you, we will win this election, and then you and I—together—will change this country and change this world.

In many instances in our careers, we met leaders and executives who spoke of change and expected people to know what to do of their own accord. But Obama knows the secret is to explicitly call for action.

If you expect a certain action, say it outright. If you say it at the height of excitement, using your voice correctly, at your speech rate and by using supportive body language, you can motivate people into action.

Obama has another secret: he serves as a role model and reference for his audience to motivate them in the desired direction. He invites the audience to do as he does; he conveys to them: when I open up to you and tell you my personal story, it's because I feel close to you and I trust you. I invite you to do the same, get close to me and trust me.

When I listen to you and take an interest in you, I'm inviting you to do the same, to listen to me and take an interest in what I have to say.

When I am optimistic and believe in my ability and yours to emerge from the crisis together, I am inviting you to do as I do, believe in my ability and yours to make a change.

When I say a kind word and see the good in you, I am inviting you to say a good word about me and see the good in me.

When I respect you, when I treat you as my friends and accept you for who you are, I invite you to do the same for me.

According to Robert Cialdini, author of *Influence: The Psychology of Persuasion,* reciprocation is structured within us as human beings, and it is one of his six "weapons of influence."

Obama uses this principle to shape and delineate the audience's attitude towards him. He provides the audience a mirror image and demonstrates how the audience should treat him. He simply takes the first step. And now it is your turn to speak and communicate with the power of dancing. Dance with the people you want to convince or persuade. After all, dancing is fun, isn't it?

> ### Joining by Putting Yourself in the Other Person's Shoes

Remember to join and pace your listeners before you lead them to a new place. You cannot lead a person unless he is willing to be led. And a person is usually willing to be led only if you joined him first.

You can pace your audience by acknowledging audience members' situations or feelings, needs, thoughts, and emotions. An efficient way to pace is putting yourself in their shoes, by applying the second perceptual position, seeing what the audience sees, hearing what they hear, and sensing their emotions.

Describe with precision and in detail facts that are not in dispute, which depict your audience's situation and the challenges they are facing. Add to that possible thoughts and feelings of the audience. Habituate the audience to agree within themselves, to nod an inner nod when you describe to them the precise situation.

After you have joined the audience and gained their trust, you can lead them to a new place—to belief, change, and action. Clarify precisely what action you want the audience to take. Never assume they understand on their own.

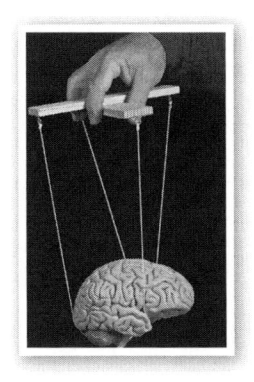

CHAPTER 19

INSPIRE PEOPLE LIKE A PERSONAL COACH – HOW TO COMPLIMENT, EMPOWER, AND CONQUER AUDIENCES

A great opportunity to learn how coaches use inspiration language is to watch Obama as a personal coach in action, when he speaks to the young generation. Education is key to success and President Obama talks to students several times. Let's go back to his September 2009 "Back to School" speech. See how Obama emphasizes that the students are the future, and like a great coach, how he focuses on realizing their potential:

> Every single one of you has something you're good at. Every single one of you has something to offer. And you have a responsibility to yourself to discover what that is. That's the opportunity an education can provide.
>
> Maybe you could be a good writer—maybe even good enough to write a book or articles in a newspaper—but you might not know it until you write a paper for your English class. Maybe you could be an innovator or an inventor—maybe even good enough to come up with the next iPhone or a new medicine or vaccine—but you might not know it until you do a project for your science class. Maybe you could be a mayor or a senator or a supreme court justice, but you might not know that until you join student government or the debate team.

A year later (September 14, 2010), he delivered another "Back to School" speech at the Julia R. Masterman Laboratory and Demonstration School, Philadelphia, Pennsylvania:

> More and more, the kinds of opportunities that are open to you are going to be determined by how far you go in school. The further you go in school, the further you're going to go in life. And at a time when other countries are competing with us like never before, when students around the world in Beijing, China, or Bangalore, India, are working harder than ever, and doing better than ever, your success in school is not just going to determine your success, it's going to determine America's success in the 21st century.

Marcus Buckingham's best-selling book, *Now, Discover Your Strengths*, emphasizes the importance of every individual realizing his or her potential by applying and developing his or her strengths. Obama, too, is aware of the secret of focusing on strengths, and he empowers his audience and motivates them towards hope and action. He reminds the people in the audience of their strengths, often speaking as a personal coach, focuses on positive thinking and connects the audience to positive experiences from their past. In October 2008, he said to an audience in Ohio:

> America still has the most talented, most productive workers of any country on Earth. You know this, Ohio. We're home to the workers who have built the largest middle class in history. We're home to workers who work two jobs or three jobs and take the last bus home at night because they want something more for their children. We're home to innovation and technology, colleges, and universities that are the envy of the world. Some of the biggest ideas in history have come from our small businesses and our research facilities. It won't be easy, but there's no reason we can't make this century another American century. Yes we can.

Obama turns the audience into a role model when he takes them back in time to their historic successes, when they confronted similar changes successfully. Thus, he creates an equation of success and is actually saying to the audience, "If you succeeded once, there is no reason why you shouldn't succeed again." Obama reminds the audience that its fate is in its hands and encourages them to act and be accountable. Let us ask you:

- How do you feel when someone believes in you and your ability?

- How do you feel when someone empowers you?

- How do you feel when the good things about you are remembered and mentioned?

- What energy do you get when someone mentions your strengths?

- How close do you feel to that person?

- To what extent do you want to be with him or her, trust that person and believe in him or her?

- To what extent do you believe what he or she is saying is true?

These questions are undoubtedly rhetorical, because the mechanism works with everyone in the same way. We will always prefer being with people who compliment us, encourage and strengthen us. Obama knows this. He often speaks like basketball coaches Pat Reilly and Phil Jackson, who evoke in their players motivation and hope, and encourage them to dream, desire, and believe. Like them, Obama reminds the audience that everyone possesses this inner resource that is hope.

In July 2009, Obama hosted the Detroit Shock women's professional champion basketball team. He addressed the winners, and through them, the American people, like a legendary coach:

> It's hard to believe the WNBA has already been around for twelve years. And that means that my daughters have never known a time when women couldn't play professional sports.
>
> They look at the TV and they see me watching SportsCenter and they see young women who look like them on the screen. And that lets them and all our young women, as well as young men, know that we should take for granted that women are going to thrive and excel as athletes. And it makes my daughters look at themselves differently; to see that they can be champions, too.
>
> So, as a father, I want to say thank you.

Obama reminds his listeners of their strength, their inner spirit. He connects to their emotions, and as a result, gets them to like him, be drawn to him, and desire mutual success with him. This is how he empowered the crowd at the 2008 Democratic National Convention:

> Instead, it is that American spirit—
> that American promise—
> that pushes us forward even when the path is uncertain;
> that binds us together in spite of our differences;
> that makes us fix our eye not on what is seen,
> but what is unseen,
> that better place around the bend.

In commemoration of forty years of the landing of Apollo 11 on the moon and the fulfillment of President Kennedy's vision, Obama met the legendary spaceship crew in 2009. Obama, who knew this meeting with them was a small step for him and a big step towards inspiring humanity, spoke like a seasoned coach and combined it with a personal story:

> The country continues to draw inspiration from what you've done. I should note, just personally, I grew up in Hawaii, as many of you know, and I still recall sitting on my grandfather's shoulders when those capsules would land in the middle of the Pacific and they'd get brought back and we'd go out and we'd pretend like they could see us as we were waving at folks coming home. And I remember waving American flags and my grandfather telling me that the Apollo mission was an example of how Americans can do anything they put their minds to…
>
> We expect that there is, as we speak, another generation of kids out there who are looking up at the sky and are going to be the next Armstrong, Collins, and Aldrins. And we want to make sure that NASA is going to be there for them when they want to take their journey.

The next time you talk to people, practice some coaching secrets that President Obama uses when he wants to connect to people and lead them. And remember Vince Lombardi's words: "Practice does not make perfect. Only perfect practice makes perfect."

We Know You Know

We know you have the capacity to empower the people around you and the people you want to motivate towards hope, change, and action.

We know you have strengths. We know you know positive thinking doesn't solve all the problems, but it surely is better than negative thinking.

We know you have dreams you can fulfill.

We know you know that what we wrote in these past lines is an illustration of the messages that were described in this chapter. But we also know you enjoyed reading these lines.

And we know you know everything we wrote is true.

Yes, you can.

Yes, you can use the simple truths and apply what you read in this chapter.

To speak like Obama—empower the people you are talking to.

We know you will love to get a standing ovation!

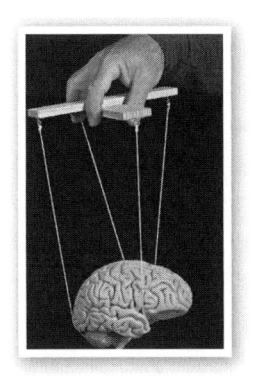

CHAPTER 20

THE POWER OF HUMOR – HOW TO LAUGH AT YOUR OWN WEAKNESSES AND WIN

"Laughter is the sun that drives winter from the human face."

—**Victor Hugo**

Obama enjoys communicating with people, so he often uses humor:

> I am just thrilled to be here tonight with some of the most brilliant, accomplished, influential women in this country. As Michelle Obama's husband, I feel very much at home.
>
> —October 5, 2010
> Fortune Most Powerful Women Summit

His family is a great source for humor in his speeches, and you can do that, too:

> I was a little confused when they told me I was coming here to address the Women's Leadership Forum, because I address a women's leadership forum every night at dinner. I just left a women's leadership forum. I have Michelle, Malia, Sasha, my mother-in-law. It's just me and Bo -- trying to get a word in edgewise.
>
> —May 20, 2011
> Women's Leadership Forum

The first time he celebrated Independence Day as president, he didn't forget to include in his brief speech a reference to his daughter Malia who was born on the same date:

> I should say that there's also one girl in particular who's just thrilled that all of you are here—and that is Malia Obama, because this happens to be her birthday, as well. When she was younger, I used to say that all these fireworks were for her.

On April 29, 2011, President Obama came to deliver a speech at Miami Dade College Commencement, and he said:

> Thank you for allowing me the profound honor of being a part of it. And thank you for my first honorary associate degree. One of the perks of this job is that degrees come free these days. Not that it impresses anybody at home. Now Michelle just says, "Hey, Doctor, go take that dog for a walk."

A smile is the shortest way to connect with people. There's nothing like the first time you smile at your baby and get a smile back. In order to influence people and lead them towards a new direction, you should know how to make them laugh. On April 20, 2011, President Obama came to launch his 2012 election campaign at a Facebook Town Hall meeting, in Palo Alto, California. He spoke with Mark Zuckerberg and said:

> Well, thank you so much, Facebook, for hosting this, first of all. My name is Barack Obama, and I'm the guy who got Mark to wear a jacket and tie.

On December 13, 2010, the President honored the NBA Champion Los Angeles Lakers at the Town Hall Education Arts Recreation Campus, in Washington, D.C., and Obama made people laugh:

> Now, I have to say that there is a longstanding tradition of welcoming championship sports teams to the White House. But here's the thing: these guys have been there so often, they were just there last year because they won the title. And Kobe and Derek have been there so many times now, they could lead tours themselves.

Obama makes people like him because he knows how to laugh at himself. As mentioned, on May 13, 2009, he was invited to speak at the University of Arizona that opted not to grant him an honorary degree. One of the reasons the university indicated was that he had not yet achieved enough in his life and he still had to prove himself with actions. This, of course, was in total contrast to the decision several months later to award him the Nobel Peace Prize, though he hadn't yet accomplished any achievements in that regard.

Obama turned the university's reason into an advantage when he addressed tens of thousands of students and family members who gathered in the stadium to listen to him:

> I come here not to dispute the suggestion that I haven't yet achieved enough in my life. First of all, Michelle concurs with that assessment. She has a long list of things that I have not yet done, waiting for me when I get home. But more than that, I come to embrace the notion that I haven't done enough in my life.

Obama does the unexpected. He laughs at himself and at his weaknesses and compliments others, even his political rivals.

On May 2, 2010, President Obama spoke at the White House Correspondents Association dinner at the Washington Hilton Hotel, in Washington, D.C.

Obama suffered from a decrease in his popularity and he said:

> It's been quite a year since I've spoken here last—lots of ups, lots of downs—except for my approval ratings, which have just gone down…

This tactic is very effective to capture the listeners' attention, because it is unexpected. Most people prefer downplaying their weaknesses or finding a rational explanation for them. Many people prefer "knocking" their rivals and exalting themselves.

But Obama knows the secrets of charisma and operates in a different way. Once again, he succeeds at doing the unexpected and, accordingly, he "knocks" himself and extols others—just the opposite of what we would expect. He undoubtedly doesn't do it all the time and, when necessary, he does know how to answer his rivals, but the use of this tactic in the proper dose grants him credit with the audience.

A person who is capable of laughing at himself proves his modesty and humanity. He also displays integrity, because he portrays himself in the right light, without embellishing reality or the "product."

A sense of humor helps one to be liked by people. In one of the surveys we conducted among our customers, we found that 78 percent believe they have an above-average sense of humor; on online dating sites, when people describe themselves, a sense of humor is the trait that appears most in the personal description, and one of the most desired traits of the ideal mate.

A sense of humor, self-effacing humor in particular, is an excellent tool with which to create rapport and human chemistry, because no one in the audience is perfect, and how nice to discover the presidential candidate is not perfect, either. This is true of any candidate for a political position in any country in the world. Obama's secret is that he says it outright, thus adding authenticity to his image.

How many political leaders do you know who said:

> I don't pretend to be a perfect man, and I will not be a perfect President.

Obama said these words in November 2007, when he embarked on his presidential path, a year before the national elections and at a time when many didn't yet know who he was.

Obama not only laughs at himself but uses humor in speeches, when answering journalists' questions, or in conversation. Like any successful sales person, he knows that when people laugh they are open to accepting ideas.

His health reform is a serious matter. However, Obama doesn't miss an opportunity to use humor, especially on serious matters such as this. At a White House press conference in July 2009, he answered the journalists:

> I will just be honest with you—I'm the President of the United States, so I've got a doctor following me every minute. Which is why I say this is not about me. I've got the best health care in the world. I'm trying to make sure that everybody has good health care—and they don't right now.

In November 2009, the Obamas hosted a classical music event at the White House. Obama opened with a humorous line:

> I'd like to welcome the many members of Congress who've joined us tonight—despite what you may have heard, they are actually a civilized bunch.

When Obama spoke in September 2009, at the Sheraton Hotel in New York in front of guests of Bill Clinton's global initiative convention, he complimented the former Democratic president with a lot of humor:

> Some of you are aware that last week President Clinton and I were here in New York together; we were having lunch in a small Italian restaurant. And we talked about the economy, we talked about health care, we talked about pressing global challenges. And then he said to me, "Would you pass the Parmesan?" And then he said to me, "Would you speak to our annual meeting?"
>
> Now, I think everyone knows what it's like when Bill Clinton asks you to make a commitment. He looks you in the eye; he feels your pain. He makes you feel like you're the only person in the room. What could I say? I was vulnerable, just as all of you have been vulnerable to his charms.

Using humor can also help alleviate stress, fear, and embarrassment. Humor as a part of a leader's repertoire can even change people's perception of grave events.

In March 1981, President Reagan was shot in an assassination attempt. The bullet pierced his left lung, merely one inch away from his heart. On his way to emergency surgery, Reagan didn't lose his sense of humor and whispered to the doctors before entering the operation room, "Please, tell me you are all Republicans." One doctor answered, "Today, Mr. President, we are all Republicans."

The examples we saw prove to what extent humor is an excellent way to surprise people.

We can summarize it in one sentence: humor is a serious tool with which to lead people and influence them.

🔍 Do the Unexpected

Do the unexpected. Laugh at yourself, turn weaknesses into a joke, and flatter others. A person who can laugh at himself demonstrates modesty, humanity, and integrity; self-effacing humor is an excellent tool with which to create rapport and human chemistry.

Laughter is not only good for the health. Laughter and unexpected messages add a lot to the relationship with the audience.

A speech is like a romantic date with a large audience. What do you do on a date to make it a success?

- Have a conversation
- Ask questions
- Listen carefully
- Eye contact
- Smile
- Create a gentle touch
- Take an interest in what you deem important to the other person
- Share personal stories and experiences
- Avoid distractions
- Balance between the talk about yourself and focusing on what the other party has to say
- Seek a connection
- Create rapport to ensure continuity

We revealed many secrets of Barack Obama's intimate communication. Now it is your turn to use them. Make your audience love you. Dance with them. Inspire them like a coach. Use words that work and make them laugh.

And now, it's time to move from ***intimate communication*** to the power of the mind in communication. We will see now how Barack Obama activates the listeners' right brain.

Despite the power of this secret, we found that less than ten percent of the people who deal in persuasion, influence, and sales use it regularly and methodically. In other words, if you want a competitive edge in the way you speak, communicate, influence, persuade, sell, inspire, and lead, learn to use the secret of activating the listeners' right brain. We are going to see how to communicate with the visual part of the brain.

PART FIVE
The Power of the Mind in Communication

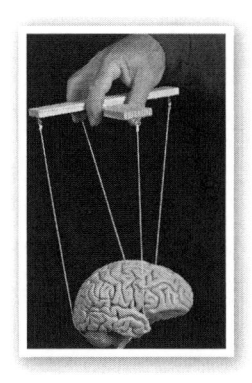

CHAPTER 21

Under the Radar – How to penetrate your audience's right brain with power stories

"Story isn't the icing on the cake, it is the cake."

—Peter Guber

Christina-Taylor Green was born in the midst of tragedy on Sept. 11, 2001, and was killed on January 8, 2011, while trying to meet Congresswoman Gabrielle Gifford at a political event.

A few days later, Obama spoke at the University of Arizona, Tucson, Arizona, and said about her:

> Imagine—imagine for a moment, here was a young girl who was just becoming aware of our democracy; just beginning to understand the obligations of citizenship; just starting to glimpse the fact that some day she, too, might play a part in shaping her nation's future. She had been elected to her student council. She saw public service as something exciting and hopeful. She was off to meet her congresswoman, someone she was sure was good and important and might be a role model. She saw all this through the eyes of a child, undimmed by the cynicism or vitriol that we adults all too often just take for granted. I want to live up to her expectations. I want our democracy to be as good as Christina imagined it. I want America to be as good as she imagined

it. All of us—we should do everything we can to make sure this country lives up to our children's expectations.

President Obama had been speaking at the event for thirty-three and a-half minutes, and the audience applauded fifty-three times during his remarks.

Obama was at his best. He talked slowly, used supporting body language, and he, himself, applauded several times for the heroes he talked about.

It was the Obama Drama, and that's the power of story.

In part four, we saw how Obama's speech preparation strategy allows him to hit his target, and we saw how he prepares to be at his best during the performance itself. We saw how he uses various secrets to get his audience to fall in love with him and magnetize them to him, and, of course, how he empowers and motivates them into action.

Now we will get to know the wide range of linguistic tools Obama uses to convey well-honed messages. A typical toolbox includes diverse tools. The trick is to know them all and know how to use the right tool at the right time.

We will see how Obama influences the "right brain" and the emotions of the listeners by using their imagination. We have compiled concrete examples to illustrate the way in which Obama seasons his speeches with personal stories and examples from life and the way in which he uses different types of stories to achieve diverse goals. If you are seeking effective ways to communicate, persuade, influence, and lead, this is the story. You, too, can tell engaging stories, as Obama does, to evoke inspiration, to build trust, to motivate others into action, to create values and belief, to share a vision, and to lead into the future.

Stories are one of the six elements that help ideas stick, according to Chip Heath and Dan Heath, coauthors of *Made to Stick*. Management guru Ken Blanchard conveys all his messages through stories. Blanchard, who wrote, among others, the bestsellers *Whale Done* and *The One-Minute Manager*, converted the story into a quick method to connect to the minds of readers and, undoubtedly, the minds of the participants in his lectures. Nobel Economics laureate Daniel Kahneman–together with his research colleague Amos Tversky, both men leaders in the study of behavioral economics–proved unambiguously that tangible examples have a far greater effect on our decisions than abstract information, even if it is more precise.

Peter Guber, author of *Tell to Win: Connect, Persuade, and Triumph with the Hidden Power of Story* writes: "For too long the business world has ignored or belittled the power of oral narrative, preferring soulless PowerPoint slides, facts, figures, and data. But as the noise level of modern life has become a cacophony, the ability to tell a purposeful story that can truly be heard is increasingly in demand."

Mark Benioff, one of the founders and CEO of Salesforce.com, was interviewed for *Business Week* magazine in November 2009, and stated that the ability to tell stories is one of the main reasons for his company's rapid success.

Obama uses this secret well. Before preparing his first speech before Congress, he sat down with Jon Favreau, his chief speechwriter, and said, "You and I always tell a story well. I want to make sure we do it again this time." Obama does it whenever he can. He turns a message into a story and combines a story in the message.

In September 2009, Obama devoted a long time to promoting his promise during the election campaign—implementing a reform in the health system, so that over forty million Americans who have no insurance will be provided what the citizens of many other countries are provided.

In his speech at the Target Center in Minneapolis, Minnesota, he used a story from his election campaign to enthuse the crowd. He related how, during the campaign, he visited the city of Greenwood, South Carolina, to speak and discovered the "warm up band" before him on stage was a lady by the name of Edith Childs who was thrilling the audience.

Obama told the mesmerized crowd what happened while he was waiting backstage.

> The lady was standing center stage and she cried out to the audience, "Are you fired up?"
>
> The audience answered in unison, "Fired up," and she asked, "Ready to go?" and they answered, "Ready to go!"
>
> And thus for five minutes Ms. Edith Childs enthused the audience.

Obama told the Minneapolis audience that, at one point, he realized this lady was a true star. She got all the attention, she created energy, and she was center stage, while he waited behind the scenes. Then Obama went on to say:

> After about a minute, maybe two, I'm feeling kind of fired up. I'm feeling like I'm ready to go.

Obama took this story and continued the momentum it created to lead the Minneapolis crowd towards his message:

> And it goes to show you how one voice can change a room.
> And if it changes a room it can change a city.
> And if it can change a city it can change a state.
> And if it can change a state it can change a nation.
> If it changes the nation it can change the world.
> It can bring health care to every American.
> It can lower our costs.
> It can make your insurance more secure.

Obama, who learned to tell stories and practiced that tactic, never misses an opportunity to wrap his message in a story about the exciting lady. Therefore, right after he conveyed a message on change, he used the same mantras Ms. Childs used and cried out enthusiastically to the crowd, "I want to know, Minnesota, are you fired up?!" and the crowd repeated after him like an echo. Obama continued, "Ready to go?" and they undoubtedly repeated after him.

Obama creates a musical crescendo at the end of his words. He creates an experience. He creates a story that all participants at the event will remember for a long time.

That's how it is when you use a good story. Obama's storytelling days began when he was a child. He grew up on his grandparents' stories and, throughout his professional career, he always seasoned his speeches with personal stories and examples from life. He knows what many leaders before him knew.

Stories are suited for the way in which people think and connect to emotion in a way no rational argument can. Stories are part of the human race's DNA. Babies hear stories from the moment they are born; most common religions in the world are based on historic stories; in every culture, stories are used to create values, to influence behavior, and create cultural unity; and throughout history, all the great leaders of change were excellent storytellers, including Martin Luther King, Jr., and President Kennedy. Life is a collection of moments, and each moment is a story. And people love stories.

The Power of Stories

Few remember the physics laws they learned in school, but almost everyone remembers the story about Archimedes who was sitting in a bathtub when he discovered the law named after him. Stories are leaders' most effective communication tools. Through them, you can convey messages more effectively than you can with logical arguments. Stories connect to people's experiences, their memories, and feelings. They enable conveying a message in an indirect way, "under the radar" and thus bypass the objections of the left brain. They present information that is perceived as more interesting and less threatening than information conveyed directly.

Stories also increase authenticity, integrity, and the humaneness of the teller and reduce the degree of objection to the message they conceal. They reach our subconscious and create a bridge from problems to solutions through exposure to new possibilities.

Stories are an integral part of our decision-making process: we see in our mind's eye different stories, and decide what story we prefer. As early as 350 BC, Aristotle wrote, "One cannot think without an image." Aristotle's mentor, Plato, and countless philosophers compared man's soul to a private projection hall, incessantly projecting complex stories with amazing power to soothe, scare, fascinate, or move.

Our memories are no more than stories made up of images, sounds, and sensations, and so are our dreams. Dreaming takes place automatically, as early as infancy; babies dream a lot before they learn to talk. When it happens to us when we are awake, we say we are daydreaming.

The most effective way to influence the soul, therefore, is to communicate with it in its basic programming language: the story. Use of the story also motivates towards effective change, because the story captures the awareness and the attention of the listener, and therefore can create within a person the intent to act.

Stories based on life experiences create an affinity. They enable the conveying of abstract and complex ideas in a simple and precise way. They arouse the listeners, extract one from stagnation, and enter the heart and soul. Since stories are perceived as logical to listeners, they manage to motivate to change—especially when they are integrated in speeches and presentations and offer a more attractive future.

A journalist from *The Harvard Business Review* interviewed famous Hollywood screenwriter, Robert McKee, in June 2003, and he was asked about the use of stories. McKee said that a most important part of every CEO's role is to motivate his employees to accomplish goals, and to do so he should connect with their feelings. The key to their hearts is using stories.

Stories and the Right Brain

Stories and metaphors (which we will see in the next chapter) transport us to a special state of awareness, a state of deep relaxation, trance-like in nature, a state where the brain is trained to identify patterns. Stories are distracting in that they load details and data, and at the same time, allow the unconscious mind to generate creative solutions and find the resources necessary and therefore provide new meaning to the situation.

When we hear a story, the left brain is also involved in the process. While the left brain is busy processing the words and other information conveyed in the story, the right brain is busy with just as important a task: it is envisioning the story, seeing the overall picture, and identifying patterns.

The processing in the left brain is organized, analytical, and separates elements. In the left brain, thinking is linear and methodological. The left brain breaks down the present moment into details, organizes them, connects them to the past and reflects on the future. The thinking in the left brain is done by language, an endless inner voice, for example, the voice that tells a person, "There is a lot more to do today." The right brain processes a lot of information at one time and focuses on the here and now. In the right brain, one piece of information can represent many things. It performs a synthesis and creates a whole from the parts.

While the left brain "speaks" about the experience, the right brain experiences it, thinks in images, and learns on the go. The left brain is programmed to see diversity and differences, and the single unit, while the right brain sees that which is similar and identifies mutual patterns. The right brain identifies similarity between people. The acknowledgment of the right brain is what makes us a human family.

Since the use of stories is so important, we are going to "brainwash" you with lots of stories that Obama uses. We believe you will enjoy reading them, and more importantly, you will feel the power stories have to trigger emotions, to inspire, to convince, and to lead to action.

That's the Whole Story

Obama grew up on stories. He actually nursed them at his mother's breast and heard stories at a young age from his grandparents. He grew up in a home of storytellers and learned at an early age that everything that happens to us is actually a story. Every experience is in fact a story that has a protagonist and a plot.

He kept listening to stories when he grew up, when he worked as a community organizer, and later, as a lawyer. As an individual connected to people at every moment of his life, he continued listening to stories, even when he became a respected politician.

Obama has become so skilled at identifying story patterns that you could say his thought language is the language of stories. He can identify with great precision story patterns that we all share, stories that cross class, culture, and race, stories that speak to many people.

His ability to think in stories is closely related to his ability to see the common denominator between people which enables him to bridge gaps. This is the same ability of the right brain to see all human beings as one human family and identify the similarities between them.

Through stories, Obama invites his audience to rise above the details and identify the basic patterns that all people share, regardless of religion, culture, gender, or race. His stories touch the foundation of human relationships everywhere in the world. He shared with readers of *Dreams from My Father* these uniting stories:

> Inside the thousands of churches across the city, I imagined the stories of ordinary black people merging with the stories of David and Goliath, Moses and Pharaoh, the Christians in the lion's den, Ezekiel's field of dry bones. Those stories—of survival, and freedom, and hope—became our story, my story: the blood that had spilled was our blood, the tears our tears; until this black church, on this bright day, seemed once more a vessel carrying the story of a people into future generations and into a larger world. Our trials and triumphs became at once unique and universal, black and more than black.

The various music events at the White House are a matter of tradition. In July 2009, Obama hosted a country music event. Obama, whose chief speechwriter is a musician, compared country music to storytelling:

After all, that's what country music is all about—storytelling. It's about folks telling their life story the best way they know how—stories of love and longing, hope and heartbreak, pride and pain. Stories that help us celebrate the good times and get over the bad times. Stories that are quintessentially American.

Obama understands that people need stories to exist. The stories people tell themselves protect them, and therefore they must be deposited in the listeners' memories and passed on from one generation to the next.

Obama tells stories from the past and stories about the future, stories about the individual and stories about the collective, direct stories and indirect stories. He tells diverse stories for different reasons: to build his audience's trust in him; to create values and beliefs; to get people to work together; to motivate his audience into action; to share the vision; and to inspire the audience to make a change in the present and in the future.

Building Trust with Stories

A large part of the stories Obama tells are personal stories about his childhood or his life as an adult. The protagonists of these stories are his family: his mother, grandmother, grandfather, and himself.

Obama opened his two most important speeches at the 2004 and 2008 Democratic National Conventions with a personal story about a half-black, half-white boy with a funny name, whose parents shared a belief that in a tolerant and generous America their son would have the opportunity to fulfill himself and realize his dreams.

Here's an example from a speech in February 2009 at the Jefferson Jackson dinner, where Obama tells his personal story. In this excerpt, you can actually see how Obama tells stories. Imagine his voice, his body language, and enter the story.

Note how he tells the story with simplicity, with short sentences, comprised of single words, how he repeats the words to give the story power. Note how he is not afraid to say that he lost, too, and how he connects his personal story to the values he wants to stick in the listeners' minds. See how simple it is to be sincere and vulnerable.

At the end of this excerpt, you will feel what his listeners felt:

I was born to a teen mom.
My dad left when I was two.
I was raised by my single mum and my grandparents.
They didn't have a lot of status.
They could give me love and education and hope.
And so I put hope on my signs.
I spoke about hope at the Democratic convention.
I wrote a book called the *Audacity of Hope*.
But I need to explain to people that hope is not a blind optimism.
Hope is not ignorance of the challenges that lie before us.
I know how hard it will be to provide health care to everybody.
Then insurance and the drugs companies are not going to give up their profits easily.
I know how hard it will be to change our energy policy.
Exxon-Mobil made $11 billion this last quarter.
I know how hard it is to live in poverty that's built up over generations.
I know how hard it is to make sure that we're lifting up our schools,
because it is not just going to involve teachers,
it's not just going to involve administrators:
it will involve parents and communities changing our mindset about our children.
I know these things because I have fought on the streets as a community organizer.
I have fought in the courts as a civil rights attorney.
I have fought in the legislature.
I have won some fights and I've lost some too.
I have seen good legislation die,
because good intentions were not enough.
Because they weren't fortified with political will.
Or political power.

By revealing his personal story, Obama builds trust with the audience and increases his credibility. Thus, he evokes empathy and is perceived as an honest, humane, imperfect man. Just like us.

On October 9, 2009, after the announcement that he was the Nobel Peace Prize laureate, Obama spoke in the White House Rose Garden and began with a short personal story:

> Well, this is not how I expected to wake up this morning. After I received the news, Malia walked in and said, "Daddy, you won the Nobel Peace Prize, and it is Bo's birthday!" And then Sasha added, "Plus, we have a three-day weekend coming up." So it's good to have kids to keep things in perspective.

Through his personal stories, Obama promotes values of equal opportunity, tolerance, and the American promise. He makes sure to give his audience the sense that he knows what he's talking about, based on personal experience, and demonstrates close and intimate knowledge of the issues that matter to his listeners, which enhances his ability of persuasion. Here is a short story he told when discussing health insurance for every person in his speech in Virginia:

> This issue is personal for me.
> My mother died of ovarian cancer at the age of fifty-three,
> and I'll never forget how she spent the final months of her life lying in a hospital bed,
> fighting with her insurance company
> because they claimed that her cancer was a pre-existing condition
> and didn't want to pay for treatment.
> If I am President, I will make sure those insurance companies can never do that again…

Do you know of anyone who doesn't know a similar story? But were Obama to have said only the last sentence, his words would have directly reached the left brain of his listeners and instantly evoked criticism and a reaction such as, "Sure, everyone promises these things when they want our vote." Obama's secret is using a preliminary personal story to reduce resistance and get straight to the listeners' right brain, while his core message travels under their radar.

He creates the pattern. "This issue is personal for me," he says, and then tells his personal story.

Another unique pattern that speech writers integrate in the relevant speeches is "*When I see/hear X, I think of/am reminded of Y.*" Then, too, Obama adds a personal story. At the 2008 Democratic National Convention, he used this pattern. Note how the speech is comprised of verses of a song:

Because in the faces of those young veterans who come back from Iraq and Afghanistan,

I see my grandfather, who signed up after Pearl Harbor, marched in Patton's Army,

and was rewarded by a grateful nation with the chance to go to college on the GI Bill.

In the face of that young student who sleeps just three hours before working the night shift,

I think about my mom, who raised my sister and me on her own

while she worked and earned her degree;

who once turned to food stamps but was still able to send us to the best schools in the country

with the help of student loans and scholarships.

When I listen to another worker tell me that his factory has shut down,

I remember all those men and women on the South Side of Chicago

who I stood by and fought for two decades ago after the local steel plant closed.

And when I hear a woman talk about the difficulties of starting her own business,

I think about my grandmother, who worked her way up from the secretarial pool to middle-management, despite years of being passed over for promotions because she was a woman.

Can you imagine the teary eyes of his listeners? This is the power of addressing the emotions and the right brain. However, many are not used to using the story tool, and they often assume it's not professional enough.

Obama knows another secret related to stories. When he speaks openly about his family, he not only conveys credibility and a sense of closeness with the audience, he associatively takes the listeners back in time to their childhood, to *their* families and *their* memories. He floods the audience with positive emotions that are related in most of us to family and childhood—feelings of warmth, security, and love. Through these personal stories, Obama also connects the audience to the innocence and optimism that characterizes children, when we are free of skepticism and cynicism, and we believe everything's possible. Another pattern Obama uses to relate memories of childhood and automatically activate the listeners' childhood memories, is the same simple pattern: "*I remember…*" Here, too, the secret is to activate the listeners' right brain. Here's an example from a speech in June 2008:

> I remember listening to my grandmother telling stories
> about her work on a bomber assembly-line during World War II.
> I remember my grandfather handing me his dog-tags
> from his time in Patton's Army,
> and understanding that his defense of this country
> marked one of his greatest sources of pride.
> That's my idea of America.
> I remember, when living for four years in Indonesia as a child,
> listening to my mother reading me
> the first lines of the Declaration of Independence…
> I remember her explaining how this declaration applied to every American,
> black and white and brown alike;
> how those words, and words of the United States Constitution,
> protected us from the injustices that we witnessed other people suffering
> during those years abroad.
> That's my idea of America.

Obama activates a trigger in his listeners, a button of which most of us are generally unaware. He opens up a window to childhood and makes his listeners feel warmth, belonging, and security. They are reminded of their childhood, and thus, they can identify with the speaker. And when he uses these patterns, it's easy for people to connect to him, like him, and accept him.

Creating Beliefs and Values by Telling a Story

A large part of Obama's stories are designed to instill in his listeners a set of beliefs and values that will support change and evoke in them the belief that change is possible. Here are three stories Obama told one after the other during his "Back to School" speech in September 2009:

> That's what young people like you are doing every day, all across America. Young people like Jazmin Perez, from Roma, Texas. Jazmin didn't speak English when she first started school. Hardly anyone in her hometown went to college, and neither of her parents had gone either. But she worked hard, earned good grades, got a scholarship to Brown University, and is now in graduate school, studying public health, on her way to being Dr. Jazmin Perez.
>
> I'm thinking about Andoni Schultz, from Los Altos, California, who's fought brain cancer since he was three. He's endured all sorts of treatments and surgeries, one of which affected his memory, so it took him much longer—hundreds of extra hours—to do his schoolwork. But he never fell behind, and he's headed to college this fall.
>
> And then there's Shantell Steve, from my hometown of Chicago, Illinois. Even when bouncing from foster home to foster home in the toughest neighborhoods, she managed to get a job at a local health center; start a program to keep young people out of gangs; and she's on track to graduate high school with honors and go on to college.

A story is like a mental program, according to researcher Annette Simmons. Therefore, planning and using a strategic story are the closest things to programming the other person's mind. Obama tells his audience stories to establish the trust that "we can" and the belief that we hold our fate in our hands. He tells stories about the values of hard work, sacrifice for a better future, hope, and mutual responsibility.

As someone who calls for leadership that will lead to change in the future, you would think Obama would tell stories about the future, too, like in Martin Luther King's "I Have a Dream" speech. But Obama knows it's not easy to get acceptance from an audience that is skeptical about the future, especially if the future is fundamentally different from the present.

Therefore, he primarily uses inspirational stories from the past that allow the listeners to envision the future. A story about the past makes the listener's brain imagine its own story about the future, and when a person invents a story himself, he believes it more and relates to it.

You can combine the future story in a sequence of positive stories, so that the listener will be ready, by way of induction, to envision a different future. Here is a classic sequence that many leaders use:

1. The story about who we were, that leads to

2. The story of who we are, that leads to

3. The story of who we will be.

The audience undergoes positive thought conditioning and accepts the sequence. Lincoln's Gettysburg Address is considered a classic speech that applies this formula, and not without reason is considered one of the finest speeches in history.

In Obama's victory speech he reviewed far-reaching changes, both in America and the world through a story about Ann Nixon Cooper, a one-hundred-six-year-old woman who voted in the 2008 elections. He used her personal story to evoke inspiration and prove the claim "Yes, we can":

> This election had many firsts and many stories that will be told for generations. But one that's on my mind tonight is about a woman who cast her ballot in Atlanta.
> She's a lot like the millions of others
> who stood in line to make their voice heard in this election
> except for one thing—
> Ann Nixon Cooper is one hundred, six years old.
> She was born just a generation past slavery;
> a time when there were no cars on the road or planes in the sky;
> when someone like her couldn't vote for two reasons—
> because she was a woman
> and because of the color of her skin.
> And tonight,
> I think about all that she's seen throughout her century in America—
> the heartache and the hope;

the struggle and the progress;
the times we were told that we can't,
and the people who pressed on with that American creed:
Yes we can.
At a time when women's voices were silenced
and their hopes dismissed,
she lived to see them stand up and speak out
and reach for the ballot.
Yes we can.
When there was despair in the dust bowl
and depression across the land,
she saw a nation conquer fear itself with a New Deal,
new jobs and a new sense of common purpose.
Yes we can.
When the bombs fell on our harbor
and tyranny threatened the world,
she was there to witness a generation rise to greatness
and a democracy was saved.
Yes we can.
She was there for the buses in Montgomery,
the hoses in Birmingham,
a bridge in Selma,
and a preacher from Atlanta
who told a people that "We Shall Overcome."
Yes we can.
A man touched down on the moon,
a wall came down in Berlin,
a world was connected by our own science and imagination.
And this year, in this election,
she touched her finger to a screen,
and cast her vote,
because after one hundred, six years in America,
through the best of times and the darkest of hours,
she knows how America can change.
Yes we can.

The motif of parents' sacrifice for their children is repeated in Obama's speeches. Through these stories, he establishes the belief that everything is possible and alludes in this way to his election as president:

> We can do this. We've done it before.
> Some of us had grandparents or parents who said maybe I can't go to college but my child can;
> maybe I can't have my own business
> but my child can.
> I may have to rent,
> but maybe my children will have a home they can call their own.
> I may not have a lot of money,
> but maybe my child will run for the senate.
> I might live in a small village,
> but maybe someday my son can be President of the United States of America.

Obama's stories about sacrifice are not related only to family, but to society, as a whole, throughout the years of its history. This is what he said in his inaugural speech:

> Our journey has never been one of short cuts or settling for less. It has not been the path for the faint-hearted—for those who prefer leisure over work, or seek only the pleasures of riches and fame. Rather, it has been the risk-takers, the doers, the makers of things—some celebrated but more often men and women obscure in their labor, who have carried us up the long, rugged path towards prosperity and freedom.
>
> For us, they packed up their few worldly possessions and traveled across oceans in search of a new life.
>
> For us, they toiled in sweatshops and settled the West; endured the lash of the whip and plowed the hard earth.
>
> For us, they fought and died, in places like Concord and Gettysburg; Normandy and Khe Sahn.
>
> Time and again these men and women struggled and sacrificed and worked till their hands were raw so that we might live a better life. They saw America as bigger than the sum of our individual ambitions; greater than all the differences of birth or wealth or faction.
>
> This is the journey we continue today. We remain the most prosperous, powerful nation on Earth. Our workers are no less productive than when this crisis began. Our minds are no less inventive, our goods and services no less needed

than they were last week or last month or last year. Our capacity remains undiminished. But our time of standing pat, of protecting narrow interests and putting off unpleasant decisions—that time has surely passed. Starting today, we must pick ourselves up, dust ourselves off, and begin again the work of remaking America.

When Obama wants to tell a positive story about the future, he asks the audience a question that requires it to build this optimistic story itself. This is what he did in his 2008 victory speech:

> America, we have come so far. We have seen so much.
> But there is so much more to do. So tonight, let us ask ourselves—
> if our children should live to see the next century;
> if my daughters should be so lucky to live as long as Ann Nixon Cooper, what change will they see?
> What progress will we have made?

This is another effective pattern that Obama applies. He asks the audience: if we were to explore the perspective of the next generation, what change will they see? How far will we have come? Undoubtedly, when he asks these questions, the hidden assumption is that, indeed, there has been a change and progress. Thus, he is inviting the listeners to envision a story about a positive future.

Stories That Inspire to Action

Obama tells the audience stories to inspire and motivate them into action. He does so directly, when he describes the listeners' situation in such a way that they can find themselves in the story. He also does it indirectly, when he tells stories about other people. In this case, the listeners hear not only Obama's voice, but also the voice within them, comparing the protagonists of the indirect story to themselves. Then the effect of the story expands to what is going on in the listeners' minds, when they make the analogy.

Generally, the stories are minimalistic. They are true stories from the past and present meant to inspire new stories in the listeners' minds to motivate them into action. The story about Edith Childs, which we mentioned earlier, is an example of that.

A story's best supporting evidence is made up of true and authentic examples. From the moment stories attract our attention, they arouse our feelings and actions and, later, repeat themselves in our mind's eye. They reinforce their effect on our behavior again and again.

What characterizes stories that the audience listens to more attentively?

1. Stories they can relate to.
2. Personal stories.
3. Stories that can be envisioned.
4. Stories that sound credible.
5. Stories that activate the senses.
6. Stories with mystery or anticipation.

Telling a Story the Obama Way

Obama uses stories, but does not overdo it. In some of the speeches, he opens with a story to get the audience's attention from the onset, and in some cases, he chooses to end with a story.

His stories are generally short. The amount of details is also small and the storylines are few. He tells a story in the simplest way, as if talking to one person, as opposed to an audience of thousands. Most of the stories are personal stories about him and his family or concrete examples from life, historic stories from the past and stories about people in the present. Very few stories are about the future.

Obama knows how to select the right story, based on the goal at hand. He understands that, when he wants to communicate a very strong message, a good story will do the job. But he also knows that a strong story will generally not save a bad message and will even work against him like a double-edged sword. Therefore, Obama includes a story only when he has a predefined goal, not the other way around, as others often do.

Stories as a Persuasion Tool

Obama has promised in the past that gay and lesbian men and women would be able to serve in the US military proudly, with no fear. One of the last things he did in 2010 was to keep his promise and let homosexuals serve in the US military.

On December 22, 2010, while signing the "Don't Ask, Don't Tell Repeal Act," President Obama used a story to strengthen his points of view:

Sixty-six years ago, in the dense, snow-covered forests of Western Europe, Allied Forces were beating back a massive assault in what would become known as the "Battle of the Bulge." And in the final days of fighting, a regiment in the 80th Division of Patton's Third Army came under fire. The men were traveling along a narrow trail. They were exposed and they were vulnerable. Hundreds of soldiers were cut down by the enemy.

And during the firefight, a private named Lloyd Corwin tumbled forty feet down the deep side of a ravine. And dazed and trapped, he was as good as dead. But one soldier, a friend, turned back. And with shells landing around him, amid smoke and chaos and the screams of wounded men, this soldier, this friend, scaled down the icy slope, risking his own life to bring Private Corwin to safer ground.

For the rest of his years, Lloyd credited this soldier, this friend, named Andy Lee, with saving his life, knowing he would never have made it out alone. It was a full four decades after the war, when the two friends reunited in their golden years, that Lloyd learned that the man who saved his life, his friend Andy, was gay. He had no idea. And he didn't much care. Lloyd knew what mattered. He knew what had kept him alive; what made it possible for him to come home and start a family and live the rest of his life. It was his friend.

As you see, a story adds power. Back in February 2005, shortly after being elected one of the one hundred US Senate members, Obama gave a speech whose purpose was to prevent President George W. Bush from passing a bill related to bankruptcy.

He quoted a study, which showed that half the bankruptcies were not a result of abuse of this law, but a result of medical problems that led to financial troubles. He related a story about Susan Gibbons, a nurse, who was forced to pay a bill of $53,000 dollars, after she suffered a stroke that led to a brief period of hospitalization. Her insurance covered only $4,000 dollars. She was forced to quit her regular job, which led to a lower income. She finally lost her home and was forced to declare bankruptcy.

Obama chose to attack the proposed bill in a very convincing way—with a story.

Story is a great tool, and you may use it when you speak face-to-face, one-on-one, or when you communicate to a group of people. Annette Simmons suggested in her book, *The Story Factor*, to tell a story that will make people wonder if you are reading their thoughts. People have a tendency to analyze facts, so they comply with what they were already thinking. Therefore, if you first present facts and only then tell the story, people will try first to see how the facts you presented connect to what they already think and know. Meaning, the left brain will act before the right brain, and you are liable to come up against resistance and concerns.

However, if you first tell your story, and only later specify the facts, there is a greater chance the audience will connect the facts to the story it heard a few moments earlier. This means that, when you tell a story first, the right brain becomes more dominant, and prevails over the reactions of the listeners' left brain, the critical side.

Story Time

In what situations can you use stories when you communicate? When you want…

- To change the listener's mood or level of energy.
- To re-diagnose a problem as a new opportunity.
- To teach in a way that is easy to pick up and remember.
- To show an approach or certain behavior from a different point of view.
- To illustrate an approach or behavior that differs from what exists, and that can be adopted.
- To emphasize a lesson in an indirect manner.
- To activate the listener's right brain and conjure up new insights.
- To create emotional involvement among the listeners.
- To make the audience tell the story to others and thus reach a wider distribution.
- To make people remember a certain message for the long term.
- To create a special experience and take advantage of the situation to lead and change an attitude, position, or behavior.
- To insert an element of humor or surprise and create renewed attention for what's to come.
- To hone and illustrate what you have in common with the listeners.
- To convey to the listeners insight that in any other way would meet resistance.
- To turn a complex message into a lighthearted and simple message.
- To connect to the child in each of the listeners.
- To wake up a sleepy audience, especially with a dramatic or funny story.

To fascinate an audience, the simplest way is to use a story on the basic level: your personal story. Such a story allows you to reveal emotions, experiences, failures, and challenges, and through it convey a message to others.

You can also ascend to the second level and use "frame" stories. Frame stories have one title, which is the main issue you want to talk about, and under this title, you can combine different stories—personal or about other people—that support the main message. Obama's frame stories during the presidential election campaign were almost always about change.

You can also ascend to the third level of stories, the meta-story or master story. Here, the level of abstraction is even higher. These are the instances Obama may choose to speak about "America's great story."

If you combine personal stories in one focused frame story, and if your frame stories are in harmony with the "big story" of the people you are addressing, people will connect to you and will feel you are in sync with them. The people in the audience will feel that you are a part of them, that you understand them and feel as they do.

The tool that complements the activation of the right brains of the listeners is a metaphor. In the next chapter, we invite you to get to know the metaphorical secrets Obama applies.

The Magic of Stories

People remember and love stories. You, too, undoubtedly remember many stories you read in a book. For example, you may remember the story about the workers and the cathedral (Chapter 6).

Stories suit the way in which people think and connect to emotions in a way that no rational argument can. With stories, you can convey messages in a more effective way than through logical arguments.

Tell short stories, and make them to the point. Connect to people's experiences, their memories, and feelings through stories. Stories enable one to get around objections of the conscious mind and convey information in an indirect way.

Stories convey personal credibility, integrity, and compassion. They reach the subconscious mind where they create a bridge from problems to solutions, while opening up new possibilities.

Remember that stories are a way to arouse, to prevent stagnation, and penetrate messages into the heart and soul.

You can tell stories from the past and stories about the future, stories about yourself, and stories about others, direct stories and indirect stories.

And don't forget to tell stories that will inspire your audience to make a change in the present or in the future.

Using personal life stories will enable you to build trust with the audience and enhance your credibility. Thus, you can achieve empathy and be perceived as human, imperfect. As we all are.

Telling inspirational stories from the past will enable listeners to envision the future. The story about the past makes the listener's brain invent his own story about the future, and when a person invents a story him or herself, he or she believes it more and can relate to it.

Stories you tell a large audience are best if they are short and concise, with a small number of details and few story lines.

A story should be told in a simple way, as if being told to one person and not a huge audience. After reading the last part of the book that focuses on nonverbal communication, you can adopt ideas that will enable you, not only to tell stories, but literally to make the people you are speaking to live the story, hear it, see it, and feel it. Thus, you can present a story, while using your voice and empowering body gestures. It will be a story about success.

Your stories will help you penetrate to your target audience's mind, under their radar, and stick your ideas for life.

Remember, Muriel Rukeyser said, "The universe is made of stories, not atoms".

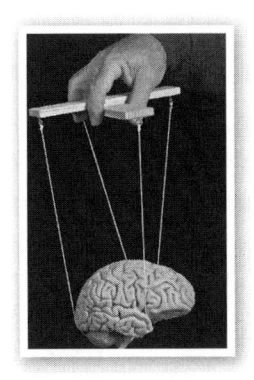

CHAPTER 22

Don't say it, paint it! – How to make messages stick with simple metaphors

"Metaphors are much more tenacious than facts."

— **Paul de Man**

Negotiations are a sophisticated game of chess. This is a metaphor, and as we will now see, a metaphor is one of Obama's winning strategic tools. If the story is the king, the metaphor is the queen in Obama's word game. Every time Obama wants to make people see his words in their mind's eye, he explores the possibility of incorporating metaphors.

When Obama incorporates metaphors, he is more than a communication wizard trying to influence and persuade; he is a painter, painting pictures in the minds of his listeners, a combination of Dali, Picasso, and Rembrandt.

Can you envision what you just read? Do you see the simplicity of using metaphors? Can you feel their power? It's so simple, yet few use this secret in their interpersonal communication with the people around them.

Why is the use of metaphors highly recommended? What can you do with them? To answer these questions, first let's see what happens in people's minds when they hear a metaphor. Metaphors help the skeptical or indifferent audience accept a new idea, because they create a connection between a new idea and something that is familiar.

The source of the word metaphor in Greek and Latin means "transformation." Metaphors have diverse definitions. For our purposes, we will define it as an equation between two different elements that have something in common.

Take, for example, the equation we made between negotiations and chess: chess is a game. Negotiations can be regarded as a type of game. Note the similarity between them in different parameters: in both there's a battle of wits; in both someone makes the first move and starts the game; in both there's a battle between the positions of the two sides, and they change throughout the game. We can go on and on with associative thinking and reach vast creativity in the parameters that can be compared. Obama likes using the game metaphor. Throughout his election campaign, he spoke of "changing the game." He says it simply: "It's not enough to change the players. We've got to change the game."

A metaphor possesses a special power. It provides a new point of reference for ideas and can also be considered a bridge between the unfamiliar and the familiar. This bridge provides a new perspective and meaning that can persuade the audience to reconsider its point of view, which is often one of skepticism or indifference.

In this book, we continuously use the metaphor that every speech can be viewed as a relationship with the audience. Think about it. Almost everything you can imagine about an effective relationship is also relevant when speaking to an audience.

When speaking of the way the human brain operates, it is convenient to use terms taken from the computer world. Despite the accelerated high-tech development, the human brain is still much more than a computer. However, when using the computer metaphor, it is easier to understand terms related to the brain's activity. For example, data that we load into a computer can also be extracted. If you enter incorrect data, you will receive an incorrect result. The same applies to the brain. What data do you want to introduce? You could say the use of metaphors enables you to introduce into the computer in the listeners' minds the data you want to share with them. The use of metaphors also stimulates audience interest and invites members to view familiar things in a new way. As you might remember, the brain has five sensory representational systems: visual; auditory; kinesthetic; olfactory; and taste. Every person has a dominant sense, and the visual people, those for whom the sense of sight is dominant, comprise 45 percent of the population. Metaphors help you communicate like a painter.

Now, we will enter Obama's mental movie theater (yes, this is also a metaphor) and see how he creates movies in the listeners' minds.

Obama often uses metaphors to illuminate one term with the characteristics of another, to help listeners see different situations in a new light. This is what he wrote on his website about the importance of the war on terror, prior to the presidential election:

> Our enemies are fully aware that they can use oil as a weapon against America.
>
> And if we don't take this threat as seriously as the bombs they build or the guns they buy, we will be fighting the war on terror with one hand tied behind our back.

Metaphors activate the imagination, and help you create an experience. Obama used this tool at the 2004 Democratic National Convention:

> I believe that we have a righteous wind at our backs, and when we stand on the crossroads of history we can make the right choices and meet the challenges that face us.

Often metaphors become overused idioms, so much so that we don't notice we are using them. An example is the common expression "crossroads." However, in these cases, the brain sees the image the speaker is presenting, and his or her thoughts reach the right brain directly, even if the listener is an auditory type and not a visual or sensory type.

In October 2009, at a funding-raising dinner for Democratic Party supporters in Miami, Florida, Obama used another metaphor:

> America is not a speedboat; it's an ocean liner. And it takes time to move a country this big, particularly because we are a democracy—and that's a good thing. We're supposed to have robust debate. Change isn't supposed to be easy. We're supposed to have to fight for it. And the fact that we've got the other party challenging us and pushing us and poking us on, that's a good thing. Ultimately, we will have a better product as a consequence of that. I want a competition of ideas. I want a strong and loyal opposition.

A metaphor can help listeners see a tough situation in a new light and provide a creative way to solve it. It also helps to easily clarify matters that are not easy to explain any other way. When we illustrated in the beginning of the book four perceptual positions and discussed them as four pairs of mental glasses, we presented the third perceptual position with the "fly on the wall" metaphor. This clear and simple metaphor prevented us from having to use many words to explain this position.

Metaphors present information that is also perceived as more interesting and less threatening than direct information. They are safe to use, noninvasive, and in the event they don't fit—the subconscious merely ignores them. Metaphors are perceived with ease and simplicity, since the brain is programmed to use metaphors from a very young age. Even babies can discern that one thing represents another.

When Obama calls the citizens of America into action, he calls them to join the renewed construction of America. To clarify the meaning of the metaphor of construction, he expands and explains. Here's the quote from the 2008 victory speech:

> I ask you join in the work of remaking this nation
> the only way it's been done in America
> for two-hundred and twenty-one years—
> block by block,
> brick by brick,
> calloused hand by calloused hand…

The adage, "a picture is worth 1000 words," is well known. However, there's another Chinese proverb, less known, but just as true, "The tongue can paint what the eye can't see." In other words—words have power.

If you want to magnetize people, influence, sell, and lead change, you should transform from just another speaker to a painter of words. A good way to do this is to use stories and metaphors. Most people feel comfortable with visual messages. A metaphor suits every age and addresses the right brain, the place where changes occur.

Obama uses dynamic images a lot, which create in his listeners a sense of forward motion. What is perceived in the brain as animated and dynamic—remains in the memory for a longer period of time. The metaphor stimulates us to enrich our perspective and invites us to reevaluate our assumptions. It also helps us shift from a problem to a solution. Obama said this simply on the website he created for the 2008 presidential election:

> If you're walking down the right path and you're willing to keep walking, eventually you'll make progress.

In his presidential election campaign, Obama often used metaphors that create a parallel between hardships in life and a journey with steep ascents, or between hope and the top of a mountain that can be observed from a lower valley. In a short metaphor, he conveys a powerful message:

> It may look dark tonight, but if I hold on to hope, tomorrow will be brighter.

In his 2008 victory speech, he continued to speak to his supporters in a metaphorical language:

> We began this journey in the depths of winter nearly two years ago,
> on the steps of the Old State Capitol in Springfield, Illinois.
> Back then, we didn't have much money or many endorsements.
> We weren't given much of a chance by the polls or the pundits,
> and we knew how steep our climb would be.

Obama's secret is simple. He not only speaks to his audience—he paints images in their mind. His images are colorful, surprising, and often ridiculous. When his message is simple, but he uses a surprising metaphor, he applies important principles that help messages stick in the minds of the listeners: the images enrich the words he says and increase the audience's experience.

They enable the audience to see familiar situations in a new light. Thus he "airs out" the standard method of thinking and shifts us to a metaphorical world, where problems become concrete and objects and expressions take on human characteristics.

Remember the story of *Alice in Wonderland*? As in this story, Obama manages to surprise us and expand our boundaries of thought. He not only involves our right brain and our creative side, he also establishes our belief that anything's possible.

🔍 Watering and Fertilizing Messages

Legendary General Electric CEO Jack Welch wrote in his book *WINNING* (which he coauthored with Suzy Welch) that every leader must view himself as a gardener, with a watering can in one hand and fertilizer in the other. You are invited to water your messages with stories and fertilize them with metaphors.

In your next speech you can, like Obama, paint colorful, surprising, and amusing pictures in the listeners' minds by using metaphors. Metaphors convey information perceived as more interesting and less threatening than direct information. Using metaphors stimulates the listeners to enrich their perspective and invites them to reevaluate their assumptions.

Metaphors are the means by which your messages stick in the listeners' minds, the arrow you shot, while speaking, that hit the bull's eye to which your words were aimed!

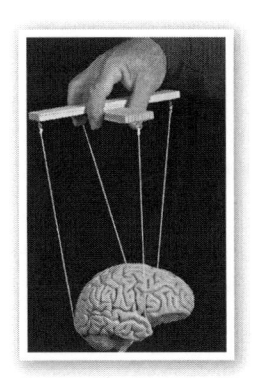

CHAPTER 23

THE MIND AS A SUPER COMPUTER – HOW TO CONNECT TO THE THINKING STRATEGIES OF YOUR AUDIENCE

During the lengthy research we conducted while writing this book, we took advantage of diverse opportunities to listen to what people of different cultures had to say about Barack Obama. There was always sweeping agreement regarding Obama's extraordinary communications ability, even among his opponents. However, during the year-and-a-half Obama managed his 2008 election campaign, and in his first two years as president, we heard different opinions as to the future in the Obama era. Here are three examples of what we heard.

1. "When I picture the future of the world in several years, I think Obama will make great changes in the world, not only in the USA."

2. "Obama talks about the future of the world, but what do I care? I want to know how he gets me back into the work force and how the value of my home will go up again."

3. "I think his opponents will ultimately eat their hats, and most people will be very pleased with him."

These very different statements reveal secrets directly from the minds of the people who said them. These people's thought styles are different from one another. And why is this important? Well, if you know what someone thinks, you can influence him or her better. We will now return to these three sentences, which represent different cognitive filters known in the NLP language as "meta programs."

Meta programs are some unconscious filters that direct what we pay attention to, the way we process any information we receive, and how we then communicate it.

Dr. Roger Ellerton wrote, "'Meta' means over, beyond, above, or on a different level—i.e. operating at an unconscious level. meta programs are deep-rooted mental programs, which automatically filter our experience and guide and direct our thought processes, resulting in significant differences in behavior from person to person. They define typical patterns in the strategies or thought styles of an individual, group, company, or culture."

To influence the people who made these three different statements about Obama and persuade them, we must understand the *meta* programs that made them say what they did.

These three people were exposed to the same Obama as everyone else. The "computer" (a metaphor, remember?) in their heads supposedly received the same data. But their inner programs, i.e., their thought processes, were different. Therefore, a totally different sentence came out of their printers (their mouths). We will read the first statement again:

"When I picture the future of the world in several years, I think Obama will make great changes in the world, not only in the USA." This is a statement that presumably represents a visual person, whose meta program is focused on the future, not present or past. Such an individual considers the overall picture and speaks in general terms about the future and the great change, without going into detail.

The second statement was, "Obama talks about the future of the world, but what do I care? I want to know how he gets me back into the work force and how the value of my home will go up again." We can see almost instantly that this person is focused on the fine details and is not satisfied with seeing the overall picture. Therefore, such a person doesn't care about the future of his world, but rather his job and the value of his home. He is focused on the present, the here and now, not the future.

And here is the third statement: "I think his opponents will ultimately eat their hats, and most people will be very pleased with him." This is a person who is presumably kinesthetic ("will eat their hats") and one of his inner meta programs is based on external judgment, i.e., what others think and what they consider right or wrong.

It is undoubtedly clear that you should speak to these people in different ways, and any attempt to convince or influence them that does not comply with their inner programs will only "jam the computer." When you know how a person you communicate with thinks, you can speak to him or her in a language that suits him or her. Thus, you can influence that person more and "program his or her mind" by identifying his or her central thinking strategies.

When communication is directed at one person, we can adapt our speech pattern accordingly if we want to influence that person. For example, if you identify that a person focuses on details, speak to him or her unlike you would speak to a person who looks at the whole picture. If you identified that the person thinks in proactive terms, speak to him or her unlike you would speak to a person who tends to react to events. When you are explaining a new subject to someone you identified as being focused on the similarity between your idea and other ideas, continue the conversation unlike you would converse with someone who is focused on the differences between ideas.

But Obama is in a different situation: he addresses many people at one time. Therefore, he should use a wide range of messages to suit the diverse thinking strategies of every person in the audience or each of the TV or online viewers.

Today, we tend to explain cognitive processes in terms of computerization. Based on this metaphor, the computer in our brain runs a complex series of programs regularly and continuously. These programs control every aspect of our existence, like breathing, walking, talking, and communicating with others, as well as our behavior and the manner in which we handle problems. In NLP terms, the meta program is, in fact, an unconscious thinking strategy that guides us on how to treat the information we get. It can be used to process different types of information, just like a computer program. Meta programs are like filters through which we take in the world around us. They guide and lead our thought processes, define our approach to specific subjects, and characterize the different ways in which we solve problems. The meta programs are manifested in the verbal and nonverbal languages in every interpersonal communication. At times, they change throughout our lifetime, but when you want to influence someone, you can definitely identify the way in which that person thinks, and speak in his or her personal computer language.

If you identified, for example, that the person to whom you are speaking always checks what happened in the past before he or she solves a problem, there is no point talking to him or her about the future, without mentioning the past. Knowing a wide range of meta programs will help you deal more efficiently with diverse people.

To speak with power, we will now penetrate the minds of the people around us. Observe caution, please!

Obama uses different and diverse meta programs to motivate people. This is one of the things he does to join people and lead them in new directions of thought. He helps the listeners enrich their "orientation maps," so they develop points of view that are similar to his and find a common denominator with him.

Audiences are naturally comprised of many people with different quantities of thought programs. Generally, an audience cannot be diagnosed and labeled in advance. Therefore, when Obama speaks before an audience, he takes into account all the different types. He builds his speech as though it were a buffet so that everyone in the audience can connect to their preferred meta program.

Obama is not a man of extremes. He does not go to extremes, but moves between extreme positions with flexibility, and according to the issue at hand. In his speeches, there are references to the different thinking strategies. Any one of his listeners can find the strategy that suits him and feel that he understands what Obama is saying.

Obama's ability to think, work, and speak in different thinking strategies and diverse combinations allows him to create rapport with the audience and increase the sense of closeness and intimacy, as well as his degree of influence on the audience.

Many speakers prepare their speech or presentation based on their own unique thought style. For example, rational people may try to influence and persuade mainly with logical arguments; people who don't like details may focus on the overall picture and forget there are many people who want to see the world through a magnifying glass; people who are results-oriented may forget that many people are focused on processes or on the people involved in the process.

When speaking to a group, you should take into account the diverse people in the audience and try to speak to each. Therefore, instead of a regular menu of your preferred dishes, you should build a message like a buffet, with a wide selection of dishes. This will enable every person in the group to choose what he or she likes. Ultimately, everyone will be happy.

We will now sketch the winning profile of Obama's principal thinking strategies as they come to light in his speeches.

Zoom In – Zoom Out (The Preference for Overview or Detail)

An issue or problem can be analyzed with various degrees of generalization and specification. Some people think and speak at a high level of generalization and you could say they zoom out with the camera until they can see the entire picture from a distance. However, too general an observation is apt to make people lose the continuity of, and disconnect from, what is actually happening.

On the other hand, some people focus on the fine details. You could say they zoom in until they see the tiniest details, down to the pixels of the image. But over-focusing on details is liable to make people lose touch with the bigger picture. It's important to mention that meta programs are not an "either/or" choice, rather they operate along a sliding scale, ranging from one preference to the other. The key is to find the right balance.

Obama knows this; he combines the two approaches in a balanced way. As we have seen, he speaks in generalizations and with simplicity and conveys optimistic messages about change, hope, and promise. But in the same breath, he also fills these general words with specific content from people's daily lives.

Here is an example from the 2008 Democratic National Convention in which he combined general words like "progress" and "economic strength" and factual details from everyday life.

> We measure progress by how many people can find a job that pays the *mortgage*;
> whether you can put a little extra money away at the end of each month so you can someday watch your child receive her college diploma.
> We measure progress in the twenty-three million new jobs that were created when Bill Clinton was President—
> when the average American family saw its income go up $7,500 instead of down $2,000, like it has under George Bush.
> We measure the strength of our economy not by the number of billionaires we have or the profits of the Fortune 500,

> but by whether someone with a good idea can take a risk and start a new business,
>
> or whether the waitress who lives on tips can take a day off to look after a sick kid without losing her job…

Obama's secret is finding the fine balance between the generalizations and the details. Almost every issue he tackles is analyzed on several levels of detailing, from the most general level to the most personal details, of stories about people or specific goals he wants to achieve. Here is more from that speech at the convention:

> That's the promise we need to keep.
> That's the change we need right now
> So let me spell out exactly what that change would mean if I am President.
> Change means a tax code that doesn't reward the lobbyists, who wrote it,
> but the American workers and small businesses who deserve it.
> Unlike John McCain, I will stop giving tax breaks
> to corporations that ship jobs overseas,
> and I will start giving them to companies
> that create good jobs right here in America.
> I will eliminate capital gains taxes for the small businesses and the start-ups
> that will create the high-wage, high-tech jobs of tomorrow.
> I will cut taxes—cut taxes—for 95 percent of all working families.

As an experienced attorney, Obama not only makes sure to utter general statements, but also provides specific appropriate and persuasive proof. He leads every audience to accept his general theory about change and hope, just as he would persuade a jury through a general line of reasoning based on details.

Break Down the Image

Remember that the general statements you make, even if they are positive, speak only to some of your listeners, the ones that think in "large chunks." To reach all your listeners, you should break down the general plans into details and cut the big picture up into small, even microscopic, pieces.

> **Stop and Reflect**
>
> - What is *your* style?
>
> - Are you focused on details or the overall picture?
>
> - What is your typical approach to details and the overall picture?
>
> - Think of a person you care for. How does his or her computer work? What does he or she prefer and when?
>
> - Practice diagnosing other people's meta programs, so you can activate them successfully.

The Carrot and the Stick (Towards/Away From)

This meta program focuses on the person's motivational energy. Is it centered on goals and achievements, on problems to be dealt with, or issues to be avoided?

Some emphasize the positives in the future, the good things they want to attain, and some focus on the negatives, the things they want to get away from or avoid.

An approach that is focused on the positives, includes the desire to achieve favored results and is characterized by entrepreneurship and pro-activeness. This is an approach that focuses on reward and compensation. If we take the carrot and the stick theory for example, this approach focuses on the carrot.

The approach focused on avoiding the negative includes a tendency to bypass potential mistakes and problems and is accompanied by conservative and less-active planning. It is focused on fears and criticism and is characterized by caution. The movement is not perceived as a way to get somewhere, it is mainly perceived as a way to avoid harm. If we take the carrot and the stick theory, this approach focuses on the stick.

Obama's meta program is of course a combination of both approaches. On the one hand, being a man of vision, he is focused on striving for a better future. We can see this already in 2004, at the Democratic National Convention:

> I believe that we can give our middle class relief
> and provide working families with a road to opportunity.
> I believe we can provide jobs for the jobless,
> homes to the homeless,
> and reclaim young people in cities across America from violence and despair.

But Obama doesn't forget the negative thinkers who tend to avoid problems, and proves to them that the change he is striving for will ensure they avoid failure and difficulties. In October 2008 and at the 2008 Democratic National Convention he said:

> And we are here because we love this country too much to let the next four years look like the last eight. On November 4th, we must stand up and say, "Eight is enough."

Obama flexibly and persuasively combines the two approaches in precise dosages and for the good of the matter. Sometimes, he uses the two approaches in the same paragraph. He began his November 2007 speech by steering clear of past failures and ended with striving for a better future:

> I am in this race because I don't want to see us spend the next year re-fighting the Washington battles of the 1990s. I don't want to pit Blue America against Red America. I want to lead a United States of America. I don't want this election to be about the past, because if it's about the future, we all win. If this election is about whether or not to end this war, or pass universal health care, or make more college affordable, it won't just be a Democratic victory; it will be an American victory…

> That's why I run in this election. I run to give my children and their children the same chances that someone, somewhere gave me. I run so that a year from today, there is a chance that the world will look at America differently, and that America will look at itself differently. And I run to keep the promise of the United States of America alive for all those who still hunger for opportunity and thirst for equality and long to believe again.

The Vision and the Fear

When people hear Obama speak, they can choose the approach they relate to the better of the two approaches he suggests. Next time you want to convince or persuade, ask yourself towards which positive goal are you leading people. What is the vision, the reward, or the desired image you want to depict in the listeners' minds?

And since there are two sides to every coin, incorporate in your message the answer to questions: What do people in your audience want to avoid? What are the failures or difficulties they want to distance themselves from? What are their true fears?

And if you don't know exactly what meta programs dictate the decisions people make—it's best to use both approaches.

Stop and Reflect

- What are you focused on when you think about the results of a certain situation or problem?

- Do you prefer avoiding risks and problems, or do you prefer being optimistic and proactive and focusing on benefits and profits?

- Consider a good friend of yours. How does his personal program work?

- If you have to persuade him, what messages must you focus on?

- It's worthwhile remembering in this regard that studies by Prof. Daniel Kahnman, winner of the Nobel Prize for Economics, and by other researchers, found that the way a problem is formulated affects the perception of risk and probability and, accordingly, the decision as well.

Past, Present, Future (Time Orientation)

With an amazing result of 9.58 seconds, Usain Bolt from Jamaica is the Olympic champion and world record holder in the 100-meter dash, as of August 2011. He is also the world champion in the 200 meters, with an incredible result of 19.19 seconds. At the 2008 Beijing Olympics, Bolt broke the world records in these categories and, in the 2009 world athletic championships in August, he broke these two world records once again.

And then, there is Haile Gebrselassie from Ethiopia, who holds the marathon world record after breaking his own personal record in the Berlin marathon in September 2008, with an amazing result of 2 hours, 3 minutes and 59 seconds. He holds another six world records and, during his career, he held all the world records starting from the 5,000 meter to the marathon.

Both these men excel in their fields, and they are both the quickest men in the world. But they have different characters and physical traits that enable them to excel in the style they choose to compete in.

Different people are focused for different lengths of time, which affects the way they interpret events and handle problems. The "sprinters"–people like Usain Bolt–are focused on the immediate short term, while the "marathon runners"–people like Haile Gebrselassie–are focused on the long term.

In his communication, Obama creates a fine balance between the two styles. When he wants to convince his audience of the possibility of making a change, he takes into account that, in every audience, there are some sprinters, whose thought processes focus on the short term, and there are marathon runners, whose thought processes focus on the long term. Therefore, he speaks the language of both groups. He presents plans for immediate improvement of Americans' quality of life in the short term, alongside long-term rescue and prosperity plans.

Our book focuses only on Obama as a role model for effective communication, but it's interesting to mention that, after only a few months in office, President Obama found that most of the American people focus on short-term results and they do not want to hear again speeches about changes that will take place in a few years while they are unemployed or suffer from the other economic crises.

We should see how Obama promised instant aid to people in the short term in those areas of their lives that concern them the most. This is what he promised at the 2008 Convention:

> America, *now is not the time for* small plans.
>
> *Now is the time to* finally meet our moral obligation to provide every child a world-class education, because it will take nothing less to compete in the global economy...

> *Now is the time to* finally keep the promise of affordable, accessible health care for every single American. If you have health care, my plan will lower your premiums…
>
> *Now is the time to* help families with paid sick days and better family leave…
>
> *Now is the time to* change our bankruptcy laws, so that your pensions are protected ahead of CEO bonuses; and the time to protect Social Security for future generations.
>
> And *now is the time to* keep the promise of equal pay for an equal day's work, because I want my daughters to have exactly the same opportunities as your sons.

Issues can be related to through the prism of the past, present, or future. Some people prefer the past; they revere history and examine everything through the test of time. They appreciate what was achieved in the past and examine what worked and what didn't. These people can try to reenact successes or avoid problems that occurred in the past. Among them, there are also people who are focused on the near past; whereas others are focused on the distant past.

On the other hand, there are people who live the moment, the "power of now." They are less focused on what happened or on what will happen. It is important to them that the situation is good here and now, and they are especially aware of the price the present demands of them.

Others prefer focusing on the future, what they can or cannot expect. Studies show that successful people tend to grant more weight to the future and speak in terms of realizing a goal and a vision.

You should remember that all people take into account the past, present, and future, but they simply do so in different doses. Obama illustrates a fine balance in his reference to time, as well. He opens up a window to the future when he speaks of change, promise, and hope for a better future; he does not forget the past and refers to events of the past to draw inspiration, to learn from failures, and prove one can overcome hardships; he also manages to bridge the gap between past and future events with an invisible line that connects historical events.

This is what he said at the 2008 Democratic National Convention:

> And it is that promise that forty-five years ago, today, brought Americans from every corner of this land to stand together on a Mall in Washington, before Lincoln's Memorial, and hear a young preacher from Georgia speak of his dream.
>
> The men and women who gathered there could've heard many things. They could've heard words of anger and discord. They could've been told to succumb to the fear and frustration of so many dreams deferred.
>
> But what the people heard instead—people of every creed and color, from every walk of life—is that in America, our destiny is inextricably linked. That, together, our dreams can be one.

In that same speech, Obama honored the present, what people are currently going through. He identified with the hardships they were confronting in their lives, spoke to them about the issues that bothered them, and promised immediate assistance:

> Tonight, more Americans are out of work
> and more are working harder for less.
> More of you have lost your homes
> and even more are watching your home values plummet.
> More of you have cars you can't afford to drive,
> credit card bills you can't afford to pay,
> and tuition that's beyond your reach…

In this way, Obama promises people with different preferences in terms of their approach to time, that they will find the program that suits them in his words.

A Plan for All Seasons

Next time you communicate with people, remember to present to your audience both short- and long-term plans, since you can never know who in your audience is focused on the long term and who is focused on the short term. If you use this insight in sales, you can tailor your presentations to the customer's orientation. Speak the right way in the present, and then you will see the results in the future, too.

Effective speeches, like Obama's, refer in a balanced way to the past, the present, and the future, and then connect the three. You, too, can apply this rule when conveying your next message.

> **Stop and Reflect**
>
> - Do you tend to refer to the past to make a decision about the present and the future?
>
> - What is more important to you—the personal results of the next year or the results you will achieve in the next decade?
>
> - Do you consume most of your income in the present, without considering what will happen in the future?

Similarities or Differences

When you came across Obama for the first time, to whom did you compare him in your imagination? Did you see the similarities between him and John F. Kennedy or the differences between them? What did you pay attention to—the similarities between him and President Clinton or the differences?

What did you notice—the similarities between Obama and Martin Luther King or the differences between them?

When you see a new product, do you focus first on the new benefits or do you say to yourself, "it's very similar to…except it is…?"

Some people tend to find similarities and point out the common characteristics. Others focus on what's lacking and what's different. In this regard, you can refer to a goal or a problem in two ways: by seeking a common denominator or by seeking the differences between the existing situation and the desired one.

Again, in order to convince people, you need to adopt your communication style to their "mind software."

Obama's Secrets

Those seeking similarities focus on what was already achieved, and those seeking differences focus on what is lacking; those seeking similarities tend to support agreement and unity, and those seeking differences tend toward diversification and innovation.

Obama often uses a similarity pattern, as part of his mediating position, which emphasizes the common denominator. He emphasizes the similarity between himself and his audience, the similarity between different people in the audience and the similarity between present and past events to draw strength from the past. In his October 2008 speech he said:

> Because, despite what our opponents may claim, there are no real or fake parts of this country. There is no city or town that is more pro-America than anywhere else—we are one nation, all of us proud, all of us patriots. There are patriots who supported this war in Iraq and patriots who opposed it; patriots who believe in Democratic policies and those who believe in Republican policies. The men and women who serve in our battlefields may be Democrats and Republicans and Independents, but they have fought together and bled together and some died together under the same proud flag. They have not served a Red America or a Blue America—they have served the United States of America.

But Obama also knows how to talk about the dissimilar. Like a seasoned marketing man, he makes sure to differentiate himself from others and emphasize the benefits of the "Obama" product and the "Democrat" manufacturer. In October 2008, he emphasized the differences between the Democratic and Republican approaches and the differences between the change and reform plans he was offering, as opposed to his opponents:

> You've heard a lot about taxes in this campaign. Well, here's the truth—my opponent and I are both offering tax cuts. The difference is, he wants to give $200 billion in tax cuts to the biggest corporations in America, and he wants to give the average Fortune 500 CEO a $700,000 tax cut. But he gives nothing at all to over 100 million Americans.

> I have a different set of priorities. I'll give a middle-class tax cut to 95 percent of all workers. And if you make less than $250,000 a year—which includes 98 percent of small business owners—you won't see your taxes increase one single dime. Not your payroll taxes, not your income taxes, not your capital gains

taxes—nothing. Because in an economy like this, the last thing we should do is raise taxes on the middle-class.

The Disparity in Similarity

Next time you want to influence people, remember that some of your listeners will want to hear about the similarities. They will want to know how things are similar, how they connect, and how they support one another.

Others in the same audience will want to understand the differences, where the innovation is, and where the difference lies between you and others or between what they hope for and the current situation.

To influence both these types of people and to give all the people in the audience the feeling you are speaking in their mental language, it's best you "supply the goods" on the two levels.

Stop and Reflect

- What do you emphasize more? The sameness or the difference?

- When you meet someone, do you consider how he or she is similar to other people or how he or she is unique?

- When you read this book, do you sometimes find yourself saying, "Oh, this idea is like something I know," or do you seek a new angle and say, "Oh, that's' a new concept that gives me a new idea I can use."

Goal Oriented or Relationship Oriented

When you study people negotiating, it is obvious that some people care about nothing but achieving the goal. Others first want to make sure the relationship between the parties is maintained and perhaps will even improve as a result of the negotiations. These are different styles of negotiation, and they also make each party behave and speak differently during the negotiation process.

If the relationship is the main factor, the chance of realizing a threat during negotiations is low; if the result is the goal—the probability increases that threatening tactics, distortion of facts, and other gambits will be applied.

During negotiations, experts recommend using the two styles at once, to achieve the best results for you and to ensure the other party is pleased. That is win-win.

However, these differences are manifested not only in negotiations. People also solve problems by using diverse filters: some are task-oriented and some are relationship-oriented. The people that relate to goals and problems in the form of tasks and are goal-oriented divide each topic into tasks. They emphasize objectives, actions, processes, and options.

On the other hand, there are people who refer to goals and problems, while focusing on relationships, observing every situation from diverse perspectives: their perspective; the other person's perspective; and from the perspective of the relationship on the whole. They consider the benefit and detriment that may be caused to the relationship.

In this case, too, it is not worthwhile going to one extreme or the other; a person with an extreme, task-oriented approach is liable to lose his human warmth, while the person that emphasizes only the relationship is liable not to focus on the task and, thus, have a hard time achieving the goals.

Obama knows exactly what he wants to achieve, and to achieve his goals he integrates the two approaches. He likes people and values relationships. He places great weight on his relationship with every audience, the relationship of the country with every citizen, and the relationship of Americans with one another. He speaks in a language of relationships. In Pennsylvania in 2008 he said to the audience:

> I will be a President who puts you first, Pennsylvania.
> Because I believe in the American people and what we can do together.

And in his 2008 victory speech he said to the audience:

> I will always be honest with you about the challenges we face. I will listen to you, especially when we disagree. And above all, I will ask you join in the work of remaking this nation…

But in Philadelphia he manifested the task-oriented approach:

> So we'll invest $15 billion a year in renewable energy to create five million new, green jobs over the next decade—jobs that pay well and can't be outsourced.
>
> And we'll provide affordable loans for our small businesses, eliminate their capital gains taxes, and give them tax incentives to create new jobs. That's the change we need.

The Goal: Relationships

In your next presentation, take into account people's different thought patterns. Break down your plans into tasks and goals, but do not short change relationships.

Remember that, apart from words that express actions, deeds, and goals, your speech should also include words that refer to relationships such as "we" and "feelings." To speak powerfully—develop your emotional intelligence. You can—and you should—achieve goals while improving relationships. Communication is like love, and true love is like a pair of socks: you gotta have two and they've gotta match.

Stop and Reflect

- Are you, most of the time, task oriented? Are you mainly focused on relationships and people?

- Perhaps you are both? When?

- And the people around you—what are they focused on? How can they be motivated into action?

- What words do you have to use to convince and persuade them?

Logic or Emotion

Dale Carnegie once said, "When dealing with people, remember you are not dealing with creatures of logic, but with creatures of emotion, creatures bristling with prejudice, and motivated by pride and vanity."

When people are busy solving problems or achieving goals, they emphasize different combinations of thought styles. Some strive to realize a vision, some are action-oriented. Some are motivated by common sense and logic, and some emphasize emotions. And there are, of course, different combinations of these styles.

Obama possesses all the thought styles. First, he's clearly a man of vision—a well-formed vision of change and better days. But as we saw, he does not make do with merely the vision, but specifies the actions required to realize the vision and proves, once again, that he is no less a performance-oriented man of action:

He specifies for his listeners how he intends to realize his vision in terms of education, health, economy, employment, and security in each area of which he speaks. Here is an example from the field of education from his speech at the 2008 Democratic National Convention:

> I'll invest in early childhood education.
> I'll recruit an army of new teachers,
> and pay them higher salaries and give them more support.
> And in exchange, I'll ask for higher standards and more accountability.

Obama is perceived as a symbol of reason and common sense. Therefore, a large part of his arguments are based on reason, statistics, and analysis of the facts. When he attacked his Republican opponent at the Democratic National Convention, he did so as a brilliant attorney:

> John McCain has voted with George Bush ninety percent of the time.
> Senator McCain likes to talk about judgment,
> but really, what does it say about your judgment when you think George Bush has been right more than ninety percent of the time?
> I don't know about you,
> but I'm not ready to take a ten percent chance on change.

On the other hand, we have seen how Obama uses stories to move an audience. That's because he knows that reason without emotion is not effective in most cases. When you mention your loved ones or your listeners' loved ones in a speech, you are adding strong emotion to your message.

Let's see how President Obama added emotion to his message, on January 12, 2011, at a memorial service for the victims of the shooting in Tucson, Arizona:

> And then there is nine-year-old Christina-Taylor Green. Christina was an A student; she was a dancer; she was a gymnast; she was a swimmer. She decided that she wanted to be the first woman to play in the Major Leagues, and as the only girl on her Little League team, no one put it past her.
>
> She showed an appreciation for life uncommon for a girl her age. She'd remind her mother, "We are so blessed. We have the best life." And she'd pay those blessings back by participating in a charity that helped children who were less fortunate.

President Bill Clinton used the same secret. Once, he said:

> You measure the impact of your words, not on the beauty or the emotion of the moment, but on whether you change the way people not only think but the way they feel.

Dozens of years of scientific research led scientists to the basic conclusion that "reason without emotion is neurologically impossible." These words were uttered by Prof. Antonio Damasio, neurologist, head of the Brain and Creativity Institute and Professor of Neuroscience at the University of Southern California. He helped to understand the recesses of the brain and wrote several bestsellers on neuropsychology, including *Descartes' Error*.

According to Steven Pinker, author of several bestsellers in the fields of the brain, emotions are adaptations, well-programmed software segments that work in harmony with the intellect and are vital to the functioning of the entire brain.

Other studies in the field of neuroscience have shown that, when leaders use only facts, listeners fill in the blanks themselves, in terms of emotion and symbols, but not always in keeping with the message that the leader wanted to convey. This happens when a leader who thought he conveyed his message in its entirety, falls into the trap of lack of understanding, lack of agreement, or lack of caring on the part of the listeners.

Obama knows this; therefore, he makes sure his audience feels exactly what he wants them to feel. This is what he said in June 2008:

> In the end, it may be this quality that best describes patriotism in my mind—
> not just a love of America in the abstract,
> but a very particular love for, and faith in, the American people.
> That is why our heart swells with pride at the sight of our flag.

Obama practiced speaking in view of activating emotions his entire life. He addresses the audience's emotions and does so in different and diverse ways. He joins the feelings of frustration, pain, and anger that the audience is experiencing because of the hard times and embraces these feelings. At the same time, he manages to evoke in the audience positive feelings of hope, anticipation for better days, and a feeling of closeness by telling personal stories about himself and others and providing inspiring examples from the past. In his direct way, he speaks explicitly about feelings and his relationship with the audience, between people and themselves, and between the country and its citizens.

Kennedy's Character

In his speech before the joint session of Congress in September 2009, in which he spoke of his health care reform, Obama read parts of a letter that the late Senator Ted Kennedy wrote shortly before he died. Ted Kennedy, a member of the legendary Kennedy dynasty, wrote Obama that implementing the reform in health care services is "the character of our nation." Kennedy, who for years fought for health insurance for the citizens of the USA, tapped into the feelings of many Americans, Democrats, and Republicans alike.

Obama incorporated a moving message and called everyone to set aside the differences and focus on realizing Kennedy's vision.

You can see—and learn from—how Obama combines logic and emotion, sometimes even in the same paragraph, as he did at the 2008 Democratic National Convention:

Now is the time to finally keep the promise of affordable, accessible health care for every single American.
If you have health care, my plan will lower your premiums.
If you don't, you'll be able to get the same kind of coverage that members of Congress give themselves.
And, as someone who watched my mother argue with insurance companies while she lay in bed dying of cancer,
I will make certain those companies stop discriminating against those who are sick and need care the most.

Speak Logically and Evoke Emotion

Influencing an inhomogeneous audience is possible only if you take into account all the standard thought styles and express them explicitly in words.

Therefore, in your next speech, ask yourself: What is my vision? How do I gear myself to present it to the listeners? What actions will be required to realize the vision?

Verify the logical considerations that support your path and how you can convince the listeners that your vision is consistent with common sense.

But keep your mind on which emotions you want to evoke in your audience and plan how you will get them to feel this way with your words.

When you prepare your next presentation, ask yourself the three "KFD" (Know, Feel, Do) questions:

What do I want them to know?

What do I want them to feel?

What do I want them to do?

> **Stop and Reflect**
>
> - How do you combine logic and emotion in your messages?
>
> - How are you affected by others when they use logical explanations?
>
> - How are you affected by them when they use emotion-provoking considerations?

Objects or People

Some people focus on objects related to an experience they went through. Some focus on a place or places related to the experience. Others focus on the actions that are performed and on what more has to be accomplished. And some focus on the people involved in the experience or on the information the experience provides.

When we go through an experience, we are generally aware of all these layers, but each one of us focuses on a different aspect.

With Obama, people are always first priority. He loves people, takes an interest in them, and talks to them. His connection is always to the people on the street.

See how he refers to people in his speech on November 10, 2010, at the University of Indonesia in Jakarta:

> I still remember the call of the vendors. *Satay*! I remember that. *Baso*! But most of all, I remember the people—the old men and women who welcomed us with smiles; the children who made a foreign child feel like a neighbor and a friend; and the teachers who helped me learn about this country.

Now see how he refers to people of different types in his speech at the Democratic National Convention:

> I believe that as hard as it will be, the change we need is coming. Because I've seen it. Because I've lived it. I've seen it in Illinois, when we provided health

care to more children and moved more families from welfare to work. I've seen it in Washington, when we worked across party lines to open up government and hold lobbyists more accountable, to give better care for our veterans, and keep nuclear weapons out of terrorist hands.

And I've seen it in this campaign. In the young people who voted for the first time, and in those who got involved again after a very long time. In the Republicans who never thought they'd pick up a Democratic ballot, but did. I've seen it in the workers who would rather cut their hours back a day than see their friends lose their jobs, in the soldiers who re-enlist after losing a limb, in the good neighbors who take a stranger in when a hurricane strikes and the floodwaters rise.

Here's an example of mentioning people and places from the 2004 Democratic National Convention:

The people I meet in small towns and big cities and diners and office parks, they don't expect government to solve all their problems. They know they have to work hard to get ahead. And they want to.

As for actions, we already saw how Obama specifies what actions he intends to take. He knows many people like to hear facts and statistics of all types, including indices, numbers, trends, evidence, and opinions. Therefore, he also includes vast information in his speeches.

In his inaugural address he said:

That we are in the midst of crisis is now well understood.

Our nation is at war, against a far-reaching network of violence and hatred. Our economy is badly weakened, a consequence of greed and irresponsibility on the part of some, but also our collective failure to make hard choices and prepare the nation for a new age. Homes have been lost; jobs shed; businesses shuttered. Our health care is too costly; our schools fail too many; and each day brings further evidence that the ways we use energy strengthen our adversaries and threaten our planet.

These are the indicators of crisis, subject to data and statistics.

Internal or External

Some people do things because that's what they're expected to do. They want to comply with other people's expectations or do what's customary in certain situations. Such people have an "external meta program," since the measure of success or lack of success is located outside them and is determined by others.

Then there are the people that do what they want to do or what they consider the right thing to do. Their feelings and inner standards are the main source of their actions. People like this have an "internal meta program," since they determine for themselves to what extent their actions are successful.

Generally, when a person combines both these approaches, while maintaining flexibility, based on the issue at hand, he manages to realize his goals.

Obama combines both approaches in a balanced manner. As a leader with a vision who leads changes, he has a strong internal meta program, first and foremost, and is motivated by inner judgment, life experience, and a personal array of values and beliefs. When he expresses what has to be done, based on his credo, he answers the need of some of the people in the audience to be led—the people with the external meta program, who deem it important to hear other people's opinions and be instructed on how to act. This is what he said in October 2008:

> But I also know this. It will take a new direction. It will take new leadership in Washington. It will take a real change in the policies and politics of the last eight years. And that's why I'm running for President of the United States of America.

On the other hand, when Obama speaks of what has to be done, based on what he has seen on the street or based on what will work or won't work for Americans, he answers the need of some of the people in the audience to act, according to their inner standards—he addresses the people with the internal meta program who want their opinions, their needs, and their preferences to be considered, regardless of what others think.

In that same speech, Obama also speaks in this language:

> There are many causes of this crisis, and it's very important that we respond using all the tools that we have. It's encouraging that Treasury is considering

dramatic steps to provide more capital to our financial institutions, so they have money to lend. This is not a time for ideology—it's a time for common sense and a politics of pragmatism. The test of an idea must not be whether it is liberal or conservative—the test should be whether it works for the American people. That's what we should all be focused on in the days and weeks ahead.

It is interesting to see the simple and intelligent blend Obama makes between the two approaches in his speeches. For example, at the 2004 Democratic National Convention, he said:

I'm asking you to believe. Not just in my ability to bring about real change in Washington…I'm asking you to believe in yours.

Inside-Out

Influencing an audience effectively requires the speaker not only have an internal approach—leadership, leading, and initiative—but also an external approach, which is considerate of what is standard and ideal and what works or doesn't work, as far as the audience is concerned. Therefore, you are better off making an effort to diagnose the thought programs of the people around you.

There's another advantage to making an effort to make such a diagnosis. It will require you to listen closely, focus on the other person, and adopt the *second perceptual position* (see Chapter 2). All these will help you speak powerfully, influence and persuade much more effectively. As we saw, Obama does this successfully. You can do it too!

The last chapter you have just finished reading will not be easy to apply. NLP experts practice it for months before they use it to help people make changes in their lives.

But now, you are more aware of the power of your brain. You know how to penetrate with stories the other person's mind, and make your messages stick in their minds.

You know to activate their emotions to stimulate action, and you can start to listen more carefully to what people say and analyze them by the words they use. If you know their meta programs, you can apply it to convince, persuade and stimulate action. And that is communication with power and a little magic.

PART SIX
Linguistic Patterns Tool Box

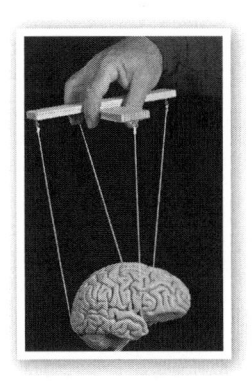

CHAPTER 24

WHY DOES IT WORK? – HOW TO ASK QUESTIONS AND LEAD TO THE DESIRED DIRECTION

"If the only tool you have is a hammer, you tend to see every problem as a nail."

— **Abraham Maslow**

For whom did Steve Jobs say he would replace all his technology just to spend one afternoon with? By the end of this chapter, you will know the answer.

In Part Six we will share with you tools that Obama uses as rhetorical devices to communicate effectively, convince, persuade, and lead his target audience to the final destiny. Obama, as we have seen, has a very large toolbox and uses an enormous array of tools to convey his messages. Bear in mind that the use of diverse techniques in different doses is what enables Obama to give people the sense that he has natural charisma and supposedly speaks without techniques.

After analyzing over three hundred of Obama's speeches, given over the course of several years, we discovered the overt and covert patterns he uses. However, keep in mind that we had identified his patterns after investing thousands of hours of research, while focusing on every syllable, word, and paragraph and actively listening to his speeches. Of course, most people who hear you are incapable of making such an analysis in real time; therefore, if you use diverse patterns and tools, you will be perceived as eloquent, charismatic, and an engaging speaker.

Obama believes in the power of words, and that is why he handles every word he says like a diamond. He knows that every word counts.

Have you heard of Socrates? Do you know what he is famous for? Do you know the reason for these questions?

Greek philosopher Socrates, who lived in the fifth century BC, was known as a scholar who taught his listeners by asking questions, to which they had to find the answers themselves. You could say Socrates was one of the first contemporary personal coaches…

Jack Canfield, co-creator of the *Chicken Soup for the Soul* book series said, "If you are not moving closer to what you want in sales (or in life), you probably aren't doing enough asking." Does it make sense?

Obama loves to ask questions. He knows it's an effective way to raise issues that interest the audience, that evoke its curiosity, and encourage it to engage in active thinking. Here's an example from November 2007:

> But the question you will have to ask yourselves when you pick up your ballot a year from today is, "What next?"
>
> How do we repair the enormous damage of these dismal years and recapture that sense of common purpose that has seen America through our toughest times?

Obama asks the questions that are on everyone's mind. He refers to issues that trouble the audience, and he expresses them in the form of questions that he was going to answer at any rate. Thus, he gives the audience the sense that he knows what's going through their minds.

People who hear a question naturally try to answer it, and this, in itself, activates thought processes within them. This is also an excellent way to develop a conversation that supposedly has two sides, a conversation in which the audience not only listens but also becomes an active partner to the issues in question. And since Obama considers a speech a type of intimate conversation with each of the participants, questions are a good way to promote this. This is what he did in his "Back to School" speech in September 2009:

> And no matter what you want to do with your life—I guarantee that you'll need an education to do it.
>
> You want to be a doctor, or a teacher, or a police officer?
>
> You want to be a nurse or an architect, a lawyer or a member of our military?
>
> You're going to need a good education for every single one of those careers. You can't drop out of school and just drop into a good job. You've got to work for it and train for it and learn for it.

Obama's questions are generally simple and short, such as, "What is the American promise?" or "Why is it important to make the change today?" and, often, it's a sequence of questions, like in the speech he delivered in June 2008:

> How do we keep ourselves safe and secure while preserving our liberties?
>
> How do we restore trust in a government that seems increasingly removed from its people and dominated by special interests?
>
> How do we ensure that, in an increasingly global economy, the winners maintain allegiance to the less fortunate?
>
> And how do we resolve our differences at a time of increasing diversity?

Using Socrates' method, Obama asks rhetorical questions that he doesn't intend to hear the answer to. These are questions for which the answer is obvious. Their purpose is to focus the audience's attention on key issues. Thus, for example, he incorporated in his speeches Reagan's rhetorical question:

> At this rate, the question isn't just "are you better off than you were four *years* ago?"
>
> It's "are you better off than you were four *weeks* ago?"

Obama also asks questions that relate to the future. Perhaps the audience wouldn't have thought of these questions itself, but "the right answer" to the questions is almost always apparent—an answer that indicates the way in which we must act in the present. Here, for example, is such a question in his 2008 victory speech:

> If our children should live to see the next century, if my daughters should be so lucky to live as long as Ann Nixon Cooper, what change will they see? What progress will we have made?

In Virginia in 2008, he used the same linguistic tool:

> Will they say that this was a time when America lost its way and its purpose?
>
> When we allowed the same divisions and fear tactics and our own petty differences to plunge this country into a dark and painful recession?
>
> Or will they say that this was another one of those moments when America overcame?
>
> When we battled back from adversity by recognizing the common stake that we have in each other's success?

Do you feel the power of asking questions?

Can you imagine yourself using more questions when you want to influence?

By the way, do you remember the question we asked you at the beginning of this chapter?

Steve Jobs, legendary chief inspiration of Apple, idolizes Socrates. In an interview he gave to *Newsweek* magazine in 2001, he said, "I would replace all my technology for one afternoon with Socrates."

Well, you don't have to get rid of your iPad or the iPhone to use this secret. Do you?

🔍 What are Your Questions?

The next time you speak before an audience, ask yourself: What are the questions your listeners are interested in? What would they like to know? What would they like to learn? What are they afraid of? What are the objections they may raise?

In the speech, ask these questions of yourself. Let your listeners first answer them in their minds, then answer them, as you had planned.

In addition, remember to emphasize key issues with rhetorical questions. You can gear any audience towards the desired action with questions that guide to the future. Don't overuse questions. This is an effective tool to influence, but it is not a substitute for a good argument, and overuse is liable to harm the effectiveness of what you are saying.

Questions can be used when you open a presentation. A question makes everyone stop thinking about other things and start thinking about the answer. That's a great way to engage any audience.

If you use a question, as we did at the beginning of this chapter, you create anticipation, which will help you to keep the audience tuned to your messages.

Now, it's your turn. Where exactly can you incorporate questions in your next speech? Can you use this secret in your attempts to influence and persuade at home? Do you like the Socratic idea of asking questions?

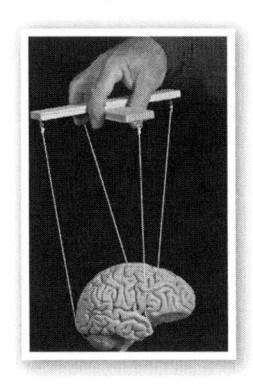

CHAPTER 25

1, 2, 3 – How to exploit the mind's preference for the magic number 3

> "No matter what some agency may say, we've always been and always will be a AAA country."
>
> — **President Barack Obama (August 8th, 2011)**

Steve Ballmer, Microsoft CEO and an extremely energetic speaker, once said, "When people ask about the company, I tell them three things." Why *three* things and not two or four? Because Steve Ballmer knows the secret that Obama knows and uses, and now you will know it too: the rule of three in rhetoric.

Speech expert Andrew Dlugan says, "Using the 'Rule of Three' allows you to express concepts more completely, emphasize your points, and increase the memorability of your message."

That's the truth, the whole truth, and nothing but the truth.

The last sentence you read is based on the rule of three: it specifies the three benefits of using the principle, it emphasizes their use, and it will help you remember the idea.

Do you agree with us that, in this way, it's clearer, simpler and more complete?

There's something *magical* about threes: "the good, the bad, and the ugly," "sex, lies, and videotape," and even three Olympic medals: gold, silver, and bronze.

Let's explore this magic and see how Obama uses it.

Studies show that our brain picks up information, stores, and remembers it better when it is presented in threes. Most people lock the gate to their brains just knowing they have to listen, and even more so when they must remember many things. But the brain opens up if there are exactly three ideas, three phases, or three reasons. The rule of three is such a strong and effective psychological principle that all the religions use it. Judaism, Christianity, and Islam all adopted it. And we recommend you use it, too.

Obama speaks in threes in many of his speeches. It could be three words, three ideas, three stories, three samples, etc.

> I will focus on *three* areas that are closely related, and fundamental to human progress—development, democracy, and religious faith.
>
> —November 10, 2010 at the University of Indonesia, Jakarta

The use of three is powerful because it creates a rhythm that is pleasant to the ear. You can use the rule of three in different ways: three words; three sentences; or three parallel paragraphs.

Obama often repeats a word or certain words three times, and sometimes, he "dances" the speech in Viennese waltz rhythm, in three steps. Here is what he said in October 2008:

> Taxpayers should not have all the downside without any of the upside.
> *That's a principle* that I've fought for,
> *that's a principle* that I'll maintain,
> and *that's a principle* that I'll stand up for as President.
> That's the choice in this election."

When he repeats the words "that's a principle" three times in a planned and conscientious way at the beginning of every sentence, what does it create in our brains?

The first time creates interest.

The second time gets people to think about the message.

The third time is a reminder to internalize.

When you say something once, the power is created through focus. One is focused and emphasized. Using a pattern of two is the best way to create an equation or negation between two messages. And when you use the pattern of three, the message is pleasant and convenient to listen to. It provides a sense of comprehensiveness, a sense that everything that had to be said was said, so the message is understood.

As we have seen, Obama "sings" speeches written by his staff, headed by "orchestra conductor" Jon Favreau. He conveys messages in three parts, often in the same paragraph, while using recurring key words or key sentences. The following example is taken from his 2008 victory speech:

> If there is anyone out there
> *who still* doubts that America is a place where all things are possible;
> *who still* wonders if the dream of our founders is alive in our time;
> *who still* questions the power of our democracy,
> tonight is your answer.

And in October 2008:

> But we need to do it in a responsible way.
> *That means* making sure that we're not overpaying for these mortgages and rewarding the very lenders whose recklessness helped cause this crisis.
> *It means* giving taxpayers a share of the benefit
> when our housing market recovers.
> And *it means* cracking down on predatory lenders
> by treating mortgage fraud like the crime that it is.

Obama sometimes uses the rule of three over three sequential paragraphs, whereas the pattern recurs at the opening of each relevant paragraph. He did this in his victory speech in 2008:

> *It's the answer* told by lines that stretched around schools and churches in numbers this nation has never seen; by people who waited three hours and four hours, many for the very first time in their lives, because they believed that this time must be different; that their voice could be that difference.

> *It's the answer* spoken by young and old, rich and poor, Democrat and Republican, black, white, Latino, Asian, Native American, gay, straight, disabled and not disabled—Americans who sent a message to the world that we have never been a collection of Red States and Blue States: we are, and always will be, the United States of America.
>
> *It's the answer* that led those who have been told for so long by so many to be cynical, and fearful, and doubtful of what we can achieve to put their hands on the arc of history and bend it once more toward the hope of a better day.

At the 2008 Democratic National Convention Obama also used the magic number 3 to attack his political opponent:

> Washington's been talking about our oil addiction for the last thirty years, and John McCain has been there for twenty-six of them.
>
> In that time, he's said *no to* higher fuel-efficiency standards for cars,
>
> *no to* investments in renewable energy,
>
> *no to* renewable fuels.
>
> And today, we import triple the amount of oil as the day that Senator McCain took office.

Obama uses the rule of three like other presidents with high rhetorical capacities.

Abraham Lincoln said in his famous Gettysburg Address:

> *We cannot* dedicate
> *we cannot* consecrate –
> *we cannot* hallow.

Now that we have learned about the rule of three, viewed examples, and comprehend it, we can allow ourselves to say the words of Julius Caesar: Veni, Vidi, Vici—I came, I saw, I conquered.

Messages March in Threes

One of the first things every consultant employed by McKinsey, the international management consulting firm learns, is that everything can be explained in threes: three words; three ideas; and three arguments. This is also one of Obama's most effective secrets linguistic tools.

You should also remember to divide your important messages into threes.

Three will do the job better—whether they're in the same sentence, the same paragraph, or whether they are spread over three sequential paragraphs.

༄

If you want to be a "AAA communicator" use this simple linguistic tool. And now, after we learned about the power of the magic number three, we can move onto Obama's next linguistic tool: repetition, repetition, repetition.

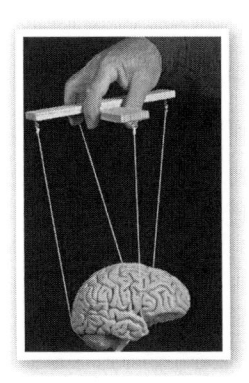

CHAPTER 26

Repetition, repetition, repetition – How to help your target internalize your key messages

"We cannot always control our thoughts, but we can control our words, and repetition impresses the subconscious, and we are then master of the situation."

—**Jane Fonda**

Obama speaks not only in patterns of threes while breaking down messages into three phases ("Together we can"), he also makes sure to repeatedly convey messages which he deems important to implant in the listeners' minds. He knows the secret of inserting messages into people's minds is a combination of a simple message with repetition, like brainwashing in commercials.

The secret is simple to apply. Nevertheless, over our years as international consultants, we have discovered that many executives tend to say important things only once in the same speech or same presentation. They assume that listeners pick up and understand their messages the first time they hear it and, therefore, it's enough. However, they don't take into account that not everyone is listening attentively or picking up things the first time or remembering the message after hearing it once.

What can sound boring and repetitive to you as a speaker may be totally new to most of the people you are talking to. This is how Obama did it in his October 2008 speech:

Now it falls to us. *Together,* we cannot fail. *Together,* we can overcome the broken policies and divided politics of the last eight years. *Together, we can* renew an economy that rewards work and rebuilds the middle class. *Together, we can* create millions of new jobs, and deliver on the promise of health care you can afford and education that helps your kids compete. We can do this if we come together; if we have confidence in ourselves and each other; if we look beyond the darkness of the day to the bright light of hope that lies ahead.

The repetitions impact upon the structure of Obama's speeches and the listeners' minds. They make every speech a song with a refrain, and often several refrains.

As we mentioned, these repetitions also enable the audience to join him, as he speaks indirectly or directly and repeat with him the key words that represent his messages. Let's see again how Obama used his winning slogan at the night of the New Hampshire Primary (January 8, 2008):

> *Yes, we can.*
> It was a creed written into the founding documents
> that declared the destiny of a nation.
> *Yes, we can.*
> It was whispered by slaves and abolitionists
> as they blazed a trail toward freedom through the darkest of nights.
> *Yes, we can.*
> It was sung by immigrants as they struck out from distant shores
> and pioneers who pushed westward against an unforgiving wilderness.
> *Yes, we can.*
> It was the call of workers who organized;
> women who reached for the ballot;
> a President who chose the moon as our new frontier;
> and a King who took us to the mountaintop and pointed the way to the Promised Land.
> *Yes, we can,* to justice and equality.
> *Yes, we can,* to opportunity and prosperity.
> *Yes we can* heal this nation.
> *Yes we can* repair this world.
> *Yes we can.*
> And so tomorrow, as we take this campaign south and west; as we learn that the struggles of the textile worker in Spartanburg are not so different than the

Repetition, Repetition, Repetition – How To Help Your Target Internalize Your Key Messages

plight of the dishwasher in Las Vegas; that the hopes of the little girl who goes to a crumbling school in Dillon are the same as the dreams of the boy who learns on the streets of LA; we will remember that there is something happening in America; that we are not as divided as our politics suggests; that we are one people; we are one nation; and together, we will begin the next great chapter in America's story with three words that will ring from coast to coast; from sea to shining sea –

Yes. We. Can.

Stylized repetitions such as these do not bore the listeners. On the contrary, they maintain their focus and enable them to follow, internalize, and deeply implant what's being said.

When someone hears a concept that is repeated several times, a learning process starts to develop, a process that can be compared to paving a path in the brain. The more the concept is repeated, the more the path is paved and deepens. In this respect, conveying a new concept is similar to an advertisement for a new product. In both cases, the message should be repeated until the potential customer is convinced.

Going back to repetition, the use Obama makes of repetition is diverse. Sometimes, he repeats one key word several times in the same sentence or throughout several sentences or paragraphs. This is illustrated in the following example, in which he wanted to emphasize the message "new" to the attendants of the 2008 Democratic National Convention:

> Change happens because the American people demand it—
> because they rise up and insist on *new* ideas and *new* leadership.
> a *new* politics for a *new* time

In another example from that convention, Obama turned the spotlight onto the audience, while emphasizing the word "you" that is an especially effective word, as noted in Chapter 3:

> For eighteen long months, *you* have stood up, one by one, and said enough to the politics of the past. *You* understand that in this election, the greatest risk we can take is to try the *same old* politics with the *same old* players and expect a different result. *You* have shown what history teaches us…

Sometimes, Obama not only repeats a key word but a vastly important key sentence, a sentence that focuses the listeners' attention on an essential message he deems important to convey. For example, in the sentence "Now is the time," he conveys a sense of urgency and the need to motivate into immediate action, as he did again in that same speech:

> America, *now is not the time for* small plans.
>
> *Now is the time to* finally meet our moral obligation to provide every child a world-class education, because it will take nothing less to compete in the global economy...
>
> *Now is the time to* finally keep the promise of affordable, accessible health care for every single American. If you have health care, my plan will lower your premiums...
>
> *Now is the time to* help families with paid sick days and better family leave...
>
> *Now is the time to* change our bankruptcy laws, so that your pensions are protected ahead of CEO bonuses; and the time to protect Social Security for future generations.
>
> And *now is the time to* keep the promise of equal pay for an equal day's work, because I want my daughters to have exactly the same opportunities as your sons.

You undoubtedly noticed that the last examples are taken from the same speech. This illustrates how Obama and his speechwriters work methodically. Once they decide upon the message of the paragraph or a series of paragraphs, they also decide on the linguistic repetition and melody of that part.

A week before the 2008 elections, Obama turned the spotlight onto this fact. He did it by emphasizing the words "In one week."

> One week.
>
> After decades of broken politics in Washington, eight years of failed policies from George Bush, and twenty-one months of a campaign that has taken us

from the rocky coast of Maine to the sunshine of California, we are one week away from change in America.

In one week, you can turn the page on policies that have put the greed and irresponsibility of Wall Street before the hard work and sacrifice of folks on Main Street.

In one week, you can choose policies that invest in our middle-class, create new jobs, and grow this economy from the bottom-up so that everyone has a chance to succeed; from the CEO to the secretary and the janitor; from the factory owner to the men and women who work on its floor.

In one week, you can put an end to the politics that would divide a nation just to win an election; that tries to pit region against region, city against town, Republican against Democrat; that asks us to fear at a time when we need hope.

In one week, at this defining moment in history, you can give this country the change we need.

The famous and historical speech that made use of the principle of repetition is Martin Luther King's speech. King, who addressed an audience of two hundred thousand people in August 1963, said the words "I have a dream" for eight sequential sentences, and the word "dream" three additional times.

King's speech was selected in the past as the finest American speech of the 20th century. The continuous repetitions in it made it so. It's interesting that the word "dream" wasn't the most recurring word in the speech: it was mentioned eleven times, and the word "freedom" was mentioned twenty times. But the word "freedom" was very scattered throughout the speech. Therefore, it penetrated more slowly in the minds of listeners who desired equality between the races in the United States.

Obama uses repetitions, not only to emphasize good, bolstering messages, but to emphasize that the situation is so bad that it can't be ignored and action must be taken immediately. Thus, in Philadelphia, he specifies the troubles of the American people while repeating key words:

It's a test we cannot fail. *Not now. Not when* we have a crisis to solve and an economy to save. *Not when* there are so many Americans without jobs and without homes. *Not when* there are families who can't afford to see a doctor, or send their child to college. *Not when* there is a generation that is counting on us to give them the same opportunities and the same chances that we had for ourselves.

Obama's repetitions can be at the beginning of a sentence or paragraph, in the middle of a sentence or paragraph, and even at the end. Here's an example from his speech in Virginia which illustrates the repetition of several words in the same paragraph that are interwoven into Obama's word puzzle:

So *I know* these are difficult times. *I know* folks are worried. But *I believe* that we can steer ourselves out of this crisis because *I believe* in this country. Because *I believe* in you. *I believe* in the American people.

We are the United States of America. *We are* a nation that's faced down war and depression; great challenges and great threats. And at each and every moment, *we have* risen to meet these challenges—*not as* Democrats, *not as* Republicans, *but as* Americans. *With* resolve. *With* confidence. *With* that fundamental belief that here in America…

In another example from the Democratic National Convention, Obama wanted to emphasize the fact that change is possible by presenting proof, based on his personal experience. He turned to all the *visual* people in the audience and repeated the pattern of "I have seen X":

I believe that as hard as it will be, the change we need is coming. Because *I've seen it*. Because I've lived it. *I've seen it in* Illinois, when we provided health care to more children and moved more families from welfare to work. *I've seen it in* Washington, when we worked across party lines to open up government and hold lobbyists more accountable, to give better care for our veterans and keep nuclear weapons out of terrorist hands.

And *I've seen it in* this campaign. In the young people who voted for the first time, and in those who got involved again after a very long time. In the Republicans who never thought they'd pick up a Democratic ballot, but did.

> *I've seen it in the workers* who would rather cut their hours back a day than see their friends lose their jobs, *in the soldiers* who re-enlist after losing a limb, *in the good neighbors* who take a stranger in when a hurricane strikes and the floodwaters rise.

Obama makes special use of repeating key words or sentences between various paragraphs, to divide the main subject into sub-topics. Obama knows that numbering arguments is ineffective when it comes to oral persuasion (as opposed to written arguments). Therefore, he creates, by repetition, a pattern of specifying information that replaces the numbering of the arguments.

It is important you know that, every time you number sections or enumerate items in a speech, you are activating the left brain, which is the logical part of the listeners' brain. If you want to activate the heart and not the left brain, don't say "one...two...three." Enumeration such as this does not activate emotions.

Obama does not say "there are *three* reasons...the first reason is..." He simply states what the reasons are. He prefers speaking as he would to a friend. In the following example from the speech in Philadelphia you can see how he repeats the words *"Change means"* at the beginning of each paragraph and thus specifies another aspect of the desired change each time:

> *Change means* rebuilding this economy. We know that it's time to create...
> and give them tax incentives to create new jobs.
> *That's the change we need.*
> *Change means* a tax code that doesn't just work for folks at the top?
> *Change means* finally fixing our health care system...
> we'll tell insurance companies, no more discriminating against people with pre-existing conditions, period.
> *That's the change we need.*
> *Change means* giving every child, everywhere the skills and knowledge...
> we will move this country forward.
> Finally, *change means* taking on the corruption...

At the 2008 Democratic National Convention, Obama specified the significance of the American promise by repeating the key sentence "it's a promise that..." and created a pattern for specifying the information:

> *It's a promise that* says each of us has the freedom to make of our own lives what we will, but that we also have the obligation to treat each other with dignity and respect.
>
> *It's a promise that* says the market should reward drive and innovation and generate growth, but that businesses should live up to their responsibilities to create American jobs, look out for American workers, and play by the rules of the road.
>
> Ours *is a promise that* says government cannot solve all our problems, but what it should do is that which we cannot do for ourselves…

And finally, it is worthwhile looking at the power of repetition combined with linguistic brilliance from Obama's speech in November 2007:

> We are sick and tired of being sick and tired.

🔍 Dress Rehearsal

Repeating key words or key sentences that reflect your important messages is most effective to persuade, whether the words recur in the same sentence or whether they recur throughout one paragraph or several paragraphs.

These repetitions make the learning process easier for the audience and help it internalize new messages and ideas.

These repetitions make the learning process easier for the audience and help it internalize new messages and ideas.

These repetitions make the learning process easier for the audience and help it internalize new messages and ideas.

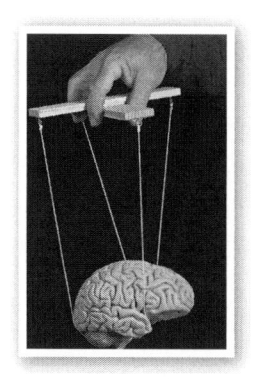

CHAPTER 27

BLACK AND WHITE – HOW TO USE CONTRASTS TO EMPHASIZE KEY MESSAGES

"I am not opposed to all wars. I'm opposed to dumb wars."

—**Barack Obama, (October 2, 2002)**

Famous cinematographer Conrad Hall said before his death in January 2003, "Contrast is what makes photography interesting." One of the linguistic tools Obama uses to attract the audience's attention and enhance tension and anticipation surrounding his words is by using contrasting ideas. The use of contrasts and opposites is effective, because it encourages the audience to think. When you say "it's not this" the audience asks itself "then what is it?"

Obama uses contrasts and opposites, while comparing ideas when they are juxtaposed. Sometimes, he does this in the same sentence and, sometimes, he builds a full paragraph or several paragraphs around an idea and its opposite, as in the 2008 Democratic National Convention:

> And it is that promise that, forty-five years ago today, brought Americans from every corner of this land to stand together on a Mall in Washington, before Lincoln's Memorial, and hear a young preacher from Georgia speak of his dream.

> The men and women who gathered there could've heard many things. They could've heard words of anger and discord. They could've been told to succumb to the fear and frustration of so many dreams deferred.
>
> But what the people heard instead—people of every creed and color, from every walk of life—is that in America, our destiny is inextricably linked. That together, our dreams can be one..."

In Virginia in 2008, he used contrast in a short paragraph:

> What we need now is not misleading charges and divisive attacks.
> What we need is honest leadership and real change.

Thus, Obama enhances the tension and anticipation for supposedly the real thing. The speech he gave in Virginia displays his control of "linguistic Aikido":

> We have risen to meet these challenges—
> not as Democrats,
> not as Republicans,
> but as Americans.

Sometimes, Obama says the two parts in a different order. First, he says something and then he adds the "it's not" part.

Let's see a short example from January 12, 2011, at a memorial service for the victims of the shooting in Tucson, Arizona:

> It's important for us to pause for a moment and make sure that we're talking with each other in a way that heals, not in a way that wounds.

When the contrast is short and to the point, the "image" of the sentence in the brain becomes simple and interesting. In October 2008, Obama said, "Together we cannot fail. Together we can overcome..." and used linguistic contrasts.

After all, everything in life is relative. If you jump into a swimming pool, you will feel you are very hot if a few seconds earlier you swam in a pool of ice water. But if you jump into a swimming pool after dipping for twenty minutes in a hot Jacuzzi, the pool water will feel cool to you. What changed in the water? Nothing. Here again, we see: it's not what you say, it's what the audience hears and feels.

Using contrasts creates a frame of reference that emphasizes what you want to stress. This is a well-known cognitive deception that can be used to influence and persuade. This effect is often used for "upsell." After you are sold a suit for five hundred dollars, it's easy to add a matching shirt for eighty-nine dollars and a tie for nine dollars.

The comparison to the contrasting idea can reinforce what comes later, as in the following example from Obama's speech (November 3, 2007):

> I believe that our party has made the most difference in people's lives
> and the life of this country when we have led
> not by polls but by principle;
> not by calculation but by conviction…

The impact of comparisons such as these is enhanced when combined with other techniques, such as repetitions and the rule of three. The method of Obama's speechwriter is clear. Here is an example of statements Obama made at the 2008 Democratic National Convention:

> Our government should work for us, *not* against us.
> It should help us, *not* hurt us.
> It should ensure opportunity *not* just for those with the most money.

This example illustrates the power of combining diverse linguistic tools. Here you can see the diversity this technique enables you to introduce into your messages, and, of course, the vast freedom of tool selection.

In our last example, taken from Obama's speech at the Democratic National Convention, note how Obama used contrasts to emphasize key messages:

> It's not because John McCain doesn't care. It's because John McCain doesn't get it.

This short example expresses the essence of this amazing tool.

Weakens? on the Contrary.

Using contrasts and opposites is most effective for persuading. Before your next speech, ask yourself not only which messages you deem important to convey, but what stands in contrast to these messages. Presenting these contrasts alongside your message will reinforce and empower your message.

The film *Twins (1988)*, in which Arnold Schwarzenegger and the significantly-shorter actor Danny DeVito played twins, is a humorous example of the contrast effect.

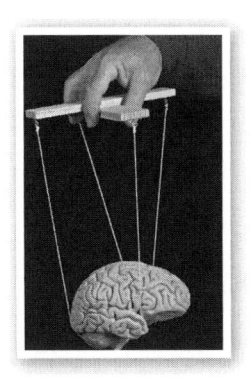

CHAPTER 28

KENNEDY SAID – HOW TO INFLUENCE BY USING GREAT PEOPLE QUOTES

Dorothy Sarnoff was a successful American opera singer in her youth. As the years went by, she developed a second career, becoming an expert on improving personal skills, mainly in terms of media training. Sarnoff, who died in December 2008, helped refine the constant smile of President Jimmy Carter. Sarnoff used to tell anyone who consulted her before a speech, "Make sure you have finished speaking before your audience has finished listening."

If you liked her quote, you must have felt the power of it, especially since it is incorporated in a short story.

An overt secret is that Obama often uses quotes in his speeches. He quotes Kennedy, Lincoln, Roosevelt, and others. He understands that quotes are a most effective way of conveying messages that were already communicated by greater and finer individuals than himself, without being considered unoriginal.

When you quote the giants, you benefit not only from the power of their words, but also from the emotions and memories that they evoke in the audience, and these are also reflected on you, the speaker.

In October 2008, Barack Obama quoted Franklin D. Roosevelt:

That's why we remember that some of the most famous words ever spoken by an American came from a president who took office in a time of turmoil—"The only thing we have to fear is fear itself."

As a master of verbal Aikido, Obama also effectively uses quotes in a reverse way. Instead of quoting the great ones to win the positive emotions they evoke, he sometimes quotes political rivals during their unsuccessful moments and thus manages to arouse among the audience criticism towards them.

Quoting competitors or political rivals' poor statements, especially if they are conveyed in a new context, guarantees the desired result. This is what Obama said in Virginia in 2008:

> Now my opponent is doing his best to change the subject and try to distract attention from the economy.
>
> Senator McCain's campaign actually said a couple of weeks ago that they were going to launch a series of attacks on my character because, they said, "If we keep talking about the economy, we're going to lose." And that's a promise my opponent has kept.
>
> He's been on the attack.
>
> That's what you do when you are out of ideas, out of touch, and running out of time.

Throughout our book, you could have seen lots of quotes we added, as part of the text and as an inspiration tool. If you liked them, you might want to use more quotes when you communicate.

A Reinforcing Quote

Next time you want to reinforce messages and connect to people's hearts, quote famous people who are relevant to the audience you are addressing.

Today, with the help of Google and other search engines, you can easily and quickly find quotes that will add power (and humor too!) to your message.

Just remember to use them correctly, and give credit to the originator.

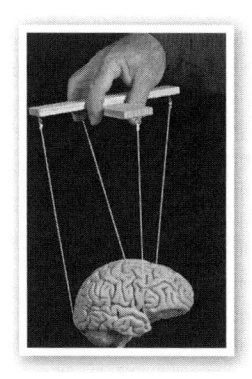

CHAPTER 29

VERBAL AIKIDO – HOW TO EXPLOIT THE OPPONENT'S MOMENTUM AND VERBALLY SUBDUE HIM

In Aikido, when an attack is delivered, rather than meeting the attack with similar force, you blend with the energy of the attacker. Rather than developing muscular force, the emphasis is on developing energy. It can appear as an alignment of your body with the other person's, or that you go *with* as opposed to *against* his or her energy. After you align or go with the energy, you then take the lead. In Judo, another martial art, you follow the same principle.

All professional judokas learn to use their opponent's movement to win by "*ippon*" or two "*wazaris*." Instead of resisting, the judoka knows how to take advantage of the opponent's movement and move him in the direction he wants him to go.

Obama has adopted this philosophy to his communication and has some verbal Aikido secrets.

Obama uses it mainly when he is required to break down restricting thought patterns or objections. The idea is simple: take the opponent's word and return it to him like a boomerang. Obama says sentences, such as "Instead of attacking me, attack the real problems, the challenges the middle class is confronting." In Virginia he pummeled his opponent when he used this Judo tactic:

> Well, Virginia, here's what my opponent doesn't seem to understand.

> With the economy in turmoil and the American Dream at risk, the American people don't want to hear politicians attack each other—
>
> you want to hear about how we're going to attack the challenges facing middle class families each and every day.
>
> That's what I'm talking about in this campaign.
>
> That's what I'll do as President.
>
> Because I can take two more weeks of John McCain's attacks, but the American people can't take four more years of the same failed policies and the same failed politics.

And in another example from October 2008:

> But here's the thing, Ohio. They can try to "turn the page" on the economy and deny the record of the last eight years. They can run misleading ads and pursue the politics of *anything goes*. But it's not going to work. Not this time.
>
> It is time to turn the page on eight years of economic policies that put Wall Street before Main Street but ended up hurting both.

Remember, sometimes to speak powerfully, you should use your opponent's messages against him when he has provided you with the rare opportunity to do so.

Another verbal Aikido move to gain support while trying to influence people is complimenting them.

Obama knows that complimenting others, especially his political rivals, is another effective act that proves integrity. When you know your rival's advantages, you are perceived as more authentic, even when you analyze their failures. Obama does this well. In November 2007, he referred to his rival for the presidential Democratic candidacy, Hillary Clinton:

> Much has been said about the exchanges between Senator Clinton and myself this week.
> Now, understand that *Hillary Clinton is a colleague and a friend.*

> *She's also a skilled politician* and she's run what Washington would call a "textbook" campaign.
> But the problem is the textbook itself…

The way he refers to rivals also enables him to suggest they join him later, just as he offered Hillary Clinton the position of Secretary of State in his administration. Obama compliments everybody: his colleagues; his staff; his family; his political rivals; and his listeners. In some cases, he compliments them at the beginning of the speech, thus creating a good and supportive atmosphere.

Many thank their supporters. Obama does one better; he knows how to relate to people specifically and speak from the heart—even if the text was written in advance—and he knows how to use eye contact. After triumphing over Hillary Clinton, he said at the Democratic National Convention:

> Let me express my thanks to the historic slate of candidates,
> who accompanied me on this journey,
> and especially the one who traveled the farthest—
> a champion for working Americans
> and an inspiration to my daughters and to yours—
> *Hillary Rodham Clinton.*
> To President Clinton,
> who last night made the case for change as only he can make it;
> to Ted Kennedy, who embodies the spirit of service;
> and to the next Vice President of the United States, *Joe Biden,* I thank you.
> I am grateful to finish this journey
> with one of the finest statesmen of our time,
> a man at ease with everyone
> from world leaders to the conductors on the Amtrak train
> he still takes home every night.
> To the love of my life, our next First Lady, *Michelle Obama,*
> *and to Sasha and Malia—*
> I love you so much, and I'm so proud of all of you.

When Obama has kind words to say about past giant leaders, like Roosevelt, Kennedy, and Lincoln, just mentioning them in his speeches projects something of their greatness onto Obama, as well. People who admire these leaders relate to Obama when he quotes them or mentions stories about them.

Obama's Secrets

This is what he did in November 2007:

> I believe that our party has made the most difference
> in people's lives and the life of this country
> when we have led not by polls but by principle;
> not by calculation but by conviction;
> when we've been able to summon the entire nation to a common purpose—
> a higher purpose.
> That's how *Roosevelt* led us through war and lifted us from depression.
> It's how *Kennedy* called on a new generation
> to ask what they could do for America.
> And *I am* running for the Democratic nomination for President of the United States because that's the kind of leadership America needs right now.

You can see Obama's virtuoso game of Scrabble in this ingenious paragraph. He knows presenting messages in three parts is perceived as very powerful, and he builds his message wisely. He compliments the other presidents that fit in with the puzzle and instantly adds himself into the equation. The structure of the paragraph is amazing in its simplicity.

> That's how *Roosevelt* led us...
> It's how *Kennedy* called on a new generation...
> And *I am* running for the Democratic nomination for President of the United States because that's the kind of leadership America needs right now.

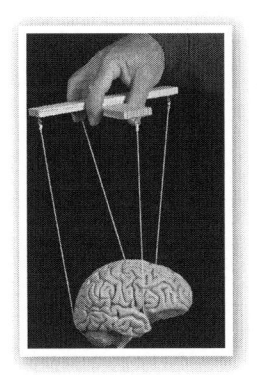

CHAPTER 30

WHO SAID IT? - HAND IN HAND WITH THE SUBCONSCIOUS

"Our subconscious minds have no sense of humor, play no jokes and cannot tell the difference between reality and an imagined thought or image. What we continually think about eventually will manifest in our lives."

— **Robert Collier**

There is something you know, but you don't know that you know.

You will discover it in this chapter. We added this chapter as a bonus chapter for those of you who want to acquire some more sophisticated tools.

Now, we will reveal several secrets of the special influence patterns that Obama uses. When we analyzed Obama's speeches, some undoubtedly written by a large staff of speechwriters and advisors, we found similarity to linguistic patterns from the Ericksonian language. It is important to note that these patterns come natural to many people, even if they have never heard the term before.

First, we will see how it all began.

What would you say if you met a seventeen-year-old suffering from polio, who the doctors believe will die in a short period of time, yet he is healing himself with the power of thought? What would you say if you knew that same young man was a late developer, dyslexic, and colorblind? What would you say if you discovered the same young man grew up and once again succumbed to polio in his fifties, as a result of post-polio syndrome and healed himself again?

The man is Dr. Milton Hyland Erickson. Erickson was born in 1902 in Wisconsin. After contracting polio and becoming paralyzed, he decided to heal himself with the power of thought, willpower, and the subconscious. He studied psychiatry as a result of his personal experience and became a specialist in medical hypnosis and family therapy. He is known to this day as the greatest hypnotherapist of all time and the developer of the short-term strategic approach.

As the years went by, Erickson developed a series of therapeutic techniques that emphasize the use of a special language of influence and nonverbal communication tools. He was renowned for his ability to generate changes in people with rapid treatment, in a few sessions. He made extensive use of metaphors and stories and referred to the subconscious as a creative place that provides solutions and has a positive effect.

Erickson also developed effective therapy methods that are not necessarily based on hypnosis, but based on effective speech patterns.

Erickson was a model of excellence in the work of Dr. Richard Bandler and Prof. John Grinder, the first developers of the NLP approach. Here are six Ericksonian patterns that can be identified in Obama's communication, in a nutshell.

Pre-Assumptions

The pattern of forming assumptions in advance is a very strong pattern. The speaker makes certain pre-assumptions that he or she doesn't want to be in question and, thus, supposedly enables the other person to make many selections. But in effect, all the options assume the same desired result.

Obama uses this pattern in two central ways: (a) assumption of a certain factual infrastructure on which his entire argument is built; (b) assumptions that attribute awareness to the listeners in advance, while using words such as "know," "expect," and "paying attention." This is what he said in his 2008 victory speech:

> I know you didn't do this just to win an election. And I know you didn't do it for me.

You did it because you understand the enormity of the task that lies ahead.

In Philadelphia in 2008, Obama incorporated in the same paragraph factual assumptions with assumptions that attribute awareness to the listeners, as in the following example:

> The times are too serious. The challenges are too great. The American people aren't looking for someone who can divide this country—they're looking for someone who will lead it.

One of the techniques related to pre-assumptions is the "double bind." With this technique, the speaker uses the word "or," but assumes in advance that at least one of the alternatives will occur. For example, in the following sentence, "I don't know if the change will be achieved this year or next year," it's obvious from the sentence that the change will be achieved. This is an early assumption underlying the proposed alternatives.

Salespeople use the double bind very often. Instead of asking a customer if he wants to buy something, they suggest two options and ask a closed question that has two potential answers, "Do you want this in red or blue?" Sometimes, even before the customer is even interested in buying, they assume he will buy and plant the assumption in his head. "How would you like your new car," they ask, "with standard seats or leather seats?"

Metaphors and Personification

As we saw in Chapters 21 and 22, using stories and metaphors is an effective influencing tool. Milton Erickson was famous for using metaphors to lead his patients towards change in a short series of sessions.

Obama, too, as we have seen, often uses metaphors and personifications. This is a very powerful influence pattern, whereby the speaker attributes qualities to something that cannot have those qualities, such as a hungry mind or a sad rock.

In this case, the listener must find some way to understand these statements and, therefore, he applies them to himself. He says to himself, the brain cannot be hungry. Therefore, it must be me who is hungry. This process, of course, is not done consciously. It is an automatic action that takes place in an attempt to understand what is being said.

For example, Obama used the technique at the 2008 Democratic National Convention when he spoke of the generosity and fairness of America. Since a country cannot be generous and fair, he in fact invited his listeners, the citizens of America, to attribute these traits to themselves.

> America, we are better than these last eight years. We are a better country than this.
>
> This country is more decent than one where a woman in Ohio, on the brink of retirement, finds herself one illness away from disaster after a lifetime of hard work.
>
> This country is more generous than one where a man in Indiana has to pack up the equipment he's worked on for twenty years and watch it shipped off to China, and then chokes up as he explains how he felt like a failure when he went home to tell his family the news.
>
> We are more compassionate than a government that lets veterans sleep on our streets and families slide into poverty; that sits on its hands while a major American city drowns before our eyes.

Statements Lacking a Source

Another influence pattern Obama uses extensively is statements that lack a source: judgmental statements from which mention of the judging or decisive factor is totally omitted.

Statements lacking a source are powerful influence patterns that act in the same way as assumptions. An example of a statement lacking a source is one indicating rules and regulations; however, whoever determined the rules and regulations is unknown. Here's a wonderful example of statements that lack a source that Obama trickled to his listeners at the 2008 Democratic National Convention:

> The greatest risk we can take is to try the same old politics with the same old players and expect a different result. You have shown what history teaches us—that at defining moments like this one, the change we need doesn't come from Washington. Change comes to Washington. Change happens because the American people demand it—because they rise up and insist on new ideas.

The best way to identify statements lacking a source is simply to ask "**who said**?" *Who said* the greatest risk one can take is to continue the same political methods with the same players and expect different results? Perhaps it is a greater risk to change players, and this will actually lead to worse results? And *who said* change doesn't come from Washington, but to Washington? Here is another example of statements without a source from Obama's speech in October 2008. To enable you to identify the pattern, we added in parentheses the question, "Who said?" after a few statements lacking a source.

> America still has the most talented, most productive workers of any country on Earth. (*Who said?*) You know this, Ohio. We're home to the workers who have built the largest middle class in history. (*Who said?*) We're home to workers who work two jobs or three jobs and take the last bus home at night because they want something more for their children. (*Who said?*) We're home to innovation and technology, colleges and universities that are the envy of the world. (*Who said?*) Some of the biggest ideas in history have come from our small businesses and our research facilities. (*Who said?*) It won't be easy, but there's no reason we can't make this century another American century. Yes we can. (*Who said?!*)

Obama uses the Ericksonian pattern of statements lacking a source because he is apparently aware of its power. By the way, the last sentence you read is a statement that lacks a source, this time ours. Who said Obama is aware of the power of statements without a source?

Abstract Nouns

What does the word "dream" mean to you? And what do you feel about the word "change?" What comes to mind when you hear the word "security?" Obama often uses abstract nouns such as promise, change, security, and hope.

In effect, we cannot see what these words represent, neither can we touch or hear them, as opposed to concrete nouns such as table, dog, or airplane.

Using abstract nouns enables one to remain vague, yet invites the listeners to conduct an inner search in their personal reservoir of experiences to fill the abstract noun with content. And, in simple words, using an abstract noun enables you to address the right brain and the subconscious of the listeners directly. The power of vague language lies in the fact that you get people into a different state. It distracts people from the outside world. When you are vague, it's easier to connect with everybody in a group of people or get rapport with someone you do not know well.

Here is an example from Obama's speech at the 2008 convention:

> It is that promise that has always set this country apart—that through hard work and sacrifice, each of us can pursue our individual dreams but still come together as one American family, to ensure that the next generation can pursue their dreams as well…

Everyone Always: Generalization

Some words create over-generalizations, such as "everyone," "always," and "never." When Obama uses these generalizations, he is actually indirectly limiting the listeners' experience and creating an effect of self-observation.

For example, when he uses the word "always," he invites the listeners to seek proof of this general statement in their experiences:

> We have always been at our best when we've had leadership that called us to look past our differences and come together as one nation, as one people; leadership that rallied this entire country to a common purpose—to a higher purpose.

Embedded Commands

In this linguistic pattern, the speaker gives the listener indirect commands by assimilating them in his words. This is an elegant and graceful way of giving orders without arousing conscious objection from the listener. Thus, instead of saying "Stand by me, fight for me, call people," Obama says, "If you stand by me, if you continue to fight for me, if you continue to call."

A message of this kind comes across much easier and therefore influences much more powerfully, since it is assimilated and indirect. See how Obama influences the audience in Philadelphia:

> And if you keep standing with me, if you keep fighting with me, if you keep making those calls, and knocking on those doors, and making sure everyone you know gets out to the polls on November 4th—if you do these things, then

I promise you, we will win this election, and then you and I—together—will change this country and change this world.

If you use this technique by adding "ifs," you will see the power of it.

We introduced just a few of the tools Obama uses to magnetize an audience, tools that can be analyzed with Milton Erickson's language of influence. Many use these tools naturally, unconsciously, and this is also the reason why it is important to know them. When you are aware of the language of influence, you can use it more correctly and you can identify instances in which others are trying to influence you.

If you want to speak and communicate with power and a little magic, then make it your goal to internalize these patterns and try to identify them in yourself and in others. And if you are slightly confused after reading this chapter, that's only natural. Read it again, after you read the last part of the book, which will be a crash course on nonverbal communication.

PART SEVEN

The Magic of Nonverbal Communication

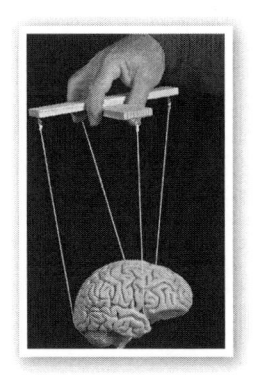

CHAPTER 31

WITHOUT WORDS – HOW TO USE MOVEMENTS, GESTURES AND EMPOWERING BODY LANGUAGE

"Words represent your intellect. The sound, gesture, and movement represent your feelings."

—**Patricia Fripp**

When Obama tells a story and mentions a knock at the door, he uses his hand and knocks on an imaginary door, so the entire audience can see what they heard. This is the essence of nonverbal communication—reinforcing the messages.

Why should we use body language while we speak?

In 2007, a neurological connection was found between verbal messages and body gestures. Jeremy Skipper, a developmental psychologist from Cornell University, used FMRI (Functional Magnetic Resonance Imaging), which measures not only the structure of the brain, but also which brain areas are showing activity. He found that the part of the brain that listens to verbal messages combined with body gestures tends to work much easier and needs to "talk" less with other brain parts to understand the verbal messages.

In simple words, if you want to influence more powerfully, you should get to know the nonverbal communication secrets and incorporate them into your verbal messages, i.e., plan *what* to say and *how* to say it.

And if this sometimes seems complicated to you, don't worry. Michael Kaschak, professor of Psychology at Florida State University, explains that it is actually speech *without* gestures that is less intuitive and demands the speaker invest more thought. He says simple body gestures often provide information that makes a long and complex explanation unnecessary.

Consider, for example how easy it is to explain what jumping is by demonstrating the action, as opposed to a mere verbal explanation.

Many people speak with their hands when they are talking to friends, but suddenly, in front of an audience, they don't know what to do with their hands. Do your hands simply move when you speak or do they "punctuate" the words?

The triangle of success for conveying an effective message includes three sides: words; tone of speech; and body language. The balance between these three components is the winning formula.

Throughout the book we have seen, mainly through examples of Obama's speeches, that choosing words is very significant, and they have a significant effect on the listeners. However, nonverbal language also has a great effect on the listeners, primarily as an important means to reinforce and emphasize your words.

Now let's go one step further and apply the nonverbal language to our needs.

Knowing the secrets of nonverbal communication in general, and the secrets Obama uses in particular, is important because we all live in a world in which other people see us.

What's the difference between a good pianist and a superb pianist? Generally, the difference comes down to personality, what the pianist brings to his playing, his soul.

Nonverbal communication is your soul penetrating your concert. Your concert is your message and helps you lead, persuade, and influence. Therefore, when you prepare a presentation, you should plan and practice not only the "what," i.e., the words you will say in your presentation, but the "how," i.e., the way in which you will say the words, so as to complete them.

The Seven Percent Myth

Let's shatter a myth. Many people who deal in mass communication erroneously quote a study by Prof. Albert Mehrabian of UCLA in which he supposedly claimed that 55 percent of the influence in interpersonal communication comes from body language and 38 percent of the influence comes from the tone of speech, leaving only 7 percent of the power to the words themselves.

Prof. Mehrabian and his colleagues conducted two studies about communication patterns and published the findings in trade magazines in 1967. Even before the dawning of Twitter, the findings were distributed in brief, leading to the "broken chain effect" and an error in the 7-38-55 rule, when it comes to public speaking. In fact, Mehrabian never claimed what is attributed to him. When he gave an interview to the BBC in 2009, he said the division into percentages didn't refer to communication in an ordinary conversation and certainly not to speeches.

Not only did the study not examine speeches, it didn't even examine the effectiveness of whole sentences. The study was based on listening to a few words and observing the subjects' attempt to understand the emotional meaning of each word, based on the accompanying body language. Instances were found in the study where there was inconsistency between the body language and the spoken word. When there's a contradiction between an emotion that is spoken and an emotion that is seen, the brain tends to believe the visual message more and be influenced by it.

Mehrabian found that only when one is speaking about emotions and approaches, and what is said and how it is said are not in line, people tend to believe the "how" more than the "what." For instance, if you tell a group, "I appreciate your efforts very much," but your nonverbal communication makes them feel you don't care at all, then your body language has a more powerful effect than your verbal message. But Mehrabian never said nonverbal communication has a stronger effect than words in a regular situation.

Like a magician who knows how to turn the audience's attention to what he or she wants them to see so they don't see what he's hiding—with effective planning of nonverbal messages, you can specifically direct the audience to your goals. Proper use of nonverbal communication will result in the audience remembering better and for a longer period of time what you want them to remember, and in many cases, they will also enjoy the experience more. This is also a way to maintain the audience's listening and alertness levels. We will see three central elements:

1. Use of body language

2. Setting and the effect of the surroundings

3. Use of voice

In previous chapters in this book, we could demonstrate Obama's verbal communication abilities by quoting things he said. However, to analyze his body language, his tone of voice, and the effect of the surroundings and the "setting" on the speech, it is more appropriate to observe his speeches that appear online. YouTube and other sites will be a great source to see him in action.

We invite you to begin a crash course on the world of nonverbal communication.

When Obama gets on stage, holding his wife Michelle's hand, you can feel the power even before the first word is uttered.

When Obama stands up straight, he conveys strength and confidence. When Obama raises his hand to emphasize an important point, he magnetizes the audience.

Body language speaks directly and without barriers to the right brain.

Words can be resisted, because the left brain may analyze and criticize them. But images that penetrate the right brain and the subconscious mind have an influence and prevent resistance, often unconsciously.

If you observe Obama speaking, you will discover that he places his right hand on his heart every time he wants to connect to the audience's emotions. When he refers to patriotism and places his right hand on his heart, the audience is left with no room for doubt, especially when the gesture seems natural.

Body language is important even before you begin to speak. When you ascend the stage, everyone is watching you. This is the moment to convey that you are calm, confident, and know what you have to do.

We once saw a CEO come up to speak with papers in his hand, and while he came up to the stage, the papers fell on the floor. This is a negative first impression that conveys unprofessionalism. We saw another CEO go on stage and adjust the height of the microphone, which of course wasn't adapted to his needs.

Before a speech, just like before a play, if you need certain props—they should be on the stage or by the speaker's podium before you get on stage. You should go on as a professional. You don't get a second chance to make an effective first impression.

Every time you speak, you should make a powerful impression right from the start. The first impression is created even before you move your lips. However, body language is important, not only to create a strong first impression, but it is also part of the message. As we said, it influences the right brain, the listeners' visual side.

You should keep in mind important information about your body language in the modern age. When you speak in front of a large audience, you have in fact two audiences: the audience that sees you on stage and the audience that sees you up close on TV or online.

In fact, you are speaking simultaneously on two different channels. You should remember that things that work well on an audience sitting at a distance from the stage are liable to look awful and horrible close-up. On TV, your every movement is seen, every lift of the eyebrow, every bite of the lips, every nostril moving. A filmed appearance before thousands of people is liable to turn into what you could call an intimate conversation, one-on-one, before millions of surfers on YouTube.

How to Create Anticipation

You often see people getting on stage who start to speak immediately.

This is a missed opportunity. It's worthwhile creating tension, anticipation, and no less important—connecting with the audience, even before you begin speaking. How is it done?

You go on stage, stand still for a moment like a statue, and look out at the audience. The goal is to connect with the audience. The trick is to look into several people's eyes; look into the eyes of a specific person, focus for a second or two, and then move on to another person in the audience.

If the audience is large, you should seek eyes in different places in the audience: someone in one of the first rows in the center, someone in one of the corners in the middle row, someone in the back row. It's best to diversify the people your gaze is aimed at and, as you do so, add a smile—like you would smile if you were to suddenly meet a childhood friend.

Obama gets on stage and smiles with confidence. Why? Because he practiced even that.

At his support conventions, when he gets on stage to the sound of the audience's applause, he joins the audience and claps, too. This is part of the rapport he establishes. And most important of all, when you get on stage, convey to the audience that you are relaxed, not nervous, because people don't tend to listen to people who are nervous.

Now we will familiarize ourselves with the secrets of *winning* body language. These include use of hands, avoiding superfluous touching, which distracts and hinders professionalism, use of eye contact, combining body movement or a look with the message, and anything else that supports the message.

In our workshops, we always emphasize to the participants that *every* body movement must support the message and not derogate from it or divert attention away from it. But before you add movements, you must stop superfluous movements, the noisy and distracting movements. Almost everyone has superfluous noisy movements, like superfluous words and sounds we use when speaking and which we mentioned in Chapter 16.

The Superfluous Gestures—What Not to Do

The main principle pertaining to superfluous gestures is: every person has natural gestures. We often tend to stop using them during an appearance before an audience. But if the gesture supports the message, use it. It is part of you. Almost everyone has superfluous gestures, like superfluous words or sounds (uh huh… and…). A gesture that is automatically repeated many times, unknowingly for the most part, harms you and the message you are conveying. We have seen instances in which the audience started counting the times the speaker made a certain gesture. Lose these gestures. Watch a recording of yourself or ask friends to tell you something you didn't know about yourself—what your repetitious and superfluous gestures include. Being aware of them is the first step. Later, practice speaking before an audience without them.

Superfluous gestures can be:

- Touching your hair many times unknowingly;

- Speaking with your hands when the hand movements have no value, when they mean nothing, when the same movement is repeated;

- Putting hands in pockets and playing with keys while speaking;

- Scratching a beard;

- Touching your ear from time to time;

- Licking your lips when you speak;

- Standing center stage and walking forwards and backwards regardless of what you are saying;

- Touching the nose numerous times.

As a rule, repeated touching of the head and face is superfluous. However, everything should be taken in proportion. We are all human. Our nose itches sometimes. It's best not to speak while your hands are in your pockets; however, there is at least one person who conveys messages very well and made hands in the pocket his trademark. His name is Jay Leno.

After cleaning up the "noise" from your body language, you will be able to focus on adding movements and gestures that all have one purpose—to support the effectiveness of the message.

Like a regularly repeated verbal message, a mantra, or a slogan, you can use a unique gesture that will be identified with you and will create an impact. For example, the victory sign, Churchill's "V," became his trademark.

🔍 How to Lose a Superfluous Gesture

1. Ask a colleague to whistle every time you make a superfluous gesture.

2. Consider in which instances you make a gesture and what purpose it serves. Consider what you can do to achieve the same goal without the superfluous gesture.

3. Before every speech, set a goal for yourself to improve one of your movements or gestures.

   Pay attention: Don't tell yourself what not to do, because the subconscious doesn't distinguish between a negative and a positive command. Formulate the goal in a positive way. What gesture will you do each time, instead of the superfluous gesture?

4. Watch a recording of yourself with no sound. Focus on your body language.

5. Take time to improve. Mark Twain once said, "**Habit** is **habit** and not to be flung out of the window by any man, but coaxed downstairs a step at a time." It takes thirty consecutive days to change a habit, and recently reported research says that, sometimes, it takes much more, so be patient. It's your personal brand for you to work on.

6. Whenever you feel you have made an improvement, celebrate it. You can give yourself prizes before every public appearance to create positive conditioning. What works with children, dogs, and dolphins will work with you, too. A personal celebration and a prize can be the slightest thing you love.

How to Add Value to a Message with Body Language

A simple way to add visual value to a message is to show the audience what you are saying. Imagine you cannot say the words. How would you express the message in pantomime? What gestures would you use? How would you express the message if you were standing before a group of deaf people?

Now, go back to talking, and at key moments, back up the word with a gesture. If you say for instance that you entered a room, show how you opened the door and entered as you say the words. If you made a phone call, demonstrate how you held the phone. If you made an effort to do something, demonstrate how you exerted your body.

When you speak before a very large audience, where many of the participants are watching you from a distance, enlarge your movements so they can be seen well from afar. Before a large audience, you should also extend your arms and place your hands higher than you would in an intimate conversation. The goal is for your movements to be seen well.

Remember, the name of the game is diversity: diverse gestures; diverse size of movements; and diversity in terms of location on stage. Diversity creates surprise and intrigue. However, you should choose one movement or gesture that is incorporated in the main message and is repeated like a refrain.

Facial Expressions and Movements

One of Obama's secrets of influence is the use of facial expressions. He uses facial expressions because he knows every speech before an audience is also a speech before millions who will watch him up close online or on TV. In such situations, you see each and every pixel of the face. Obama's expression generally conveys leadership, serious intent, and power. This is his basis. He diversifies this expression when the texts and message change. Your expressions are important. If you say one thing, but your face says another—the audience will tend to believe the emotion manifested in your face. A face conveys emotion and, as mentioned, based on Albert Mehrabian's study, every time there's a contradiction between emotion that is uttered and emotion that is visible, the brain tends to believe the visual message more and be influenced by it. Using the face is especially important if you are seen up close at intimate presentations or every time you are being filmed.

In the modern era, when it's likely your appearance is being filmed, your face is of the utmost importance. We live in an age in which everything is close up, with no restrictions of time and place. People in the audience may even be recording you on their smart-phones and upload it to the net!

However, as mentioned, we are not always aware of our gestures. Do you smile too much to the extent you convey a lack of credibility? Do you use facial expressions to reinforce the emotion you are expressing? In video footage of yourself, you will be able to see, for example, if your eyes shift from side to side unknowingly. Such an action is often perceived as lack of confidence.

Be aware of how you use your facial expressions to support messages, sometimes even to the extreme.

The simplest expression is a smile. Many remember to get on stage and smile, but forget to keep smiling while they speak. Smiles can serve as punctuation marks in a message and have another important advantage: when you smile, the audience smiles too.

A smile is one of the simplest tools with which to create rapport. It helps create, preserve, and maintain the relationship with the audience. When someone in the audience laughs and you laugh and smile back at him—you've connected.

But not only can a smile come to your aid. Almost every emotional situation you address can be backed up with a facial expression—for example, expanding the eyes and opening them wide, raising or lowering an eyebrow, expressions of happiness, sorrow, joy, disappointment, despair, fatigue, surprise, and many more.

If you are being filmed, and your image is projected onto giant screens, using facial expressions is critical. Although the audience is large, everyone sees you up close, as if they were viewing you on TV, and every movement can be seen as a close-up. The camera can be your best friend or your worst enemy. It is a unique tool that enlarges everything.

Be careful!

Consider the difference between watching a theater actor on stage and watching a TV or movie actor. In TV and cinema, you can see the tiniest expression on the actor's face in close-up footage.

Eye Contact

Obama looks out into the audience and straight into people's eyes. He knows how to use the teleprompter well so that people feel he is looking at them; he knows the text he is reading well and therefore he can quickly look at the teleprompter and say the text while looking at the audience, too.

Obama generally says one sentence—or part of a sentence—and looks at one part of the audience. Then he reads the second part from the teleprompter located on the other side and looks at the other part of the audience and so on and so forth like a metronome.

The audience senses that he is doing this naturally. But he controls the texts and practices them until he doesn't really have to read them. He just glances quickly at them to remember the precise words he planned to say and then picks up the next message and says it.

The purpose of using the teleprompter is so you don't seem to be reading a text—especially if the speech is filmed so that the TV cameras do not pick up the teleprompters and home viewers see you speaking without them.

Obama, who practiced using this tool, does so correctly and precisely. If you don't know how to use this aid, you are liable to convey to the audience that your words don't come from the heart, that they are artificial. This is also the downfall of many people who read a speech from their speaker's notes, or use computerized presentations that cause them to focus on the computer instead of on the audience.

The right way to create eye contact with the audience is to focus every time on someone else and "talk to her." The idea is to create a type of rapport for two to five seconds, each time with someone else. Also, when the audience is at a distance and is comprised of dozens, hundreds, and perhaps even thousands of people, find a specific person and talk to her for a few seconds. After you have spoken to that person, move on to another person in the audience and talk to him.

Be relaxed, scan the audience in the shape of a W. Speak once with someone on the far left then speak to someone closer, then to someone sitting near the middle and so forth, until you reach the right-hand corner of the room. Then repeat your scan of the audience in the same way. Every time you want to diversify or emphasize messages, shift your gaze from side to side in a less subtle manner.

Remember Obama's secret: A speech in front of hundreds of people should be built as if you are speaking intimately each time to one person in the audience. The time you devote to a specific person can include a full sentence, part of a sentence, a word, or even a syllable.

If, for example, you decided to say, "The word peace is comprised of five letters: p; e; a; c; e;" say instead, "The word peace is comprised of five letters" to one person in the audience. Then turn your gaze and say, "p" to another person in the audience, "e" to a third person, and so on. Speak only to one person at a time, and remember to turn your gaze towards the next person, only after you finish saying the word or the sound. Make a brief pause and, only then, look the other way and continue speaking. This will also create a dramatic effect.

How long should you "speak to a specific person?" Generally, not for more than five seconds, so that person will not feel he or she is being stared at. Take into account also that there are differences between men and women. A study shows that, on average, when you talk to women you may look them in the eye a longer period of time than when you talk to men.

You can choose the W method or any other method; just make sure your method remains unnoticed. When Obama is forced to read speeches with teleprompters on both sides, he tries to shift from side to side so that it seems natural. When he speaks without a teleprompter, he does exactly what we recommended. He speaks naturally with different people in the audience, avoiding the method that stems from using a pair of teleprompters.

Also take into account that the audience has a hard time watching a quick game of table tennis, where the ball shifts quickly from side to side. If you shift your gaze too fast from side to side, you're not making it easy on the audience. And if you add a walk from side to side on the stage, you will look like a caged lion seeking to escape.

We know some presentation-skills trainers who suggest not looking directly into people's eyes, but at the spot between their eyebrows. They claim that, in this way, a person will think you are talking to him, but you won't be distracted because of his eyes.

But that's exactly what we suggest you shouldn't do.

You must be genuine, not fake, and look directly into people's eyes in order to talk to them. In most cases, you don't have to plan who you will look at, at every given moment. Thus, you will appear more natural, not robotic. However, every time you speak to an audience, there are special moments when you want to accentuate a certain message to a specific participant, a specific group or whoever's watching you on

TV or online. These are moments that should be planned in advance. Direct your gaze directly at the person you intended to talk to at that moment.

If the audience you are speaking to is comprised of diverse groups of affiliations and you know how to identify where they are seated, these are the moments you should combine a message designed for specific participants.

Corporate presentations, for instance, are attended by decision-makers in different job positions. When you present the message or your solution, we recommend that you speak each time to the person the message is most relevant to; when you emphasize the vision of the solution, this is the time to look at the president or CEO and not the CFO. But when you emphasize cost effectiveness and budget control, this is the time to speak directly to the finance people.

Now, you may ask how to maintain eye contact when you don't have a teleprompter and are reading a printed speech. It's likely there will be instances when you will stick to the text you wrote in advance and won't be able to use aids such as a teleprompter. How will you create eye contact with the audience instead of the page on which your speech is printed (in a large font)?

Here is one of the well-kept secrets, the simplicity of which many world leaders are unaware. Even if you don't use it, you will no longer be able to say you didn't know.

We like to call it "Ronald Reagan's secret." Though Reagan didn't invent it, and Churchill and Roosevelt and others used it, Reagan controlled it better than all the presidents that preceded him. He was familiar with the technique from his auditions during college, when he said a sentence and looked at the director, as opposed to other students who read off the page.

The secret is simple and is comprised of three parts: *look; pause; say*.

Every time you look at the next line in the text, pause and raise your eyes to the audience, saying aloud what is written in the text. In this fashion, you are not really reading a speech, you are saying it.

The key rule to success is to never let the words out of your mouth when your eyes are looking down. When you speak, always look at the audience and create a connection.

Pay attention to the pause. It is an important factor in your voice, and we will expand on the subject when we tackle voice power later.

One of the advantages of Reagan's secret is that the pause you make between sentences is an opportunity for the listeners to digest what you said in the previous sentence. It helps the brain pick up messages, and this is an important goal of every speech. The pause between sentences also gives the audience the feeling that you are not reading the text, rather peeking at comments and important notes you wrote to yourself. The pause conveys you are choosing the right words with which to express your next idea. It conveys that you are speaking naturally and only using what you prepared for yourself as a "road map" for your speech.

When you incorporate a personal story or anecdote you find easy to recreate, write a reminder about the story and highlight the important messages you want to illustrate through it. These are also the messages you will undoubtedly want to repeat after you finish telling the story. In this way, you will tell the story from your memory of emotional experience.

Don't be concerned that the audience will think the technique of you looking, pausing, and speaking will seem too lengthy; it will actually add a ***dramatic dimension*** to the message and will allow you to elegantly divert your gaze every time in a different direction and also **emphasize the most important** word in each sentence (that you already **highlighted,** obviously, with large font or a marker).

We mentioned that Jon Favreau writes "musical speeches" for Obama that are well heard, well remembered, and influence the listeners. You can apply Reagan's secret if you print your speech in a special format, like a song. Most songs are written in short lines as compared to regular text.

You can divide the speech into brief sentences. What will be the length of each line? Every message you want to convey in sequence, without having to glimpse at the page, will appear on one line. Therefore, the line can include several words and you will often want to highlight only one word. In any case, the rule is simple. Jump to the next line after each comma.

This means, after each comma, you will pause, and this is what you should do so your speech seeps well into the listeners' brains.

> ### You Are the Star
>
> Let us remind you of an important tip. Reading a presentation or a speech is not recommended, unless you are a politician who needs to do it for other reasons.
>
> We see communication as an intimate experience, a love story between you on stage and the people who listen to you. You "dance" with them, you create rapport with them, and you lead them. You should be natural in order to nurture them. "Hug" your listeners. Be close to them. Practice your presentation, so you do not need to read it.
>
> Remember that *you* are the star, not the computerized presentation.

Use of Hands

In most of Obama's appearances, due to security constraints, he stands in a relatively small and restricted space, an area from which he can read the speech that is projected on the teleprompters on either side of him with ease. He must use his hands because he can hardly move around on stage. So his hands do the talking. They move in unison with his messages, emphasizing and interpreting his intentions. Sometimes, he moves each hand separately, and sometimes he moves them simultaneously. He divides his hand movements into three areas: right; left; and center.

Obama is careful not to make the common mistake people make who speak with their hands—they raise their hands every so often, regardless of the message. Obama does the opposite; every time he wants to instill a message into his listeners' minds, he lowers his hand, as if he's going to hammer the message in hard. Obama has several other typical movements:

- A hand on the heart in a moment of sincerity, for instance, when he said, "I was given an African name";

- Use of two fingers (the thumb and index finger) touching each other to emphasize statements;

- Open arms to convey openness;

- Use of a fist every time he wants to convey strength;

- When he wants to talk about similar or common issues, he raises his open hands with palms facing one another as if they were friends.

A Message Accompanied by Airplanes

Often we are asked, what should I do with my hands?

It seems they just get in the way for most people who speak in front of an audience, not knowing how to use their hands. But for the audience, hands are significant, because they can be used to emphasize statements, as Obama does.

As people, we naturally speak with our hands during a routine conversation. But when it comes to a presentation or lecture we don't know what to do with our hands because we are nervous. The best way is to use hands naturally, as part of the message. When speaking in front of an audience, imagine your hands are two airplanes on either side of your body.

The hands are awaiting take-off. When you want to emphasize certain words, you can lift your hands or make any other movement to emphasize the message. Remember, the use of your hands is important for the success of your message.

As they say, you hold the seeds of success in your hands.

Be Mindful of the Nonverbal Messages

Here are some facts worth remembering when it comes to the nonverbal messages of your body.

Openness: You can convey openness if you smile a warm smile, create eye contact, avoid folding your legs and hands and avoid leaning forward in a chair.

Aggressiveness: You are liable to convey aggressiveness if you aim your glasses at someone in the audience, point an accusing finger at someone, put a hand on your waist or behind your back, or infiltrate a person's private space.

Boredom: You are liable to convey boredom if you stare into space while you are speaking, drum your fingers on the table, close your eyes, or create limited eye contact.

Nervousness: You are liable to convey nervousness if you touch your hands to your mouth as you speak, hide your mouth, scratch or drum your fingers.

Bill Clinton's Smart Move

Here's an example that illustrates the power of one small gesture. In 1992, during the second television debate between President George H. Bush, and presidential candidate Bill Clinton, President Bush was caught on camera glancing at his wristwatch. This gesture was very brief and conveyed to the viewers that Bush was impatient, bored, and wanted the debate to end. The damage was intensified when, just at that moment, one of the audience members asked President Bush a question and he momentarily lost his concentration, didn't really listen, and fumbled his answer.

Bill Clinton immediately took advantage of the situation, got up, and approached the woman who asked the question. The camera picked it up. Clinton was filmed from the back and the camera focused on the woman agreeing with him. Her body language conveyed she agreed with his message.

This small incident was valuable and had a great impact on millions of Americans who watched the debate. It is important to remember that even when we say nothing, we are communicating with our surroundings.

When you are speaking in front of people—every movement has meaning. It's not *what* you say, it's what they see.

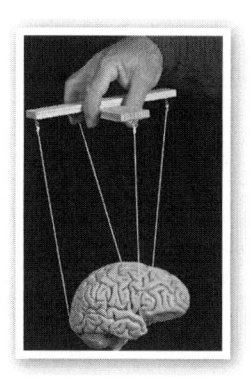

CHAPTER 32

ALL THE WORLD IS A STAGE – HOW TO USE THE SURROUNDINGS, THE SETTING, AND PROPS TO EMPOWER YOUR MESSAGES

You are the choreographer of your speech, and the entire auditorium is your stage. One way to fascinate the audience is to plan where you will stand and where you will move as you speak. The more important the speech, the more important it is to plan the choreography down to the last detail, like directing an actor in a play. In a play, the location of the actors is not improvised. Every actor knows exactly where to stand at any given moment. But with a speech or a presentation, usually it's enough to plan the critical positions in advance.

Contrary to Obama, who for security reasons must stand in a specific area, limited in most cases, you surely have a much larger space in which to maneuver. You can choose to move on stage, get off the stage, talk from within the audience, sit down, stand, or bend down.

Every movement your body allows you to make is an option. All that's left is to decide what's right.

The diversity concept is relevant here, too.

The conspicuousness that is created as a result of adding movement or moving from one side of the stage to the other is what will make members of your audience remember what you wanted them to remember. The simple tendency of most inexperienced speakers is to focus mainly on hand movement. But the name of the game is diversity and unexpected moments for the audience.

For example, you can emphasize once with a hand movement, once with a look, with different facial expressions, by standing at a different angle towards the audience or at a different height or location, or by sitting on a chair that was set out in advance.

You want to do a dance step as part of the message? Dance! You want to make your messages stick in your audience's minds, don't you?

When you design your presentation, do not ask yourself, "What should I say." Instead, ask, "What can I show them to create the experience that will lead them to action?"

You want to highlight how your opinion changed from one extreme to another? Illustrate this by quickly moving from one side of the stage to the other. As long as you don't exaggerate in a way that will harm how you are perceived as professional and deter from the message you are conveying—everything's possible.

In one of our seminars, we wanted to demonstrate to the participants how limited the brain is in its capacity to take in many new messages all at once. Gil decided to use a pitcher from which he poured water into a glass, which is a metaphor for the participants' capacity of absorption and attention.

Almost everyone remembers the water that was spilt, thus the message that was conveyed through the demonstration.

The most common mistake is assuming "the scarecrow position" behind the podium. Of course, there are instances when you will want to stand there, for example, if you want to read a printed message in which every word is important. But in many cases, standing in such a position creates a physical distance that creates a mental block between you and the listeners. The subconscious separates you and the participants at the event. That's not intimate communication.

The Smiling Moles

In many of Obama's speeches, you can see at the edge of the camera shot, people sitting behind the stage while he speaks. They are always smiling and nodding. In many cases, these are people who were instructed to do so, since the viewers' eye is also influenced by the body language of the people beside or behind the speaker. This is generally picked up by the TV camera and also by the ultimate camera, the viewer's subconscious.

If you present to a group of people, it's likely you aren't attending alone. In this case, remember the viewers are not only affected by the speaker's body language, but also by the body language of the people in the audience. Therefore, while you are speaking, the people you want to influence will also be influenced by the body language of members of your group. Remember, you are a team, even if only one of you is the main player. Therefore, the co-players should convey that they are listening to you and agree with what you are saying. They will nod every time you make a strong argument. It will help influence the audience's subconscious.

Supportive Setting

If you have a supportive setting, you will go on stage with a different energy level. If you watch Obama getting on stage to speak at the 2008 Democratic National Convention in Denver, Colorado, you will see the extensive efforts placed in the surroundings, including a stadium designed to communicate that the next president of the United States is about to speak here. The decision to conduct the speech in a football stadium with 75,000 seats is a message in itself. A football stadium is an open venue (as opposed to a closed basketball arena, for example). Seventy-five thousand seats must be filled, and this conveys that this is a movement that has many supporters and, thus, has a great effect. The more you see people, who prefer a certain idea, the easier it is to influence those that are not so easily convinced.

Influence by "social proof" is very effective, as proven in the studies of Dr. Robert Cialdini, and Obama's team knows it.

When Obama chose a stadium, he took a calculated risk. He created high expectations and, for this reason alone, his messages were received as more powerful. He conveyed to his supporters, and in fact those who still hadn't joined him, that he was a rising star, that he fills stadiums, that he was as popular as a rock star. It's no wonder that, just days before the election, he attended an event in which Bruce Springsteen performed.

We recommend you watch the 2008 Democratic National Convention speech online.

Observe how Obama gets on the stage to speak with confidence. He smiles and claps his hands with the audience when they applaud him even before he speaks.

Obama knows that every detail counts. One of his secrets is to create influence, not only in the speeches themselves, but also in their overall perception. Obama wanted to be compared to John F. Kennedy, who took upon himself the candidacy for presidency at the Coliseum in Los Angeles. We assume that the date of the event, August 28, was selected on purpose. Martin Luther King, Jr. delivered his famous speech on that same date, forty-five years earlier, in front of two hundred thousand people in Washington. King had a dream. Obama fulfilled it.

Let's go back to February 2007, when Obama first announced that he would run for president. He did so in Springfield, Illinois, on the steps of the "Old State Capitol," which instantly evoked memories of President Abraham Lincoln.

He wanted to be compared to Lincoln and connected to him both on the conscious and subconscious levels, thanks to the setting of the speech.

Obama also used these memories in his spoken text, meaning, he also connected on a perceptual level to the revered president. No doubt this was the right way to start the run for presidency on the part of a person who, until that time, was unknown to many people who believed Hillary Clinton was the sure candidate of the Democratic Party.

Sometimes, Obama gets on stage to the sound of rhythmic music. When is the last time you saw a CEO getting on stage to the sound of music? We saw Microsoft's Steve Ballmer, but that's because he understands showmanship, too. He is another role model for an energetic speaker. And in March 2, 2011, Steve Jobs unveiled the iPad 2 with the music of the Beatles. Jobs came on stage with "Here Comes the Sun" and finished with the music of "Hard Day's Night". Music is very important, because it activates the right brain. Remember that the next time you go for shopping and hear some music…

The location and setting are part of the extended nonverbal communication of the speech. They create a mood that influences the subconscious. They aren't something you do, but if you make the right choice, they can help you influence others.

After we saw the influence of the combination between body language and surroundings, we can go on to another important one of Obama's skills: using his voice to convey charisma, to influence, and to lead to change.

Don't Say it. Show it

Adding a special hat, scarf, or any other props that will evoke a chuckle raises the attention bar during a presentation and the prospect of conveying a powerful message.

Remember, you own the stage. You can convey messages powerfully if you use props that will assist the message and support it. Everything around you affects your messages. If you are about to speak about organizational change—know that the setting, the music, and the colors influence the right brain of the people you want to influence, therefore also their perceptions, attitudes, and behavior.

If you host a group of clients before an important presentation—there is significance even in the room where the presentation takes place, including its structure, the music that's playing while you are mingling, the setting, the chairs the guests will sit on, and the food that will be served. Everything makes an impact. The entire world is a stage.

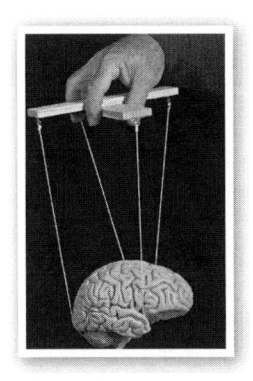

CHAPTER 33

Voice Power– How to thrill and influence an audience by varying voice tones

If y-o-u w-a-n-t to p-u-t an a-u-d-i-e-n-c-e to s-l-e-e-p s-p-e-a-k in a m-o-n-o-t-o-n-o-u-s v-o-i-c-e.

The name of the game is vocal variety. Be interesting, surprise the audience, refresh, change tempo and intensity, change the voice itself, and whisper at times. Obama uses his voice with such diverse measures as speech tone, changing the speaking pace, pausing between words, sentences, and paragraphs, diverse volumes of the voice, and emphasizing words.

In fact, the charisma many people attribute to Obama stems from, among other things, his ability to use his voice. If you watch his speeches, you will see (or rather, hear) how Obama plays with his voice. He changes the intensity, at times speaking loudly, at other times speaking softly; he changes the pace from a standard pace to a faster, more energetic pace, or to a very slow pace; he uses the range of his voice and uses a low or high voice pitch.

Why does he do it? Obama wants to keep the audience alert, and no less important, because he emphasizes conveying emotions. Music, like our voices, conveys emotions. Every song you listen to puts you into an emotional mood, primarily because of the melody. Next time you watch a film, pay attention to the soundtrack. Pay attention to the sounds of the drums, the violins, and the piano. Pay attention to the melody itself, its intensity, and how it reflects the same mood with the plot. Sometimes, you can envision the plot when you listen to music. Use of various instruments and types of music is also designed to convey tension, fear, and calm.

In this regard, Obama's secret is twofold:

First, he knows how to use his voice well. He learned, practiced, and studied how it is done correctly and adopted techniques for voice usage, which are used by the leading motivational speakers and experts in the world. Second, his head composer, his chief speechwriter, is Jon Favreau, a musician in his soul and by vocation who knows how to compose concerts full of charisma for Obama.

Obama's Composer

Obama is experienced in writing effective speeches, but like every leader who must perform many important tasks, he delegates authority and leaves the speech writing to a professional team. At the head of the White House speech writing team is the man who accompanied him, even before he entered the White House, Jon Favreau. Favreau was born in 1981. In his childhood, he learned to play the piano, and like Obama, he too was the editor of his college magazine. Obama and Favreau work as such an effective team that Obama doesn't call him "my speech writer." He calls him "my mind reader." They say Favreau often used to write for sixteen hours a day, during months of the presidential campaign. He sometimes worked until 4 a.m. and stayed awake with the help of a double espresso and energy drinks.

In the past, Favreau was John Kerry's speechwriter, the Democratic Party candidate for president in 2004. Favreau met Obama before he delivered his famous speech at the 2004 Democratic National Convention. Over the years, the two men have created an effective speech-writing process. According to Favreau, when he writes for Obama, he can actually get into Obama's shoes and write what he knows Obama himself would say. According to Favreau, the trick is to write so that your intelligent words will sound as if they came out of the speaker's heart.

When we were born, we instantly made the sound our parents must have thought was the finest sound they had ever heard—our first cry. But we weren't born charismatic speakers. Therefore, it's worthwhile that we become familiar with the five Ps to diversify the voice in order to captivate an audience and influence it: Pause; Pace; Pitch; Power; Punch.

Pause: The Silence before the Storm

Mark Twain said, "The right word may be effective, but no word was ever as effective as a rightly timed pause."

The pause, the temporary halt, the momentary silence works like magic. We say nothing, but as a result, everyone suddenly hears words, as if they were highlighted with a magic marker.

For example, when Obama mentions the sequence of the words "The United States of America" in his speeches, he utters the words slowly and creates a clear separation between the words. Thus, he creates emphasis, and in this case, a true feeling of loyalty to the country. Obama's pauses are often designed to obtain applause, and this indeed influences the audience to act in the direction he is striving for. Someone in the audience, presumably a mole, starts clapping, and the rest happens on its own. A good pause has extraordinary power. During the pause, especially if supported by matching body language, such as eye movement, the audience sees a film in their minds; that is, they are completing the details they invent.

Obama uses pauses consciously and precisely. He senses the rhythm of the words and knows how to space the message with pauses. It seems simple, but at our seminars worldwide, when we gave very experienced people exercises to change the pace of speech or incorporate pauses, they learned how hard it is to keep silent, even for a moment.

It's not easy to incorporate pauses in the right place in every sentence. It takes practice. At first, it's best to plan them. It requires that you decide when there will be pauses and indicate with a marker or large font on the text the word you choose to emphasize by pausing before and after it. If you do this, you will be in good company. They say President Bush, Sr.'s speech writers showed him when to pause, and so that it would be totally clear, at times they explicitly wrote the word "*pause*."

Pauses, Pauses, Pauses

The length of the pause can be diverse: a pause of a second or two is designed to give breathing space and emphasis, and a slightly longer pause is designed to indicate to the listeners that the speaker is moving on to another topic. Here are several types of pauses:

- The sandwich method: pause before—and after—the word you want to emphasize. The important word is the meat in the sandwich, and the pauses are two slices of bread that cover the meat. The quiet before—and after—creates emphasis. Thus, the word is powerfully taken, and the audience remembers it better.

- A pause before and after a sequence of words serves as a vocal comma with which to emphasize an entire message, as opposed to only one word. The pause before indicates to the listeners that they are about to hear something important. The pause after enables them to think about the message and internalize it.

- Pauses between syllables of the same word emphasize the word. When you want to emphasize a word, you can break it down into syllables. In this case, slow equals fast: you speak slower and the message enters the listeners' brains faster.

- Using a pause at the end of a sentence or paragraph enables the listeners to take in what they heard, to think about the information, and then process it. Many speakers fear that, if they say nothing, the audience will start talking. But a pause of a few seconds in a speech actually reinforces the chance that what you said will enter the mind better. At classical music concerts, long pieces also include several parts, and, at the end of each part, the listeners get a few seconds of rest to change positions, to say to the person beside them, "What a great performance," and even to cough…It is worthwhile allowing your listeners to internalize the information and share the experience with the person beside him or her, and for you to create tension towards the next part.

- Before you answer a question, pause. The pause is important not only to formulate the best answer to a question; it also makes people think you are contemplating the answer, so that your words will be perceived as having greater weight and as more intelligent. You will be perceived as someone who tends to listen well and isn't quick to answer before the questioner finishes the question.

How to Create Pauses

The pause can be accompanied by a change in where you stand. The combination adds drama. Obama often makes dramatic stops that are designed to convey to the audience that he is about to say something very important. His body language also supports the message when he signals "stop" with his hand. The dramatic combination achieves the desired effect.

A pause can also be created by taking a sip of water. This way, you make sure your throat isn't dry and allow the audience to internalize the message and understand that you're about to talk about a new subject. In fact, every combination of a pause with a nonverbal action will create a dramatic effect. During the pause, you can pick up an object that you will soon use, to emphasize the next message. You can make a pause that looks natural to the audience if you glimpse at the written material on which the speech is based. A combination of rhetorical questions also creates a powerful effect. You ask and then say nothing, without expecting an answer. Thus, a dynamic conversation with the audience is created, instead of a speech before the audience.

It's important to pause after a linguistic flash of brilliance. Remember, even if the audience is listening, most individuals are not as focused as the speaker. Therefore, if you said something brilliant like a word that has two meanings, you should give the audience time. Some pick up the message quickly, as soon as you speak, and some need a few more seconds. The pause helps, doesn't it?

You made them laugh? Now is the time to say nothing. A combination of moments of humor, not necessarily jokes, during a long presentation, is a good way to maintain the audience's alertness. When the audience is having fun, it is also more open to pick up new messages and less prone to resist. Therefore, it is important to say nothing to enable the audience to laugh, and it's worthwhile to maintain silence until you feel the laughter is on the decline. At first, part of the audience laughs, then the rest join in, until a climax is reached.

When the laughter dies down, there are two options. One is to sense when the laughter is dying down and then continue conveying the message. Thanks to the microphone you can speak over the noise. The other option is reserved for special circumstances where you have another surprising punch line, after the first punch line: wait until the first round of laughter has almost died down and "the lemon has been squeezed," and only then utter the next strong and funny message to cause an even bigger wave of laughter than the first, just like excellent comedians.

🔍 A Classic Secret

Frederic Chopin is considered one of the romantic composers of classical music. During the forty years of his life in the first half of the 19th century, he composed over two hundred thirty musical compositions.

Arthur Rubinstein, one of the greatest pianists of the 20th century, was once asked what the difference was between the way he so magically played Chopin's two concertos for piano, his three sonatas, and twenty-six preludes and the way other great pianists played them. And he answered, "We all play Chopin's notes. The difference is in the slight pause, the split second before I touch the piano keys." The right pauses can transform regular text into a memorable experience that will empower and motivate any audience.

How to Combine a Pause and Eye Contact

Here is a simple method to use a pause to establish eye contact. It requires relatively little practice and creates a dramatic effect for the person speaking before an audience. Every time you speak and pause, this is your chance to choose whether or not to continue speaking to the same person in the audience or to divert your gaze to another audience member.

The more people feel you are speaking directly to them, the more you will establish rapport with them; and through their looks and nods, you will pick up that they are on your wavelength.

The concept is simple: while you divert your gaze to another person, say nothing. It can be after a comma, at the end of a sentence, a pause before or after an important word, and, of course, every time you inhale. Divert your gaze only at "intervals" between the words.

And now, after we have examined the power of silence that is introduced before and after important messages, we will move on to speech *pace,* the second P of vocal variety.

Pace

When you increase your speaking pace, you convey to the audience enthusiasm, passion, and belief in your messages. Obama changes his pace all the time, which helps him maintain the listeners' level of concentration and also emphasizes certain words. The variety in pace maintains the listeners' alertness and powerfully influences them.

When you combine the pace variety with the other elements of nonverbal communication, your words are more powerful. A combination of several elements creates a more powerful effect.

Increasing the pace: a person's speech pace is sixty to one hundred and eighty words a minute on average, while the brain is capable of listening, picking up, and processing at a rate three to six times greater than that. This is why we can understand sports commentators who speak at a very rapid pace.

Increasing speed is designed to add energy and momentum to the words and attain dramatic emphasis of the speaker's feelings and emotions or of the emotions the audience experiences as a result of listening. Obama increases his pace towards the end of his speech, every time he wants to motivate people to join him in action. If you want to end your presentations powerfully, increase the pace and the tone of speech.

The end of your presentations should sound like the endnotes of Tchaikovsky's masterpiece "1812 Overture" that are often accompanied by fireworks. When you want to motivate people into action, don't speak the same way and at the same pace as the rest of the speech. Enthusiasm is infectious; rhythm is infectious. In most cases, your body language will also change and enthuse the audience when you speak faster. The intensity will increase even more if you focus the increase in pace on the most important moments, the *fireworks* moments. Remember that you shape your messages, and every word or message also has a "how."

Slowing down: when people are nervous, they tend to speak fast. President Obama generally speaks calmly, slowly, and with many pauses. In his speech at the 2004 Democratic National Convention, he spoke slowly and with confidence. When you want to insert every word into the listeners' brains (even every syllable), that's the time to s-l-o-w d-o-w-n.

The combination of a slow pace with pauses, and often also a quiet and confident voice, creates a strong, dramatic effect that remains in the memory. Slow speech with a relatively moderate tone connects well with the listeners' subconscious minds.

Exaggerated speed: intentionally speaking more quickly at certain moments enables you to speak successfully. However, be careful of the following landmines:

1. **Speaking too fast in a manner that is ill-suited to a certain audience**: When you speak a language that is not the mother tongue of most of the listeners, they must translate in their minds and process the messages. This is the time to slow down the speech pace, as opposed to an audience that speaks the same language as you. The problem is similar when you speak to an older audience; they pick up more slowly and, at times, their hearing is impaired. To create rapport with an audience such as this, you must adapt the speech rate and the intensity. Also, when using diverse professional terms that most of the audience is unfamiliar with, slow down to allow the listeners to pick up and digest them.

2. **Being unaware of the speech pace**: People who talk fast tend to speak this way to an audience, too. But while in a regular conversation most words can be taken in, in a presentation the words are taken in differently. You are liable to swallow words and syllables when you speak too fast, and this is likely to hinder your perception as a professional and undermine the understanding of the messages. Ask for feedback regarding your speech pace.

3. **The second part of the presentation trap**: Many have a tendency to speak calmly during the first half of the presentation, to speak for a long time, to divert from the planned outline, and assume there's still time to refer to comments from the audience. Suddenly, you discover a lot of time has gone by and you didn't have a chance to present most of the message, so you rush in an attempt to say everything you had planned. This is a mistake. Speed will make you not only swallow words and make mistakes; it will also make you be perceived as stressed out and nervous. Instead, prevent this mistake at the beginning. Don't speak extensively when you don't have to and reduce the number of messages. If you have fallen into the time trap, verify what the important messages are and what messages you can forego. Remember, the audience doesn't know what you planned to say, so it's best to skip a topic or give fewer examples than speak quickly and in unclear sentences. In most

cases, less is more. Always consider the listeners, not yourself. It's within *them* that you want to make a change.

༄

Pitch

The third P of vocal variety is your pitch. Are you familiar with the musical piece, "Peter and the Wolf?" Imagine you are listening to this piece by Sergei Prokofiev. You can envision the relevant animal or any other protagonist of the piece when the orchestra plays, correct?

You imagine the bird every time you hear the flute. You envision Peter every time you hear the violins. And you envision the hunters every time you hear the kettledrums.

Each instrument has its own unique sound. When you speak in public, you are not making orchestra sounds, but you can certainly change your sound wave frequency, the sounds other people will hear.

To diversify your messages, you can diversify the sounds you use to express them. A great example of changing pitch can be heard in Obama's speech in Springfield, Illinois, when he announced he was running for president. In that speech he began telling a personal story. As the speech went on, his voice went up, the tone intensified, and the pace became enthralling, until he literally shouted when he announced his candidacy.

It was a concert with crescendo and a powerful ending.

If you want to enthrall people, you can't expect that just because your message is important, they will follow you. You need music that will emerge from your heart and directly reach the listeners' hearts, not just their ears.

If you are demonstrating a dialogue, you can speak in your own voice when you are telling your side of the story. Every time you play the part of the other person, change your voice. In certain cases, you can be like an actor and combine diverse elements of nonverbal communication so the audience can envision the dialogue; every time one party speaks, stand at a different angle towards the audience—once on the right and once on the left—and the audience will imagine two people talking. If you incorporate a story with several characters, you can "act" the parts and speak every time in the voice of a different character. If it's a child, you can speak in a childish voice and crouch down. This way, you'll not only tell a story, you will also be presenting a story—its quality will improve and its effect will increase. Be the characters; emphasize their individualism. They will speak at a different pace, in a different way, and will stand differently. This is nonverbal communication at its finest.

Power

If you want to speak and communicate with power, you should use the fourth P of vocal variety: Power.

Obama has open, wide, and powerful mouth motions. Why? So the sound can be heard well, you must create a sound box in the cavity of your mouth, as you do when you learn to sing. Most people don't do this when they talk, but you can practice it, and you will quickly hear the difference. Let's practice first. Read this page aloud, in your normal speech. Then read it again, this time with an awareness of wider movements and the opening of the mouth. Did you hear the difference? Good job!

Do you speak in a loud voice, normal voice, soft voice, or a whisper? You undoubtedly won't convey an entire speech in a whisper. But imagine the intensity of a speech where you speak of "three secrets of success in our organization," and every time you say the sentence, "secret number X is…" you whisper into the microphone, while slowing down the speech pace. Like pauses, the diversity in the voice's power enables one to also emphasize messages through a quiet voice.

Obama changes the power of his voice throughout the entire speech. He can speak fairly quietly to prepare the audience for more power to come, and then he diversifies again.

We said diversity is the name of the game. Obama has a simple secret in this regard. Emphasis is mainly created when you use the contrast effect. If you speak in a loud voice, then suddenly, speak in a much lower voice, you attract attention. If you use a loud voice and increase the speed, in many cases you can enthrall the audience emotionally. If you use a quieter and softer voice, you can convey emotions such as sadness, empathy, and love.

The use of your voice will enable you to bring out the actor in you, even without movements, gestures, or props.

Punch

We met four elements of vocal variety: pause; pace; pitch; and power. Now, let's move to the last element. Imagine saying a word while you punch. Now, imagine saying a word, emphasizing a syllable or a sound, and giving a punch at the same time. This is how the punch is used, accentuating a word or a syllable so they sound stronger and emphasized.

It's likely this reminds you of the combination between a pause and the power of the voice. However, you don't have to raise your voice so the word sounds emphasized. Nor do you have to emphasize a whole word; you can give a punch just to one important syllable in the word. And by adding a supporting hand movement, where your arm lands on the podium while you say the word you wanted to emphasize, you will feel, hear, and see how powerful it is.

If we take Obama's classic campaign speech in 2008, in which he incorporated "Yes we can" for the first time, we will see and hear him saying this slogan in different ways: once with power and once quietly and softly. On the one hand, the repetition of the slogan created a refrain effect. On the other hand, no one likes feeling he or she is being brainwashed, so the diversity with which Obama said the sentence blurred the effect. The result was that the audience started chanting with him and answering him in the refrain.

As we said, a speech is like a concert, and these are its climaxes, when the speech becomes a sing-along. You will know the message was unmistakably understood and was stuck in their minds if a moment comes when, instead of the speaker uttering the words, the audience utters them itself.

Speak and Envision a Caress

A good text can hold an audience's interest. But when you diversify and make frequent changes in the way things are said, the text sounds much more interesting.

Here's a technique that was inspired by Russian director Constantin Stanislavski, who developed a unique method for training actors.

Instead of thinking what you will do with your hands, head, and the rest of your body at any given moment, imagine what type of action you will do while speaking. You don't have to perform the action itself, just envision it, so it affects your body language and your voice. Your thought process will make you change your body language and your intonation. For example, imagine that, at the highpoint of your speech, you are enthusing basketball fans; at another moment imagine you are speaking to children who got into a fight. The thought will influence the way you speak. The concept is simple; instead of focusing on what you physically do, you focus on the type of action, to create emotion naturally. If you practice this, you will also be able to change the type of action you convey numerous times as you speak, and at times even in the course of a sentence.

For example, the minute you want to speak with contrasts, imagine that, in the first part of the sentence, you're banging on the table and, in the second part, you are caressing with love. Try it and see how the words come out of your mouth in a totally different way.

We saw the five Ps of vocal variety and many examples of potential uses in nonverbal communication that will support your messages. Before we finish that part, here is a warning. After training hundreds of executives for over twenty years, we learned that, occasionally, people who are exposed to the importance of using body language make a fatal mistake you should avoid:

They try to shift from practically no use of the voice and body to using them almost incessantly, artificially. They exaggerate the use and intensity. As a result, their message is impeded. Therefore, don't overdo it and don't be quick to use all the tools you learned at one time. Refer to the ideas as supporting the message and learn to gradually improve your body language. Actors need years of daily practice. There's no reason you should skip from kindergarten to high school.

We are now approaching the end of the journey, during which we familiarized ourselves with Obama's secrets. We got to know the secrets of how he thinks and the way he acts, and we also learned the way in which he speaks to everyone in two languages at the same time: the language of words and the language of nonverbal communication. Together, they enable him to communicate with power and a little magic.

AFTERWORD

We've come a long way. You now have a deep understanding of President Barack Obama's communication profile. You have become familiar with his street smarts and the personal experiences that shaped him as a speaker.

You were exposed to a wide range of strategies, tactics, and tools that make him such a powerful speaker and that serve to attract the audience to him.

In conclusion, we want to emphasize what we said at the outset. We believe anyone can learn Obama's secrets and realize them in many aspects of their lives.

We believe all people can improve their influence and persuasion skills and speak powerfully, if only they are provided the right tools and practice them consistently.

However, we believe it is important to maintain individual authenticity. In that respect, we provided you in this book an abundance of secrets and techniques, so you can uncover your authenticity, your personal charisma, and what makes you unique.

Remember the power of personal experience? Remember the power of the personal story? Remember the importance of vision, identity, beliefs, and values? All these are ways in which you can discover your motivating force, your uniqueness, and your charisma.

The better you master the techniques and the more you learn, practice, and repeat the secrets revealed in this book, the more skilled you will become at the methods of influence and persuasion. In time, you will be freer with the use of the secrets divulged in this book, and you will be able to expose and discover your unique communicative self and your special secrets of influence.

This is what Obama does. His control of the ensemble of techniques to the point of an art form grants him the freedom to be who he is, connected to his life experience, vision, and identity.

True professionals, in every area, study, learn, and practice well-known techniques and methods, but they don't stop there. They add ideas, insight, and improvisation that they have created during their professional experience.

Famous painters such as Dali, Rembrandt, and Picasso learned to paint in their youth. They all had the same canvas and paints, and they all learned the same fundamentals. But each developed his own unique artistic style. Therefore, this book is like a recipe for a great cake. You are invited to use it as is, but you are more than welcome to add your special ingredients so it becomes your specialty cake. Ultimately, like your family members, your audience too will prefer to accept your messages with the special spices you use.

Now, it's time to implement Nike's legendary slogan: Just Do It.

We are confident that, if you dare to jump into the deep end and try out an idea or technique you read about in the book, you will discover that…yes, you can.

Whenever one learns a new skill, the first step to success is the desire to learn and the commitment to the learning process. Perseverance is another trait professionals share. If you have the will to adopt Obama's secrets, and if you are committed to practicing and improving their use—you will discover how far you can incorporate these secrets into your life and to what extent these secrets will change your communication and influence skills. It will be interesting to discover how fast all of this will happen.

Perhaps as early as next week you will find yourself telling a moving story at your board meeting, incorporating a slogan that causes the message to stick in your listeners' minds, or speaking in threes.

We believe everyone has an area in which they can excel. Everyone has something special about him or herself. Professional or personal charisma isn't something we are born with. It is a result of a continuous journey of discovery—discovering our strengths, what makes us unique, discovering the skill we are especially good at.

We hope and believe the tools you read in our book will help you on this fascinating journey of discovery. Remember that one of the reasons for Obama's success stems

Afterword

from the fact that he is in tune with the power within himself and skilled at using different and diverse tools. These tools enable him to activate his secrets of charm and influence in a way that people interpret as personal charisma.

We don't know what an American president will say in another twenty, fifty, or one hundred years about Obama's influence on the United States and the world. And it makes no difference. But we are sure of one thing: Obama will always be perceived as a master of words and will be mentioned in the same breath as other eloquent leaders such as Washington, Lincoln, Kennedy, Reagan, Clinton, Churchill, Roosevelt, Gandhi, and Nelson Mandela, who understood the power of words to motivate people and made exceptional use thereof.

And now we will end, not surprisingly, with a story.

George Gershwin is one of our favorite musicians. He was born in Brooklyn in 1898 and, in his youth, he fell in love with music. He learned to play and compose music virtually on his own and is considered as having the most unique style of the early 20th century.

Shortly after composing "Rhapsody in Blue," he traveled to Europe to complete his formal music studies. He applied for composition classes with French music teacher Nadia Boulanger and with Maurice Ravel, well known for composing his "Bolero." They both turned him down, claiming formal classical music studies were liable to hinder his unique jazz style. Gershwin asked Ravel to tutor him.

Ravel asked, "Why do you want me to teach you?"

"Because I want to be the second Ravel," Gershwin answered quickly.

"And why do you want to be the second Ravel, if you can be the first Gershwin?" Ravel concluded. Shortly thereafter, Gershwin composed his amazing "An American in Paris."

This is the essence of our professional approach to personal development.

You came all this way with this book to become a powerful communicator, applying the style and approach that suits you.

Thank you for giving us your precious time and reading our book. It will be our pleasure to speak at your organization and to train your people. And most of all, it will be our pleasure to stand up and applaud you when you stand on stage, and communicate with power and a little magic.

Sincerely Yours,

Gil and Nili Peretz

www.ObamasSecrets.com

GIL PERETZ

International speaker Gil Peretz is one of the world's leading authorities on communication and sales training. With more than 25 years of experience, Gil has coached and trained thousands of CEOs, entrepreneurs, sales experts, coaches, political leaders, and diplomats.

Since 1986, Gil has delivered more than 2,600 keynote speeches, presentations, and seminars. He is considered both a "motiv-actional" speaker and a results-driven trainer covering a range of topics including communication, presentation skills, whole-brain selling, negotiation, intimate marketing, and training for impact.

Gil has helped a wide range of organizations unleash their sales teams' potential. Global Fortune 500 companies engage Gil for their keynote addresses, breakout sessions, and to coach executives on their presentations.

Gil's clients include international organizations such as Microsoft, Motorola, Coca-Cola, IBM, Allergan, Merck, Teva, Pfizer, Philip Morris International, Swiss International Air Lines, HP, Hertz, Orange, Ericsson, Hilton, British American Tobacco, Manpower, Dun & Bradstreet, M-systems, Comverse, Peugeot, Citroen, Lee Cooper, Delta, and many more.

As a highly respected member of the American National Speakers Association, Gil has been invited to deliver his *"unforgettable presentations"* many times across the globe at conventions and conferences attended by thousands of participants.

Since 2009, Gil has been invited to deliver his seminars about *Obama's effective secrets of communication* and the ways in which they can be utilized for presentations, sales calls, and even in education.

Gil is considered a high-energy, virtuoso intimate speaker with rare presentation talents and a special ability to bond with any audience. Participants at his lectures feel that he speaks to each of them, individually, as if it were an intimate talk. The participants always leave with ideas for immediate implementation and, no less important, with a sense that they have taken part in a special intellectual and emotional experience.

Gil has been teaching "Marketing 101" and "Sharpening Your Presentation and Speech Skills" at the University of Tel-Aviv's Faculty of Management – The Leon Recanati Graduate School of Business Administration.

Gil is the author of the best-selling instructional novel *Intimate Marketing*.

To explore the possibilities of bringing the power of Gil Peretz to your organization, contact international@ObamasSecrets.com

www.gilperetz.com

www.ObamasSecrets.com

www.IntimateMarketing.com

NILI PERETZ

NLP expert Nili Peretz has brought to this joint writing endeavor her experience of over a decade as a business attorney, during which time she has worked as Defense Attorney, preparing dozens of defendants for the most important presentation of their lives—the one that would determine their innocence in front of a judge.

In addition to her BA and MA degrees in Law (completed with honors) and her training as a certified mediator, Nili has contributed her expertise as a Master Practitioner NLP (Neuro-Linguistic Programming) to the research, as well as the knowledge and hands-on experience she has accumulated in helping people make significant changes in various areas of their lives through the use of NLP tools.

Nili also conducts "Excellence Studies" projects - as a role model and as a means to improve business performance.

To explore the possibilities of bringing the power of Nili Peretz to your organization, contact international@ObamasSecrets.com

RECOMMENDATIONS FROM LINKEDIN ®

"Gil is an exciting and charismatic speaker. He manages to produce a rare blend of practical management and business principles laced with humor, memorable examples and intelligent wit. As a professional presenter and trainer myself, I very much enjoyed his lecture series and gained personal benefit from his special approach."

"Gil is a brilliant speaker. His presentations are both informative and fun. As Gil so successfully preaches to convey complex messages in simple terms, all that needs to be said is, "don't miss Gil's presentations"!"

"Gil is an outstanding keynote speaker with exceptional presentation skills. The crowd was hypnotized! Gil uses innovative tools to convey his key messages thus ensuring active participation on the part of his audience and thorough assimilation of the aforesaid messages. Gil understands the cultural difference among international audiences and has shown the ability to carefully craft the appropriate messaging and tools to use upon each separate engagement."

"Gil helped me optimize my presentation to a very high level. His open and constructive critique, in a very pleasant yet precise manner was extremely beneficial for me in my preparation before a large audience presentation."

"Gil is an energetic speaker who embodies forward thinking. Gil's approach to issues is straight to the point, no-nonsense, and infused with humor and ease. If you are looking for someone to inspire your organization and open the door to better communication inside out, Gil delivers!"

"Gil Perez is a great speaker. I have had the pleasure of attending a number of his presentations at various events. I was impressed and highly inspired. I will strongly recommend Gil as a consultant for seminars on presentation/communication skills."

"Gil is a talented, creative, visionary entrepreneur with energy and discipline to match his vision. Not only does he have great ideas – he knows how to bring those ideas into reality! If you're looking for a guy who can deliver the goods, Gil is your man. I recommend him highly."

"I have hired Gil to guide me through a 'once in a life time' presentation to the management of one of the biggest FMCG (Fast Moving Consumer Goods) companies in the world. Gil helped me transformed a boring, data based presentation to an emotions-burst of the esteemed audience. Gil's outside the box ideas together with an excellent understanding of how to influence the audience is highly appreciated!"

"Gil deserves every possible superlative that's out there. He is one of the most professional business persons I have come across. I would recommend Gil for any type of project related to personal training, coaching and business advisory."

To explore the possibilities of bringing the power of Gil Peretz to your organization, contact international@ObamasSecrets.com

Made in the USA
San Bernardino, CA
03 July 2013